1990

RENOIR ON RENOIR

OTHER BOOKS IN THE SERIES

Paul Clark, *Chinese Cinema: Culture and Politics since 1949*
Sergei Eisenstein, *Nonindifferent Nature: Film and the Structure of Things* (trans. Herbert Marshall)
Vlada Petrić, *Constructivism in Film: The Man with the Movie Camera – A Cinematic Analysis*
Eric Rohmer: *The Taste for Beauty* (trans. Carol Volk)
William Rothman: *The "I" of the Camera: Essays in Film Criticism, History, and Aesthetics*
Paul Swann: *The British Documentary Film Movement, 1926–1946*

RENOIR ON RENOIR

Interviews, Essays, and Remarks

JEAN RENOIR

Translated by
CAROL VOLK

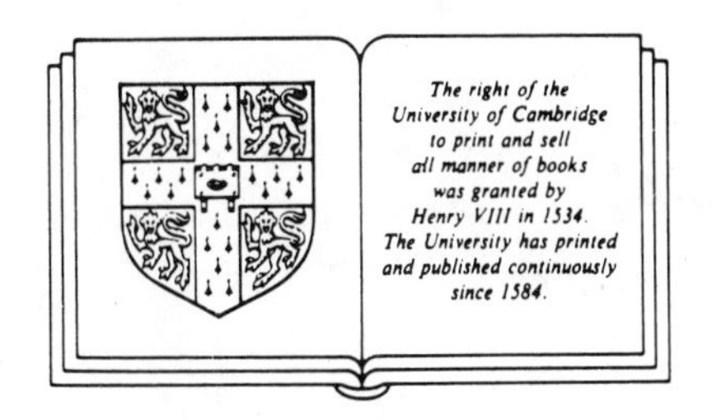

CAMBRIDGE UNIVERSITY PRESS
CAMBRIDGE
NEW YORK PORT CHESTER MELBOURNE SYDNEY

Published by the Press Syndicate of the University of Cambridge
The Pitt Building, Trumpington Street, Cambridge CB2 1RP
40 West 20th Street, New York, NY 10011, USA
10 Stamford Road, Oakleigh, Melbourne 3166, Australia

First published 1989

Printed in the United States of America

Library of Congress Cataloging-in-Publication Data
Renoir, Jean, *1894–1979*
[Entretiens et propos. English]
Renoir on Renoir ; interviews, essays, and remarks /
Jean Renoir ; translated by Carol Volk.
p. cm. – (Cambridge studies in film)
Translation of : Entretiens et propos.
Filmography : p.
ISBN 0-521-35151-0 (hard covers)
ISBN 0-521-38593-8 (paperback)
1. Renoir, Jean, 1894–1979 – Interviews.
2. Motion picture producers and directors – France – Interviews.
I. Title. II. Series.
PN1998.3.R46A5 1989
791.43'0233'092 – dc20 89–17413

British Library Cataloguing-in-Publication Data
Renoir, Jean, *1894–1979*
Renoir on Renoir : interviews, essays and remarks. –
(Cambridge studies in film).
1. French cinema films. Directing. Renoir, Jean, 1894–1979
I. Title
791.43'0233'0924

ISBN 0-521-35151-0 (hard covers)
ISBN 0-521-38593-8 (paperback)

Foreword to the American edition,
by Henry Breitrose — *page* vii

Preliminary note to the French edition,
by André S. Labarthe — ix

Foreword to the French edition, by Claude Gauteur and Jean Narboni — xi

Acknowledgments to the French edition — xiii

Part One Interviews in *Cahiers du cinéma* — 1

I First interview, by Jacques Rivette and François Truffaut — 3

II Second interview, by Jacques Rivette and François Truffaut — 53

III Third interview: My next films, by Michel Delahaye and Jean-André Fieschi — 112

IV Fourth interview: The progression of ideas, by Michel Delahaye and Jean Narboni — 124

Part Two Television interviews — 145

V Jean Renoir talks about his art — 147

VI Jean Renoir the boss — 168

The search for relativity — 168

The rule and its exception — 190

Part Three Remarks — 211

VII Jean Renoir presents twenty of his films [for television] — 213

VIII Hollywood conversations [from *Cahiers du cinéma*] — 248

Afterword: The love of Renoir, by Jean-Louis Comolli — 259

Filmography — 264

Name index — 281

Title index — 286

Frontispiece – Jean Renoir at his home on Leona Drive, 25 August 1957. (Photo by Jacques Raynal, a photographer friend of Jean Renoir. Its reproduction in any form is prohibited.)

Foreword to the American edition

Henry Breitrose

There are very few filmmakers who have been as influential, as widely respected, as aesthetically and intellectually provocative, and as good as Jean Renoir. The publication of this American edition of his interviews with *Cahiers du cinéma* is intended to bring his insights and ideas to an English-speaking audience.

As a group, filmmakers aren't particularly disposed to write about their methods and work, preferring, it would seem, to let the films themselves communicate method, philosophy, and intention to the audience. There is good reason to honor this and to recognize the primacy of the artist and the work.

Jean Renoir was an exception to the rule. He was as generous with his time as he was with his spirit. He had what seemed to be total recall of the conditions of production of all of his films. He could be quite specific about his intentions and methods, and quite critical, in retrospect, of his own work. Whether the questions came from journalists, fellow filmmakers, or the students at UCLA where he taught for several years, Renoir answered seriously, specifically, and generously – regardless of the questioner's level of sophistication.

I had the opportunity to meet Renoir in California during his last years when the late James Kerans, who taught at Berkeley, Stanford, and UCLA somehow organized the Drama Department at UC–Berkeley to stage Renoir's play, *Carola,* with Renoir himself in residence. Renoir knew that the text would probably never make it to the screen, and it struck me that he didn't seem particularly concerned, as long as it was performed, brought from text to action. He didn't in the least seem concerned that the work was being staged by a university drama department rather better known at the time for its work in dramatic literature and theory than for acting and directing. I cannot imagine how Renoir could have been more involved, more energetic, more adventurous if the production were to have been a fully budgeted commercial film production, with a name cast. In this, as in all other things, whatever he did he did with a full measure of intensity, enthusiasm, and commitment.

The interviews with Renoir in this volume span several decades, and one can sense the ideas ripen and develop over time. Renoir had a love for paradox as well as a strong Cartesian streak. The text is full of his playing with ideas, developing them, putting them into conjunction and counterpoint, and ordering his replies so that, frequently, they provoke good-naturedly as well as inform. From time to time he will reply to the interviewer with a response not to the question that was asked, but rather to the question that *should* have been asked. All this is done with grace, good humor, wit, and immense style.

Most of the *Cahiers du cinéma* interviews were done during the heyday of the *politique d'auteurs,* the so-called auteur theory, when the young French cinema was rejecting the established criteria of cinematic merit, which had much to do with literary orthodoxy and which celebrated such cinematically barren but financially successful films as Marcel Pagnol's popular prewar trilogy *Marius, Fanny, Cesar.* The *Cahiers* critics favored a cinema of authorial primacy for the writer-director that ignored the pedigree of literary antecedents. The critical impulse that brought auteurism into vogue prepared the way for the intensely personal cinema of the *nouvelle vague,* the New Wave of critics-turned-filmmakers who shocked the bourgeoisie and energized the French cinema.

That the *Cahierists,* who hoisted the auteurial flag and gave the world the New Wave, venerated Renoir above all other French filmmakers is not a surprise. Renoir took chances, made films on risk and instinct, insulted some serious political sensibilities, challenged the Hollywood studio system during his wartime exile, and actually managed to make some interesting films in America despite the best efforts of the studio managers not to understand him.

Jean Renoir was a man of great wit, style, and passion who could look into the complexity of social structure and morality and see the world made manifest in the interaction of social structures and human relationships. His imagination was his intelligence: subtle, immensely complex, prophetic, transparently stylish, astonishingly lucid, and always eager to engage in a dialogue with an audience.

Publisher's note: This American edition includes a filmography and two indexes that did not appear in the original French edition. Footnotes added by the translator end with her initials (CV).

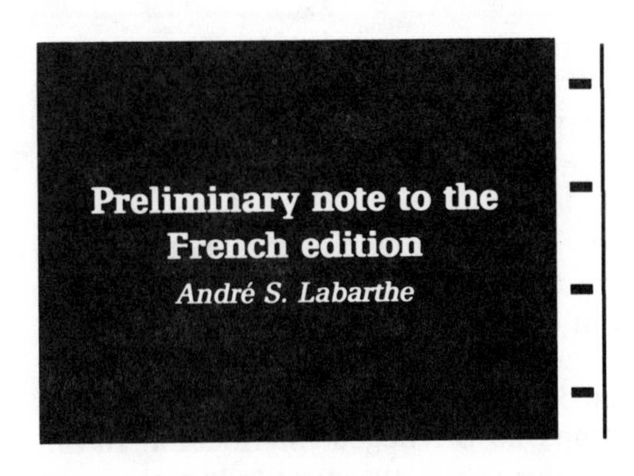

Preliminary note to the French edition

André S. Labarthe

The evolution of *Cahiers du cinéma* resembles that of all historical epochs: One fine day, you notice that the landscape around you has changed and that, in addition, the same people are no longer taking stock of it. Of those who left on their crusades with typical ardor, some settled in the conquered territory (the New Wave); others continued their travels but seem to have given up on the destinations they had set for themselves. Like travelers who trek for too long, they forgot the reasons for their journeys.

The history of *Cahiers* functions rather like a movie camera, with the blinking shutter admitting samples of light, the starts and stops of intermittent movement, certainties, and doubts, which make it – at least for those of us who have followed its course – one of the most exciting postwar adventures. The *Cahiers*'s fidelity to itself resembles that which gave life to (and destroyed) surrealism between the two wars or that to which Renoir refers when telling how the impressionists prolonged the great Western pictorial tradition by opposing those who believed they had been entrusted with it.

Despite all the changes over time, there is one practice that *Cahiers* has never abandoned: the tape-recorded interview.

(A paragraph is missing here that discusses the first uses of the portable tape recorder; the golden age of journalism immediately following the war; the creation of large photo agencies; neorealism; and, finally, how the tape recorder became the journalist's alter ego and how it restores for us, at the end of a questionable process of transcription, the voice and the very thought patterns of directors we love: the voices of Buñuel, Hitchcock, Welles . . . The voice of Renoir . . .)

The use of the tape recorder at *Cahiers* was perhaps never more appropriate than in these conversations with Renoir, milestones in a twenty-eight-year friendship.

If one looks at them closely, they are strange conversations!

They could hardly be more different from the usual commentary, which provides an overview of someone's work, explains it, or draws a lesson from it.

This teacher, however, teaches nothing. He preaches nothing. He has no advice to give.

He is no more a man defending an idea than he is an advocate of a cause.

He neither forces his ideas nor opposes those of others. Listen carefully: This old friend of *Cahiers* has no privileged interlocutor. In answering Bazin, Rivette, or others, the same discourse takes root and subsists peacefully, overcoming any obstacles, but not without having tasted and appreciated their consistency and contours: "Yes...of course...you're right...I would go so far as to say...what you say is true...etc."

In fact, Renoir doesn't converse at all. He doesn't try to convince his interlocutor, but rather, he tries to *overwhelm* him. Whoever met Jean Renoir was struck by his way of always embracing more, by his gestures, like those of a dancing bear whose trainer has just fled. Thus Renoir speaks of nothing that he does not, in turn, overwhelm with a flood of contradictory propositions, as if truth were always across the way or, rather, could be glimpsed only in the process of turning around, which of course renders it elusive. But this continual motion holds everything together: the spinning top of ideas driven by the string of an ever-active mind.

Renoir's thoughts have an unusual biological character, which permeates both his work as a filmmaker and his "literary" attempts. In the interviews gathered here, there circulates the warm blood of an unfettered mind. And we can guess the type of death that awaits such unstable discourse: it's gallstones, hardening of the arteries, blockage of the circulation of meaning. Basically, it's the same kind of death that never ceased to haunt *Cahiers* throughout its tumultuous history and that, every evening, on a thousand spots on the globe, threatens to interrupt the projection of a film in progress.

There is therefore nothing to learn from reading these transcriptions except of the pleasure Renoir took in savoring the world in each of its parts and in offering, to those who listened, his unique and inimitable vision.

André S. Labarthe

This volume of *Interviews and Remarks* by Jean Renoir contains two kinds of talks by the filmmaker, both of which took place between 1954 and 1967: those that were done for the review *Cahiers du cinéma* and those that were done for television. We are thankful to the Institut National de l'Audiovisuel for authorizing us to reproduce the segments included in the "Television interviews."

In February 1954, *Cahiers du cinéma,* "cinema and tele-cinema review," published an interview with Jacques Becker by Jacques Rivette and François Truffaut. Neither of the parties had any doubt that they had just inaugurated what would become a veritable genre: the tape-recorded interview. The tape recorder was, at that time, a most cumbersome apparatus.

In April and May of that year *Cahiers,* nos. 34 and 35, published a lengthy interview with Jean Renoir, by the same interviewers. With great ease, they went from *The Rules of the Game* (*La Règle du jeu*) to *The Woman on the Beach* (*La Femme sur la plage*) and then from *The River* to *The Golden Coach* (*Le Carrosse d'or*), films and periods that were virtually unknown at the time.

In 1957, the Christmas issue, no. 78, was devoted entirely to Jean Renoir. It contains a very long "New Interview," by Jacques Rivette and François Truffaut, who start with *Orvet* and end with *Nana,* by way of *Eléna et les hommes* (*Paris Does Strange Things*) and *The Human Beast* (*La Bête humaine*), following a quite uneven progression.

Twelve years later, Michel Delahaye and Jean-André Fieschi brought a conversation with Renoir (no. 180, July 1966) on his upcoming films to the Cahiers office at 5 rue Clément-Marot. Most of this conversation centers on *C'est la révolution!,* a project that was never completed.*

In 1967, practically invisible since its release in 1938, *La Marseillaise* reappeared in its full version (two hours and fifteen minutes,

*In fact, it became *The Little Theater of Jean Renoir* (*Le Petit Théâtre de Jean Renoir* [1969]) – CV.

compared with the one hour and thirty-five minutes in which it was first released). This resurrection became an occasion for Jean Renoir to explain his intentions in a long conversation with Michel Delahaye and Jean Narboni (no. 197, July 1967).

These were the circumstances under which the *Cahiers du cinéma* interviews with Jean Renoir occurred. They have been organized in the order in which they appeared and in their entirety.

Members of the *Cahiers* team, first Jacques Rivette in 1961 and then Rivette again with Janine Bazin and André S. Labarthe in 1966, interviewed the "Boss" (Paulhan's description of Braque, which was used for the Renoir programs in the series "Cinéastes de notre temps") for television. These comments, televised in 1962 and 1967 but never published, fit this homage, as does Renoir's conversation with Jean-Louis Noames in 1964 in Los Angeles (which appeared in *Cahiers,* no. 155, May 1964).

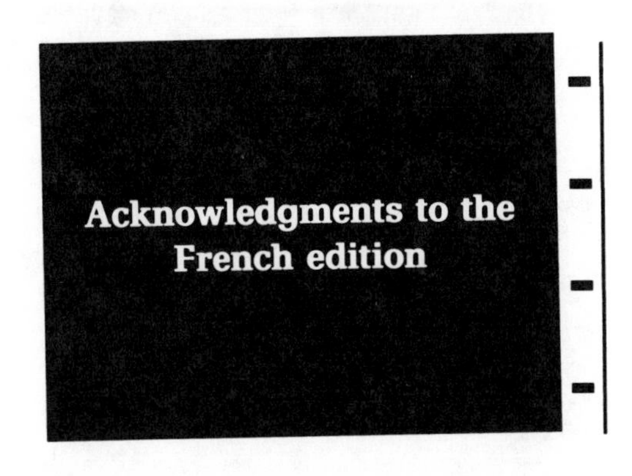

Acknowledgments to the French edition

The French text of this volume was compiled for *Cahiers du cinéma* by Jean Narboni, with the assistance of Janine Bazin and Claude Gauteur.

We would like to thank the following people for their help on this volume: Mmes Anne de Saint-Phalle et Micheline Gardez, MM. Claude Beylie, Jean-Marie Coldefy, André S. Labarthe, Gérard Lebovici, and Jacques Rivette, as well as the Centre National des Lettres, the Centre National de la Cinématographie, the Compagnie Jean Renoir, the Institut National de l'Audiovisuel, and the Ministry of Culture and Communications.

PART ONE
Interviews in Cahiers du cinéma

This section contains four long *Cahiers du cinéma* interviews with Jean Renoir, which took place between 1954 and 1967. The numbers first, second, third, and fourth were added for convenience.

The first interview, by Jacques Rivette and François Truffaut, was originally published in two consecutive numbers of the review (nos. 34 and 35, April and May 1954). The current division into two parts represents the division of these two issues. The short introduction and notes also date from that time, unless otherwise indicated.

The second interview, also by Rivette and Truffaut, appeared in a special edition of *Cahiers* that was dedicated to Jean Renoir (no. 78, Christmas 1957). It also appeared in *La Politique des auteurs*, published by Champ libre in 1972, which has kindly authorized us to reprint it.

The third interview, by Michel Delahaye and Jean-André Fieschi, took place while Renoir was preparing *C'est la révolution!* (which never materialized)* and was published in July 1966 (no. 180) and entitled "My Next Films."

Finally, the fourth interview, by Michel Delahaye and Jean Narboni, centers on *La Marseillaise* and took place in 1967, after the film was first released in its full version) (two hours and fifteen minutes, compared with one hour and thirty-five minutes in the 1938 version). It was published in *Cahiers* in December 1967 (no. 196) and was entitled "The Progression of Ideas."

The illustrations are not those that accompanied the original publication of these interviews.

*It became *The Little Theater of Jean Renoir* (*Le Petit Théâtre de Jean Renoir* [1969]) – CV.

CHAPTER I
First interview
Interviewers: Jacques Rivette and François Truffaut

PART ONE

The work of Jean Renoir is too extensive to attempt to address all of it in this interview. We therefore decided to question him on the most recent period of his life, which is also, paradoxically, the least well known. The most conflicting comments have circulated about his stay in America, and we are aware that our interview contradicts many of those that have been published. Allow us simply to point out that we had the benefit of an impartial tape recorder and also that we had no desire to make Jean Renoir disavow any of his films.

In short, we had no greater goal than to continue the famous article that appeared in *Point* in December 1938, in which Renoir summarized the first part of his life. It was therefore only natural that our first question touched on *The Rules of the Game* (*La Règle du jeu*).

JEAN RENOIR: I had wanted to do *The Rules of the Game* for a long time, but this desire became clearer while I was shooting *La Bête humaine*. This film, as you know, was taken from a novel by Zola and is essentially a naturalist work. I remained as faithful as I could to the spirit of the book. I didn't follow the plot, but I have always thought that it was better to be faithful to the spirit of an original work than to its exterior form. Besides, I had some long conversations with Madame Leblond-Zola, and I did not do anything that I was not certain would have pleased Zola. Yet I didn't feel obliged to follow the weave of the novel; I thought of certain works like *L'Histoire du vitrail*, *La Cathédrale*, *La Faute de l'Abbé Mouret*, or *La Joie de vivre*; I thought of Zola's poetic side.* But in the end, people who like Zola declared themselves satisfied.

*Compare these comments with this excerpt from a 1951 interview with André Bazin and Alexandre Astruc:
Question: When you read a book with an eye to adapt it, do you know exactly what you will do with it?
Answer: No. You see pieces of it, and when you see clearly enough, you can go ahead. What helped me do *The Human Beast* were the hero's explanations of his atavism. I

Nevertheless, working on this script inspired me to make a break, and perhaps to get away from naturalism completely, to try to touch on a more classical, more poetic genre. The result of these thoughts was *The Rules of the Game*.

Since one is always inspired by something (after all, you have to start somewhere, even if there is nothing left of that somewhere in the final work), I reread Marivaux and Musset carefully in order to get ideas for *The Rules of the Game*, but with no intention of even following the spirit of their works. I think that reading them helped me establish a style, halfway between a certain realism – not exterior, but realism all the same – and a certain poetry. At the very least I tried.

A bouquet of flowers

CAHIERS: Rumor has it you started with an adaptation of *Les Caprices de Marianne*.

RENOIR: No, I had no intention of doing an adaptation. Let's just say that reading and rereading *Les Caprices de Marianne*, which I consider to be Musset's most beautiful play, helped me a great deal, but it obviously had only an indirect effect. That is, these writers helped me more to conceive of the characters than to develop the form and the plot.

CAHIERS: You wrote several versions of this script. Jurieu, for example, was an orchestra conductor in one of the first versions.

RENOIR: Yes, of course, but that's always the case. I am rewriting the same play* now for the third, even the fourth time. It doesn't even resemble my first draft; the characters even have different identities.

CAHIERS: Did you also change *The Rules of the Game* during the shooting?

RENOIR: On the set? Yes, I improvised a great deal. The actors are also the directors of a film, and when you're with them, they have reactions you hadn't foreseen. Their reactions are often very good, and it would be crazy not to take advantage of them.

CAHIERS: In what way did you change things?

RENOIR: Well, the changes based on my contact with actors are the same in all my films. I have a tendency to be theoretical when I start working: I say what I would like to say a bit too clearly – a bit like a

said to myself: This isn't really beautiful, but if a man as handsome as Gabin were to say it outdoors, with lots of horizon behind him and maybe with some wind, it could have some value. That's the key that helped me make this film.

Orvet.

lecturer – and it's extremely boring. Little by little (and my contact with the actors helps enormously), I try to get closer to the way in which characters can adapt to their theories in real life while being subjected to life's many obstacles, the many minor events, the many little sentiments that keep us from being theoretical and from remaining theoretical. But I always start with theories. I'm a bit like a man who is in love with a woman and who goes to see her with a bouquet of flowers in hand. In the street he goes over the speech he is going to make; he writes a brilliant speech, with many comparisons, talking about her eyes, her voice, her beauty, and he prides himself in all this, of course. And then he arrives at the woman's house, hands her the bouquet of flowers, and says something completely different. But having prepared the speech does help a little.

CAHIERS: And the last-minute sincerity?

RENOIR: That's it. There is one other thing: It's difficult to be sincere when you're all alone. Some people manage to do it, and they are gifted writers. I'm much less gifted, and I can only really find my own expressions when I'm in contact with others. And I'm not talking about criticisms so much; I'm mostly talking about the kind of ball game that seems necessary to me. It's exactly the same in all walks of life. For example, in politics, you see politicians go into a meeting having prepared a very "clever" statement. They completely forget that the other side has also prepared a very "clever" statement, and so they never agree. But if the two sides came to this political meeting in the state of mind I try to bring to my work, perhaps they could get along.

CAHIERS: In short, you prepare your work with the idea of abandoning everything on the set.

RENOIR: Yes, absolutely. Yet I cannot completely improvise, I can't work like the great pioneers, like the great film pioneers, like Mack Sennett. . . . I often went to see his little studio, which is still standing in an old neighborhood between Los Angeles and Hollywood. It's no longer a studio, there are offices there now. I spoke to some old stagehands, some old electricians who were working at that time. I also met a few old cameramen. There's a Frenchman, for example, whose name is Lucien Andriot, who is very familiar with that period. You know Lucien, he did *The Southerner* with me. Old Mack Sennett used to tell everyone to be there in the morning, and those who were at least getting paid came, and he would say, "What are we going to do this morning?" Someone would say, "We could take a policeman, the seal, a lady dressed as a milkmaid, and we could go to the beach." And they went to the beach: They thought about it on the way, they shot something, and it came out well. I obviously couldn't do that. I have to know what I'm going to shoot, but even when I do, what I wind up shooting may be different. But it's never different as far as the props, the set, and the general feeling of the scene go – only the form changes.

The field and the poplars

CAHIERS: To get back to *The Rules of the Game*: Weren't you surprised by the poor reception it got?

RENOIR: Well, I wasn't expecting it, I never expect it, and for a very simple reason: I always imagine that the film I'm going to make will be an extremely marketable film, which will delight all the distributors and will be considered rather ordinary. I try my hardest to make as marketable films as possible, and when exceptions like *The Rules of the Game* occur, they occur in spite of my efforts. Besides, I'm convinced that this is always the case, that theories follow practice.

I just told you that I begin by being too theoretical and that the practice, the contact with life, changes my writing completely; that's true. So when I say that theory follows practice, I'm not thinking of the theories that the characters express on the screen and that disappear little by little from my writing. I'm thinking of general film theories, the conclusions one can draw from a film, the lesson – the message, as they say – that it may hold. I have the feeling that this message can be truly meaningful only if it hasn't been planned in advance, if it appears, little by little, by itself, just as a certain light effect springs forth from a landscape: You see the landscape before you see the light effect. You can walk in the country, knowing that you are going to come to a specific place near a road and that a field with poplar trees will be there. You see the field and the poplars. Then, little by little, the more subtle details – the lighting, certain contrasts, certain relationships – appear, which are the essence of the landscape and are much more important than the field and the poplars. Sometimes – and this happens with many artists – one completely forgets the field and the poplars and preserves only its consequences: That's what we call abstract art. In reality, I believe that all great art is abstract. Even if a bit of the field and poplars remains, they must be different enough so as not to remain mere copies.

CAHIERS: And so it was later on that you discovered everything in *The Rules of the Game* that foreshadowed the approaching war?

RENOIR: Oh, no! I thought about that, but I thought about it only indirectly. I didn't say to myself, "This film must express this or that, because we are going to have a war." And yet, even so, knowing that we

The Rules of the Game.

were going to have a war, being absolutely convinced of it, my work was permeated with it. But I didn't establish a relationship between the impending state of war and my characters' dialogues or words.

The complex interplay of Italian baroque

CAHIERS: And your next film was in fact interrupted by the war.... But what were your reasons for going to shoot *La Tosca* in Italy?

RENOIR: Well, there were several reasons. First, I really wanted to shoot in Italy; next, I was asked to shoot in Italy. It was before the war, but people had a sense of what was going to happen, and many French officials wanted Italy to remain neutral. It so happened that the Italian government, and even Mussolini's family, wanted me to go to Italy. My first instinct was to refuse. So I refused, and I was told, "You know, this is a very special time, and one must forget personal preferences. Do us the favor of going there," not only to film *La Tosca*, but also to give a few lessons on stage setting at the Centro Sperimentale di cinematografica in Rome, which is what I did.

That's the real reason, the practical one. Intellectually, I might say, I went because of *The Rules of the Game*. You know you can't think of Marivaux without thinking of Italy. One mustn't forget that Marivaux started by writing for an Italian troupe, that his mistress was Italian, and that essentially, he took up the thread of the Italian theater. I think he can be put in the same category as Goldoni. Working on *The Rules of the Game* brought me fantastically close to Italy, and I wanted to see baroque statues, the angels on bridges, with clothes with too many folds and wings with too many feathers. I wanted to see the kind of complex interplay of Italian baroque. I should add that, later on, I quickly learned that the baroque was not the essence of Italy. I am now much more drawn to previous periods, even those before the Quattrocento. If I were invited to visit one place in Italy, I think I would choose to return to the National Museum in Naples to see the Greek paintings of Pompeii, yes, that would still be my choice. But at the time of *La Tosca*, I didn't know all that. I've learned it since.

CAHIERS: You shot only the first sequence, I think, in which the taste for the baroque is so apparent?

RENOIR: Yes, a few gallops at the beginning, a few horses. I don't know if they're in the film, I've never seen it. Koch, my friend and associate and assistant, shot the film for me when Italy entered the war. I've been told that the film followed my script rather closely; Koch told me that himself.

CAHIERS: It's a very good film, in any case.

RENOIR: Oh really? That's good. It proves that I can write scripts; that's very flattering.

The façade at Tournus

CAHIERS: Shouldn't we be sorry that Koch hasn't shot other films?

RENOIR: We certainly should. He's a remarkable man, one of the most intelligent men I know . . . in the world. He came to film in a strange way: Instead of coming to it from the technical end, as so many people do (which in my opinion creates a whole race of very ordinary directors), he came to film through the study of medieval architecture. He's

Imperio Argentin and Michel Simon in *La Tosca*, by Karl Koch (the film's first five shots are by Jean Renoir).

a man who knows medieval architecture as no one else does. When we started working together, we went to some churches.... I remember being surprised the first time. We arrived at a church, Koch looked at the façade, got his bearings, and said, "Let's see, north, south, okay, I've got it." And he told me everything we were going to find in the church, he knew the capital of the least important column – everything – by heart.

CAHIERS: He was Lotte Reiniger's husband.

RENOIR: Yes, he still is. I hope to go see them soon in England. He has a hard time working because he wasn't able to get permission from the

English unions, I think. It's awful to see a man who has all of film in the palm of his hand – and not like a theoretician but like a very cultivated man with experience – it's really a pity to see that he's not making any films.

CAHIERS: He was also your associate on *The Rules of the Game*.

RENOIR: Yes, we worked together all the time. We were separated by Italy's entry into the war. That's what indirectly sent me to America.

CAHIERS: Now we're getting to the main part of this interview: your experience in America. We'd like to hear as much as possible about this period.

RENOIR: Lots of people have probably already told you what it's like to work in an American studio. I would have nothing new to tell you, and my particular case is not very different from the others. Nevertheless, I can divide my American films into two categories: a few attempts with the large studios, and some others with independents. The results with the large studios were not bad, since I shot *Swamp Water*, which isn't a bad film – it's an enjoyable film in any case. The only reason I was able to shoot it, however, is because I was new. My other advantage at that time was that I spoke English very poorly, and so I couldn't understand anything. I wasn't yet able to be influenced.

In fact, everything that is said about the large studios is true, but I think that the main reasons that make it difficult to work there for a man like me, an improviser, have not been touched on: The large studios have enormous expenses; films cost a great deal there; and they cannot risk all that money without having what they call security – the security is the script, it's the work outline. Each detail of a film is decided in advance by a kind of board of directors to which the principal members of the studio belong, as well as the producer and the director. If you're eloquent, you can do just about anything you want as a director, but you have to know in advance, you must be able to convince people beforehand of what you're going to do, and I can't do that. What often happened was that I would convince people that we had to do this or that, and once I was on the set, I found that it was a stupid idea and wanted to do something else. In other words, what people say about the tyranny of the large studios is sometimes true, but it depends on the individual. Personally, I could have worked there without being tyrannized at all – if I had known beforehand what I would want on the set, but I couldn't.

In any case, when I decided to leave Twentieth Century–Fox after *Swamp Water*, it all happened in a very friendly way. I explained to Zanuck what I am explaining to you now, and he said to me, "Of course we can't; we have to know where we're going; we're very sorry." I said to him, "Well, do me a favor, break my contract." He said to me,

"Of course." We're the world's best friends. I just don't think my type of work fits in with a large administration. In any case, I think my type of work is going to disappear, not just from Hollywood, but from the whole world, because films cost too much today. The price of a film is outrageous. That's why I am convinced that people in my category – and these people have to make films too, after all – may be able in the future to make only less expensive films, in black and white, less industrial, maybe in 16mm; it's possible....

Picasso born in China

CAHIERS: Was the script for *Swamp Water* your own idea?

RENOIR: No, not at all. Dudley Nichols wrote it, maybe a year beforehand, and in a different form. At that time Nichols had left Hollywood and was in the east, in Connecticut, where he was writing other things, but not for film. When I arrived, Fox gave me many scripts to read and asked me to choose the one I wanted to shoot. I read piles of them, and to me, they all were too much like European stories. I'm still convinced that it is extremely difficult to make films that are not tied in with the place they are made. I think that the artist's origin is not very important, but...I often use the comparison with the French school of painting, which was, all in all, as important an event in the world as the Italian Renaissance. These people were from every possible country, but just the same, they painted in the French style and were in close contact with everything that came from French soil. Picasso may be Spanish, but because he paints in France, he's a French painter. Even if he had been born in China, he would be a French painter.

That's why, because I was a Frenchman, Fox gave me a lot of films on France or on Europe, thinking, "He knows France, he knows Europe, he's going to do fantastic things." But I wanted no part of it. Finally I found this essentially American story, and I was enchanted. In addition, it gave me the opportunity to meet Dudley Nichols, who has remained an extraordinary friend – I could say a brother – with whom I correspond and with whom I planned other films, which were never made.

It was also because of *Swamp Water* that I was able to see America. Here's what happened: The film took place in Georgia, and so I asked the studio, "When are we leaving for Georgia?" They were quite surprised. They said, "Do you think we built a studio worth so many millions, in which we can reproduce anything, so that we would have to go to Georgia? We're going to build Georgia right here." I didn't buy this, and protested mightily. The problem was presented to Zanuck, who squirmed. He said to himself, "Boy, these French people have

Swamp Water

some crazy ideas." I told him, "I may have some crazy ideas, but I'd rather do nothing than do this film in the studio. It seems to me that in Georgia we'll at least find some exteriors. I'm not saying we shouldn't do the interiors here, or even some atypical exteriors – Why not construct the front of a house in the studio? – but everything that expresses the character of the Georgia countryside, I want to do in Georgia." So we went to Georgia, and I was able to see this swamp, and I must say that it was quite enjoyable and I had a good time.

I'm a slow director

Another thing happened: The film took longer to shoot than we had estimated. I was supposed to have shot it in – I don't know – forty days, and it was already the forty-fifth day and we were far from finishing it. I had a very slow cameraman, but it wasn't his fault; I was the one who was taking my time to shoot the film. One day they called in the cameraman to complain about his slowness. I protested: "Listen, the cameraman isn't slow, I am, I'm a slow director, and if you don't want a slow director, don't use me." The cameraman became a very good friend of mine, by the way; he was very pleased with my attitude....*

Here's what had happened: I had refused a story adapted from a well-known novel, and I had refused to use a star, although I certainly had some very good actors. I had Walter Huston; Dana Andrews, who played a stock boy; Anne Baxter, who played a stock girl; and Walter Brennan, who had received an Academy Award and was very well known. But they were character actors who played supporting roles, and at that time, the star system was very strict in Hollywood: A film that cost a certain amount had to offer audiences a star, a young lead of some importance. Since I had refused, my film automatically fell into the category of films that were to be made with only a limited amount of money. They therefore asked me to stop shooting, and so I stopped shooting the film and went home. That night, I received a phone call from Zanuck, who said to me, "No, no Jean; of course they were kidding, but I'm taking responsibility for it. I explained to the board of directors that despite the added cost, you're going to continue the film." So the next morning I went back to continue shooting, and I received a show of affection that moved me tremendously, that shows that film people are really the same all over the world, and that they understand one another. When I arrived at the studio, at exactly 9 o'clock, which was the starting time of the shooting, I found the entire team in the middle of the set. Instead of being at their lights, the elec-

*It was Peverell Marley.

Swamp Water: Anne Baxter.

tricians were down below. The cameramen, the actors, the extras – everyone was there standing very formally, almost as if I were arriving at Elysée to visit the president of the republic, and when I opened the door, they all applauded me. There was a great deal of applause, and then we went to work. It was very nice.

I had another cameraman during this same film who was a very interesting young man, Lucien Ballard. He's an American Indian, and like a lot of American Indians, he has a French name, because in the eighteenth century, the French had close contacts with the Indians. Many of them lived with Indian tribes or in Indian territory, or married Indian women. There was a great Indian–French mix. Lucien Ballard was a marvelous person. Because he made a good living, he tried to help other Indians, who often are very unhappy living on the reservations. He brought me with him to a reservation, where we spent several days with the Hopi Indians, in an absolutely charming school, from which I brought back many watercolors done by young Indians, almost all of which had pictures of Santa Claus with a white beard.

CAHIERS: *Swamp Water* was very successful in the United States.

RENOIR: Yes, it was. Later, Zanuck often told me that. Several films came out that year, and five or six were big films with very big stars and had cost millions. But *Swamp Water* made much more money than any of them, and so they were very happy. Nonetheless, despite this good relationship, I didn't continue working at Fox.

Deanna, Koster, Saint-Exupéry

CAHIERS: Rumor has it you began shooting a film with Deanna Durbin.

RENOIR: Yes, after leaving Fox, Universal offered me this film. I met Deanna Durbin, and I liked her very much. She's a charming girl, and at that time she was going from being a young girl to being a woman. She had just gotten married, she was particularly ravishing, and I was very excited about it.

The reason I didn't finish the film is that Deanna Durbin was imprisoned by the genre that made her a success. It's a genre that I admire very much, and it was invented by someone whom you know well and who lived for a long time in Paris – Henry Koster. Koster was originally a script writer, and he's the one who had the idea for *Three Smart Girls*. It was a charming film, and he had really discovered an extraordinary genre for Deanna Durbin. Besides, when I started this film, I had asked to see all the Deanna Durbin films – and I must say there were a lot of them – and Koster's films were, of course, much better than the others. But I wasn't good at this genre, and so it was better for the film to be shot by people more familiar with it than I was. Deanna Durbin's success had literally saved Universal Pictures, which was close to bankruptcy when Koster arrived there with his ideas and shot Deanna, who was unknown at the time, in *Three Smart Girls*, which was an immediate success for them. Deanna Durbin had become as good as gold, and this film's script was once again the usual type.... Although – I repeat – I could have done things the way I wanted, but in the end, each decision was so important. Even a smile, a wink, was discussed by ten people around a green rug. It was difficult for me to work with so much seriousness.

CAHIERS: It was a little like changing the laws of the Byzantine mosaics.

RENOIR: Yes, something like that. After that, I wanted to shoot *Terre des hommes* (*Wind, Sand and Stars*). I still have some recorded conversations with Saint-Exupéry, by the way, mostly about literary subjects. We wanted to do this film, and we had established not really a script but a project, and we had found a style, a formula for making *Terre des hommes*. But I still couldn't interest anyone in the film, despite the book's success in the United States.

I must tell you that since then there has been a great turnabout – Zanuck did a great deal to make it happen: It was the agreement to shoot on location. When I arrived in Hollywood, everyone shot on sets. The idea of shooting on location came about with the war. When I wanted to do *Terre des hommes*, they were still in the intensive-studio stage, but this film had to be shot at the locations described in the book. I think that's the main reason that no one accepted it.

An extraordinary man

CAHIERS: That's when you decided to do *This Land Is Mine*, which was an independent production.

RENOIR: It's an independent production distributed by RKO. But note that the word *independent* is one of the many labels that indicates fifty different ways of making films in Hollywood. This film was independent in the sense that the studio left us in total peace, Nichols and myself, but it was financed by RKO and distributed by RKO, and we had to answer to the studio for the film's budget, its expenditures, and its results.

I must tell you that at that time RKO was directed by Charlie Korner, who was an extraordinary man. Unfortunately, he died, and I was very sorry about that. If Korner hadn't died, I think I would have done twenty films at RKO; I would have worked my whole life at RKO because he was an understanding man, a man who knew the film market, who understood the workings of it very well, but who allowed for experimentation just the same. In addition, the people who preceded him at RKO were also extraordinary people: They enabled experiments like *Citizen Kane*, which would have been impossible at any other studio. RKO was truly the center of the real Hollywood during the final years, until Korner's death, which was in 1946. Korner died while *The Woman on the Beach* was being filmed, and I finished it under the temporary heads of the studio.

CAHIERS: You produced *This Land Is Mine* in close collaboration with Dudley Nichols?

RENOIR: Very close, we wrote the script together, completely together; which is to say that we closed ourselves off in a small room – he, my wife who was helping us, and I, and we wrote everything, the three of us. At that time, Nichols didn't think about the stage setting. I was the one who made him think about it. He has since abandoned it once again, but at that time, he didn't want to get involved in camera angles. I was therefore alone on the set. At the same time, everything concerning the writing of the script, as well as the discussions with the set designers, we did together. By the way, I had brought Lourié from France with me to be the set designer.

CAHIERS: This film has a style rather different from that of your other American films.

RENOIR: Maybe with more action–reaction shots, fewer scenes filmed at length? Well, I'll tell you, this is a strange film. In order to talk about it you have to consider the period during which it was shot. It was shot during a period when many Americans allowed themselves to be influenced by a certain propaganda attempting to represent all of France as collaborationist. Therefore I did this film, which was not intended to be shown in France, but only in America, to suggest to Americans that daily life in an occupied country was not as easy as some people may have thought. I must say that the results were extraordinary, and I'm pleased. Not only did the film have a good shelf life, but I also received many letters of approval and many shows of affection and esteem for France. I think the film fulfilled its goal.

Nevertheless, because it was a bit of a propaganda film – I hate the word *propaganda*, but... in any case it was meant to persuade people of something. So I thought we'd better be cautious so as to be able to change the editing. Usually I am very certain of my editing on the set, and I take risks. That is another reason for my divorce from the large studios, because their method is not to take any risks, whereas I like to take them. If I know that I have to throw myself in the water and that it's either sink or swim; if I know I can't eventually save myself with editing tricks, I feel that I shoot my scene better. But in the large studios – once again for financial reasons; when a product is expensive, you must be sure it will satisfy the client – the only method is a secure method, and that is why you have to have shots, reaction shots, master shots, medium shots, so that with just a few retakes you can make almost another film if the editing doesn't work. I never did that. I did do it in *This Land Is Mine* because the stakes were too high. It seemed to me that I was somewhat responsible.... You know, many French people in the United States during the war indulged in patriotic talk that was totally incomprehensible, completely private and sometimes even a bit hostile, and I had the feeling that this wasn't the right way to represent our country. I therefore had a great responsibility, and so I adopted the mind-set of a large studio that wants to be very cautious, but for different reasons. I composed the film carefully; I wrote a shooting script as if it were a commercial film, so that if need be I could change it during the editing, and with the help of previews, I could find the correct dosage to produce the desired effect on the public I wanted to influence.

CAHIERS: When seeing *This Land Is Mine*, we couldn't help think of Daudet's "Monday Tales" and especially "The Last Class."

RENOIR: I thought of that. Listen, my first idea when I left France was to do a film about an exodus of children from Paris to the South. . . . In fact, I was thinking of [François Boyer's] *The Secret Game*,* but without the bit about the cemetery, of course; and then I thought that, with the children we would find to act in it, it wouldn't go over abroad. That is, we would have to use French children speaking French. A film like this therefore had to be done by established actors, who could artistically – which is to say, through their talent – translate certain feelings for the American public. I often talked about it with Charles Laughton, who is one of my good friends – we see each other constantly – and in retelling the tale by Daudet to each other, one day I thought of this story, which I wrote.

CAHIERS: In any case, that proves Daudet's effectiveness over the years.

RENOIR: Yes, it's astonishing.

CAHIERS: You also are said to have fathered a short film entitled *Salute to France*, which we have never seen.

RENOIR: Listen, I cannot say I was the father of *Salute to France*. I have done many films in my life, which were more or less propaganda films, to help various causes, or very often to help technicians who were my friends and who said to me: "We're doing such and such a film, come help us." As for *Salute to France*, a few friends were working at the Office of War Information in New York: Burgess Meredith, for example, and Philip Dunne, who is now a well-known writer – he did *The Robe*. They said to me, "You should come to the Office of War Information to help us do a film for American troops, to explain to them that in France people drink wine, that they do this, that they do that, so as to avoid conflicts (which were inevitable, in any case) and to explain what French people are like to the Americans who are going to land there." I then received an official invitation from the Office of War Information. I felt that I couldn't say no and that it was my way of doing my part for the American and French governments. I went there and participated in the film, but I didn't make it. There is a little of me in this film, very little.

The greatest director in the world

CAHIERS: We've now come to *The Southerner*, which I suppose marks the beginning of the independent producers.

*Later filmed by Clement as *Forbidden Games* (*Les Jeux interdits*) – CV.

Poster for *This Land is Mine.*

RENOIR: That's right. *The Southerner* was Robert Hakim's idea. One day he brought me a script that was . . . well, that wasn't very good. It was pretty much the standard script for large studios, and Hakim said to me, "I'd like to shoot this film with a very small budget." I read the script. To shoot it would have required millions. I told him this, and he believed me, but I added, "There are nevertheless some fantastic things in this story, and I would like to read the book" (because it was already an adaptation). So he brought me the book, which is charming. It's a series of short stories that take place in Texas, written by a fellow named Sessions Perry, about characters like those in *The*

Beulah Bondi, Betty Field, and Zachary Scott in *The Southerner.*

Southerner. The stories, however, are much more varied – you could make ten films from this book. And after reading it, I said to Hakim, "I'm interested in it, provided I can forget the first script and write another one." It happened that Hakim had proposed *The Southerner* to another producer, David Loew, which enabled me to become friends with this extraordinary character. He's really a wonderful man who was extremely courageous. So I wrote another script, which he liked, and said, "Okay, let's do it." I told him, "I'm warning you, I'm going to change it during the shooting." He said, "OK." I said to him, "Besides, I'd like you to come to the shootings; that way when I change it, we can talk about it together." He said, "I'd love to." He understood my work methods very well.

But when the script was given to the film's two stars, who were used to a very different type, they didn't mince their words. Even though they covered me with flowers, adored me, and said, "Oh, Jean, the greatest director in the world," and so forth, when I showed them my script, the compliments turned into criticisms and they told me, "We don't have to shoot a script like that, and we won't." So David Loew told them, "OK, you refuse. I couldn't care less. Jean and I will find somebody else." And once again, we chose some unknown actors, and we embarked on an adventure.

The film was supposed to be distributed by United Artists, but they told Loew, "We can't distribute it because you promised us a film with stars. Because there aren't any, you can keep it." Loew told them, "OK, I have a rather large share in about thirty films that you distribute, and I'll give them all to Columbia." So United Artists said, "In that case, we'll take *The Southerner*."

It's a film that I did with complete freedom, and right from the beginning it was a rather ambitious film. Of course it was more ambitious in Hollywood than it would have been here, because we had already told stories like that in France, and we'll continue to tell such stories. But at that time the war was on in America, and there was a kind of tacit understanding that Hollywood had to present a rather glamorous image of the United States to the world. In any case, the film wasn't shown in Europe. It came to France much later, by a bit of a fluke. United Artists hated the film. Because they had been forced to take it, they distributed it with little effort. Even so, it ended up making money. I know, because I had a share in the profits, and I received some money, so there must have been profits. In any case, the film currently belongs to David Loew and me. Right now, we're starting to show it on television.

Florence, Pisa, and Ravenna

CAHIERS: We may be wrong, but it seems to us that *The Southerner* marked the beginning of an evolution in your conception of film.

RENOIR: That's true – it's an extremely accurate idea – and for one simple reason: It was the end of the war. The liberation took place while I was shooting *Diary of a Chambermaid*, which I started a few weeks after *The Southerner*, and right away, new ideas started coming to me. . . . Many people considered this war to be just a war, but it was much more than a war; it was a veritable revolution, an absolutely uncontrolled reshaping of the world. I think that people will be separated much more by civilization than by nation. I don't mean that nations will disappear. Nations existed in the Middle Ages; in fact, there were more of them. For example, instead of Italy there was Florence, Pisa, and Ravenna, but the citizens of Ravenna, Pisa, or Florence were first and foremost part of a civilization, the Western Christian civilization. They were Roman Christians and represented certain ideas that were a continuation of Greek ideas altered by the Christian revolution altered by the Roman organization and altered especially by the beginning of the Middle Ages. The divisions among nations were much weaker than the division by interest, by profession, or by intellectual tendency. For example, a medieval clerk – a man whose profession it was to be educated, to try to learn – was not specifically an Italian or a French intellectual but, rather, an intellectual who belonged to the great Western civilization. This clerk was therefore just as much at home at the University of Bologna as at Caen or Oxford. The first great French work known to us – there may have been others that haven't been preserved – the only version known to us of the *Song of Roland* (the one that was translated into modern French by Bédier) was written at Oxford. It could just as well have been written in Milan. In the Western world, there was a kind of international society of intellectuals, and there were also international societies for other interests. For example, a cooper was a cooper belonging to this Western world. He was a cooper in Nuremberg as well as in Bordeaux, and he traveled, by foot, from Nuremberg to Bordeaux and then continued down to Sicily.

I have the feeling that this kind of interpenetration awaits us. I believe this. But it doesn't prevent me from believing even more in local influences than in national ones. I think that it's a mistake, for example, to make a film in Provence that is supposed to take place in Paris. One should make Provençal films in Provence and Parisian films in Paris. To repeat what I said before – and we have proof of this even after the Middle Ages – I think that the origin of the artist is only of secondary importance to the work he creates. Soil is so strong that it naturalizes you, not in a few years, but in a few weeks. Benvenuto Cellini, who worked on Fontainebleau, or Leonardo da Vinci, remained Italian, yet there is something in the works they did for the kings of France that makes them French works. I feel that we are going to return to this kind of international society, in certain professions in any case, and that it was a more arbitrary desire that separated people.

In the meantime, I don't know whether this is good or bad. Personally, I think I'd feel comfortable in a world divided in such a fashion, but I'm probably the only one who thinks this way today, because nationalism has almost never been so strong. Minor details, the most secondary events, are suddenly translated into a waving flag. I believe that these somewhat ridiculous manifestations are precisely the last signs of a dying nationalism and that we will eventually have worldwide categories. That's not to say that there will be only one world, as Mr. [Wendell] Willkie said, but in any case the world we will know will probably be larger, vaster, and wider than our childhood world, which was limited to our borders. I remember when I was a kid (and I assure you the world was much smaller than when you were young yourselves), when I went to my village school in Bourgogne, we didn't think there was anything worth knowing beyond our borders. Besides, we naturalized everything in good faith. For example, I was convinced – until I was at least twelve years old – that Mozart was French, simply because I had seen some prints of engravings that showed him playing the harpsichord for Marie Antoinette, and I had come to the conclusion that because he was playing the harpsichord at Versailles, he must be French.

The sympathizers

So I believe that if we think in this way, if we think in terms of being citizens of the motion picture culture before thinking of ourselves as citizens of such and such a nation, it will change our attitude toward film more and more. It will also allow us to create certain kinds of film for a certain public, for specialized audiences. I think that this kind of film will be better and will be possible because it will be shown in several countries. It will therefore be able to pay for the cost of making it – not as a result of large audiences in one place, but because of smaller audiences in many places. I truly hope that this will come about, because I'm convinced that film is a more secret art than the so-called private arts. We think that painting is private, but film is much more so. We think that a film is made for the six thousand moviegoers at the Gaumont-Palace, but that isn't true. Instead, it's made for only three people among those six thousand. I found a word for film lovers; it's *aficionados*. I remember a bullfight that took place a long time ago. I didn't know anything about bullfights, but I was there with people who were all very knowledgeable. They became delirious with excitement when the toreador made a slight movement like that toward the right, and then he made another slight movement, also toward the right – which seemed the same to me – and everyone yelled at him. I was the one who was wrong. I was wrong to go to a bullfight without knowing the rules of the game. One must always know the rules of the game.

The same thing happened to me again. I have some cousins in America who come from North Dakota. In North Dakota, everyone ice-skates, because for six months of the year there's so much snow that it falls horizontally instead of vertically. It's cold; everything is frozen; and everyone there skates very well. Every time my cousins meet me, they take me to an ice show. They take me to see some women on ice skates who do lots of tricks. It's always the same thing: From time to time you see a woman who does a very impressive twirl: I applaud, and then I stop, seeing that my cousins are looking at me severely, because it seems that she wasn't good at all, but I had no way of knowing. And film is like that as well. And all professions are for the benefit of – well – not only for aficionados but also for the sympathizers. In reality, there must be sympathizers, there must be a brotherhood.

Besides, you've heard about Barnes. His theory was very simple: The qualities, the gifts, or the education that painters have are the same gifts, education, and qualities that lovers of painting have. In other words, in order to love a painting, one must be a would-be painter, or else you cannot really love it. And to love a film, one must be a would-be filmmaker. You have to be able to say to yourself, "I would have done it this way, I would have done it that way." You have to make films yourself, if only in your mind, but you have to make them. If not, you're not worthy of going to the movies.

Aristotle and Plato

This idea of the world about which I've spoken to you inspired me to travel to India. It convinced me that if I can lovingly apply myself to the exploits of a fisherman on the Ganges, then maybe I can also identify with him because I am a man of the cinema, and though a foreigner, I am still the brother of the man of the cinema who works in Calcutta, and there is no reason I can't talk about the Ganges as he does.

CAHIERS: It seems you are seeking greater conciseness, greater density.

RENOIR: That's right, a greater density in the location. Right now I am trying to forget ideas, formulas, and theories, but at the same time I am trying to identify with the only thing that remains truly solid after all these turnabouts, catastrophes, and stupidities that we have witnessed, and this one thing is our civilization. God knows I adore India, and I admire Hinduism; I know a little about the Hindu religion, which is fascinating to study. Yet I think that if I want to work properly, I would be better off reading Aristotle and Plato, and following in the wake of all the people who are in my situation, whether in Washington, Oxford, Palermo, or Lyons. That is, following Greek civilization, by way of Christian civilization.

CAHIERS: In essence, you seek a certain classicism?

RENOIR: Exactly.

In total freedom

CAHIERS: Your next film, *Diary of a Chambermaid*, was rather poorly received in France.

RENOIR: Very poorly.

CAHIERS: As far as we're concerned, it's very good, and we might even prefer it to *The Rules of the Game*.

RENOIR: I'm very proud of it. Oh, you know what I'll ask you to do? Since you feel this way, some day, if you don't mind, let's get together and send a note to Paulette Goddard; she'll be pleased because she feels the same way; she likes the film very much.

CAHIERS: It was a rather old project.

RENOIR: It was a very old project that had been completely changed, because I made it at the beginning of the period when I envisioned scenes in a more concentrated, more theatrical manner, with fewer action–reaction shots. I envisioned the scenes more as small vignettes added one to the other. My first attempt was during the silent era, and I conceived of it, at that time, in a very romantic way, very *Nana*-esque.

CAHIERS: The scenes in the servants' quarters in *Nana*, in fact...

RENOIR: Well, listen, each person embodies all that he will do later in life, which changes all the time. Obviously, no one knows what one will do tomorrow, but it is likely that a shrewder observer than ourselves would see it in us. The possibility is certainly there. Anyway I went back to this project because I wanted to make a film with Paulette Goddard. In fact, I was looking for a part for her, and I thought she would be very good in the role of Celestine. That's the only reason.

It was an independent production. Burgess Meredith, a few friends, and I were a small group of associates. Benedict Bogeaus found the money. He was the owner of an independent studio that works like the studios in France. That is, it rents its sites to individual producers and doesn't even have a sound department; you have to rent the sound nearby, at Western Electric. It's a studio like the old ones in Hollywood. In any case, it's a very old, charming studio, called General Service. Bogeaus was the owner, and he had connections that enabled us to find a small down payment and the necessary bank loans to make the film. It's also a film that was shot in total freedom and with a great deal of improvisation.

CAHIERS: And yet a few years ago, many people in France said, "Jean Renoir wasn't able to do what he wanted, he was bullied."

RENOIR: No, not at all. This film may be good or bad, but if it's bad, I alone am responsible for it. Notice that I was influenced – I'm the most easily influenced man in the world – because people say, "You may be wrong in doing that; why are you doing it?" And then, well, you tell yourself that maybe they're right, and you're cautious. Obviously, you can be influenced in good ways or bad ways, but that's true of all films. Even if you do films the way Chaplin did, with his own money, without making any concessions to anyone else's interests, you're still influenced.... But I repeat, I always did what I wanted to in Hollywood, and if I made mistakes there, I would have made the same ones in Paris.

CAHIERS: Is it true that the final lynch scene was entirely improvised on the set?

Paulette Goddard and Judith Anderson in *The Diary of a Chambermaid*.

RENOIR: Naturally it was improvised, it wasn't in the script, but it's not the only improvised scene; there are many of them.

CAHIERS: It seems as if you're seeking a mounting climax in this film. You're trying, as they say, to go all out.

RENOIR: Yes, of course, and I was interested in seeing an actress work toward this, an actress who doesn't normally do this in her films and whom I like very much. She's an extraordinary working companion, a really good associate, and so I wanted to push her in this direction. . . . I also wanted to do scenes that were almost sketches, to leave them undeveloped, to simplify them to an extreme. I wanted them to be like sketches or rough drafts.

Preview in Santa Barbara

CAHIERS: Finally we come to *The Woman on the Beach*, a film in which you met with a few difficulties, so they say.

RENOIR: It was quite an adventure. It's a film that one of my friends, Joan Bennett, asked me to do. She said to me, "RKO has asked me to do a film; come do it with me." RKO also asked me. I had been very happy with this studio, and I was pleased to go back. At the beginning, the producer of the film must have been Val Lewton. I'll say a few words about Val Lewton, because he was an extremely interesting person. Unfortunately he died several years ago. He was one of the first, maybe the first, to have had the idea of making inexpensive films, films using the budget allocated to B pictures, but with a certain amount of ambition, with high-quality scripts that tell higher-caliber stories than was typical. Not that I don't like B pictures. In principle I like them better than the grand, pretentious, psychological, big-budget films; they're much more fun. Whenever I go to the movies in America, I go to see B pictures. First, because they demonstrate Hollywood's high technical quality. In order to make a good western in one week, as they do at Monogram – to start it on Monday and finish it on Saturday – believe me, you have to have extraordinary technical capacities. And the adventure films are done just as quickly. I also think that the B pictures are often better than the so-called important films, because they are done so quickly that the director is necessarily free: There's no time to watch over him.

Val Lewton, then, gave RKO a list of films that were inexpensive but that told more ambitious stories. I'll name one, a successful one that was done with Tourneur's son [Jacques] and that starred Simone Simon: *Cat People*. It was a very good story and a very good film. Anyway, Val Lewton very kindly helped me begin *The Woman on the Beach*, and then he had other projects that conformed better to his list and in which he was probably more interested, so I found myself all alone. I was practically my own producer, in association with a friend, named Gross, for the practical side of things. In fact, I was entirely responsible for *The Woman on the Beach*. No one interfered, and I was able to do exactly what I wanted. I have never shot a film for which so little was written, which was so improvised on the set. I took advantage of the situation to try something that I had wanted to do for a long time: a film based on what we call today *sex* – maybe we called it sex then, but we talked about it less – but envisioned from a purely physical perspective. I wanted to try to tell a love story based purely on physical attraction, a story in which emotions played no part. I did it and I was very pleased with it. It may have been a slow film, but it had some rather strong scenes. It was acted admirably by Robert Ryan, whom you know – you saw him in Wise's *The Set-Up* and in many other films, but this was his first important part – and Joan Bennett, who was wonderful.

The directors of RKO, the actors, and I all were very happy with the film, but we had some doubts about the public's reaction to it, so we all agreed to show some previews. We showed them, mainly in Santa Barbara, to a very young audience, mostly students. They reacted very poorly to the film; they weren't interested in it at all. I felt that my way of presenting these sentimental questions shocked them, or maybe it didn't correspond to what they were used to. In any case, the film was very poorly received, and we returned to the studio very depressed.

You know, a preview is a horrible test. You sit in a theater, and it's as if someone were stabbing you with knives all over your body. I must admit to having been very discouraged after returning from this preview, and I was the first to suggest cutting and changing the film. The film had been rather expensive, because to achieve this somewhat different style, I had to work slowly. Joan Bennett kindly lent herself to what was almost a personality change. I even asked her to change her voice. I worked to lower its tone – she had a rather high pitched voice, and in this film she had a low voice – all that took time, therefore money, and I was the first to fear a financial catastrophe for the film, to feel responsible, and to become a little crazy. The studio graciously offered, "OK, we'll make changes, but you'll make them." I asked for a writer to help me so that I wouldn't be alone, so that we could talk and bounce ideas back and forth. At the same time, Joan Bennett's husband, Walter Wanger, also came to see a screening and to give me his opinion. In sum, it seemed to me at the time that I didn't have the right to take all the responsibility for the film by myself. I think, by the way, that I was wrong and that this fear didn't help the film.

So I went back to a number of scenes very cautiously, that is, to

The Woman on the Beach: Joan Bennett.

about a third of the film, essentially the scenes between Joan Bennett and Robert Ryan, and I finally released a film that I think was rather middle-of-the-road, which had lost its reason for existing. I think I allowed myself to be influenced too much by the preview at Santa Barbara, which was decisive. All of a sudden I was afraid of losing contact with the public, and I gave in. But once again, the people who criticize this film should not criticize the influences on me. I'm responsible for the changes, just as I was responsible for the film beforehand.

The truth is I think I tried something that would have worked today. If I were to shoot *The Woman on the Beach* now, in America, with the ideas I had in mind when I made it, I think it would work. I'm afraid I was ahead of the public.

Deep-sea fishing

CAHIERS: You were saying that you were looking for a certain style.

RENOIR: The word *style* is rather ambitious. What I wanted, without using that exact word, was to suggest that my characters were very physically in love, and to express this idea with different words, with very ordinary words, for example, with memories. Thus Joan Bennett recounted her childhood memories and spoke of a certain Italian professor who had taught her music, and these very common memories were told in such a way as to suggest a mutual desire by both Joan Bennett and Bob Ryan. These things, of course, are very difficult to express, and it took time. Another thing is that it's the kind of film that requires facial expressions that the audience can easily grasp, and that calls for many close-ups, and close-ups take time in film and are expensive.

CAHIERS: There's the cigarette scene, for example. I personally would be unable to pinpoint what makes it so remarkable.

RENOIR: It's probably because of the quality of the actors in the close-ups. It's also a scene in which the conversation has no relationship to the interior action. The conversation in the scene you mentioned is about deep-sea fishing. God knows no one there could care less about deep-sea fishing, but anyway, they talk about it. In the meantime, the only question in the mind of the new guest, the man who desires Joan Bennett, is "Is that man blind or not?" That's all, but it isn't said.

PART TWO

Add a few maharajas

JEAN RENOIR: After *The Woman on the Beach*, I was confused. I realized that this film hadn't touched the public as I had wanted, and I had many more projects. For instance, I had formed a small company with a few friends, which I called the Film Group, and I wanted to try to shoot classical plays on a small budget. I wanted to create a kind of film revival using young stage actors' groups that had been very successful in Hollywood at the time, not financially successful, but very respected. Moreover, these theatrical enterprises were valuable in America. There were many of them: notably the Circle, which operated out of the first floor of an old house. Because there was no stage, they placed the audience around the actors, as in a miniature circus. These different groups performed all the time, and their actors, their members, were often very interesting. I therefore had the idea – with many rehearsals and working with classics or with good modern texts – of trying to create a kind of classical American film. I must admit that I didn't succeed, and for one simple reason: Bank loans started to become more and more difficult to obtain, and because this was a new enterprise, the American banks were less amenable to taking a risk than they might have been one year earlier when all films were making money. I don't know if I told you what my friend Charles Korner said to me one day, shaking his head, "Jean, all films are making money these days, even good ones." Those days were gone.

Seeing that things weren't going to work out, I started thinking about other things. One day, by chance, in the book section of the *New Yorker*, I read a review of a book by an English author, a woman named Rumer Godden, and the name of the book was *The River*. The review said something like this: In terms of its language, it was probably one of the best books written in English over the past fifty years, and it added that the book would most likely not make a cent. It was encouraging enough for me to go out and buy the book. I went to a bookstore right away, bought it, read it, and I was immediately convinced that it was a top-notch film subject. I wrote to Mrs. Godden through my agents, so that everything would be done by the rules, and she agreed to sell me an option on the book. At the same time, I wrote to her saying that I thought her subject was a tremendous inspiration for a film but was not a film story, and so she would have to rewrite it with me, change the events and maybe even the characters, while keeping the general idea of the story, which, in my opinion, had the makings of a great film. She agreed, and I found myself with an option on *The River*. Then I went to see lots of people, but I wasn't able to interest anyone in my project.... Because to many people, a film on India means charging cavalries, tiger hunts, elephants, and maharajas. People said to me, "Now if you could add a few maharajas and a few tiger hunts, it would be a beautiful story, but we think that people who go to see a film on India expect something else. After all, we do have to give the public what it wants."

Pandit Nehru's niece

In the meantime, I didn't get discouraged, and this is what happened: A man who wasn't involved in films wanted to make them and had found a group that could finance him in India. What he lacked was any knowledge of film, a subject, and a director. He knew people in the Indian government, and it happened that one day he had a conversation with, I think, Pandit Nehru's niece, who told him, "You know, making a film in India isn't easy for a Westerner. If you want to shoot an Indian subject, you might fall flat on your face and say things that aren't true. If I were you, I would start by making a film in which there were some Westerners. This would permit a director capable of understanding India to establish a kind of bridge between India and Western audiences." And she added, "As far as I'm concerned, the English author who knows India the best today is Rumer Godden. She wasn't born in India, but she came here when she was a few months old, she grew up here, she speaks some Indian languages, and she knows India as if it were her own country." This gentleman was very impressed and inquired about *The River*, asked if he could buy the rights, and came to me because of my option. He asked me, "Do you want to do *The River* with me?" I told him, "Yes, but on one condition: You have to send me to India so that I can find out whether I can really do something interesting." So I took my first trip to India, and I was convinced. I returned with a great passion for the country. I wrote the script with Rumer Godden – we rewrote it on location, by the way, while we were shooting – and that's how I shot *The River*. Very roughly, this was the practical story of it.

CAHIERS: So Rumer Godden was with you.

RENOIR: She was with me during the shooting, and she watched two-thirds of it. She helped me both decide on the script and rewrite a story that is different from the book, and of which she is the author as much as I am. She also helped me with many other things. For example, we used many inexperienced actors, especially for the leading role, the little Harriet, who is an English girl we found at the school in Calcutta. I must say that the professional actors I had in *The River* also helped a great deal with these inexperienced ones. We had to train them. I don't believe in total inexperience, I don't believe in luck, I believe that everything is learned. In the villa that you see in the film, which was our headquarters, our everything, we set up a little acting school and even a dance school, because Rumer Godden was a dance teacher. We had to teach these young actors and actresses a new profession. She helped me give a professional side to these young people's acting.

The Indian scale

After the film was shot, the producer and I were, of course, wondering how it would be received. My last experience had been *The Woman on the Beach*, and the poor reception at the previews had been a great surprise to me. So I asked myself if we weren't going to have a problem with a subject that, according to some very intelligent people who know their profession in Hollywood, doesn't give an audience inter-

Jean Renoir during the filming of *The River*.

ested in India what it wants. The India that I was supposedly showing in this film was – how can I say – a bit colorless. Because of all this, I wanted to be cautious, and as I worked on the editing, I constantly monitored the audiences' reactions. I screened it in an old studio in Hollywood – now almost entirely used for television – called Hal Roach. Hal Roach was a place for pioneers; the first comical films were shot there. It has a very large screening room with more than a hundred seats – it started to feel like a real audience – and I gathered people in this room quite often, people purposely chosen from certain categories. From time to time, for example, I had people who worked in industry, in the neighboring factories, or sometimes people who worked in business, in the shops in Beverly Hills, or professional people, designers, and, once in a while, very mixed groups. At each step of my editing, I showed the film to small groups like that.

This was all the more dangerous a test because the cutting copy was in black and white, although it was shot in color. I made up for that sometimes by showing certain color samples, either before or after. I had what are called *pilots*, which Technicolor sends to help you imagine what the film will be like while you're editing it. You could print the work print all in color, of course, but it would be very expensive, and you save an enormous amount when you do the editing in black and white. In addition, it's an especially ugly black and white, since it's printed from one of the three color separation negatives. It therefore lacks some of the values, other colors aren't visible at all, it's not even orthochromatic [lacks red]; altogether, it's quite disappointing.

I was very worried about one thing: the music. I was lucky enough to make many friends in India, especially with young film people, technicians, journalists, or actors, who introduced me to the Calcutta art world, and especially to the music world where I was able to meet some very good musicians. In addition, I had a wonderful adviser in *The River* in regard to India: Radha, the dancer who plays the role of the half-Indian, though in reality she's a pure Brahmin. Anyway, she plays the role of a half-caste. And obviously, as a dancer, she was familiar with music, especially that from the South (she's from Madras). So, on the one hand from my friends in Calcutta, and, on the other hand through Radha for the South, I was able to understand something about this music and to hear a good deal of it. And with the help of these friends, I was able to tape some exceptional Indian music, very classic, very pure, and not at all influenced by Western thought. The music in Indian films is often very bad. Indian producers think they will make a hit by adapting European instruments and often by forgetting the old Indian scale. You know that the Indian scale – like that of European music in the Middle Ages, before all the great revolutions brought on by Bach and the seventeenth-century Italians – had between forty and seventy notes, or even more; it was infinite. Indian music is still like that, and many Indian producers don't hesitate to rewrite old songs on the modern scale, with modern instruments, which are, so they say, more vivid, but it's very contrived in my opinion. It winds up sounding like fake Mexican music, and it's not very good. I therefore avoided that. But the music I used is unusual just the same, and I wondered how European and American audiences would react to it. My previews helped me a great deal here, as I tried mixing the dialogue and this music.

A counterbalance

I must say that the previews helped me establish a bridge to the public more easily, but right from the beginning I realized that I hadn't been wrong about *The River*. The reactions were good right from the start: People were engrossed in my characters but had varied reactions. From time to time we had them fill out questionnaires, and the responses were very different. Part of the audience was interested in the English people in India and saw in them a picture of themselves had they been there; others, on the contrary, were interested only in the life-style of the natives. It soon became clear that there were different topics of interest in this film and that I could "go ahead"; so I opened the flood gates and asked the producer not to make any musical recordings for the film, following the modern principle that music underlines the images. In any case, I'm against that, I think the music should act to counterbalance the film, I'm against having it repeat the action and sentiments. The producer accepted this, and even the European music was taken from classical pieces, [von Weber's] *Invitation to the Dance*, for example. I also used some piano airs by Schumann, a little air by Mozart somewhere.

Anyway, the question of the music had worried me a great deal, and these previews helped me confirm my opinion. They were very valuable, especially because they gave me the courage to make the film as a whole as I had conceived of it, as I saw it, and as Rumer Godden and I had imagined it. The editing was done in the same way: My first previews were very cautious. In my first cut, I simply tried to follow the film's action. Then, little by little, I understood that it was a film in which I could allow myself to add a few purely poetic morsels that had no relationship with what we call the action, for example, the passage on the stairs, which I liked very much but which I dared to insert only when I had finished the editing. So to a large extent because of the moral support that these audiences gave me, *The River* is a film that fully represents what I had imagined at the beginning.

Breaking down the walls

CAHIERS: In what way was the adaptation of Rumer Godden's novel different from the novel?

RENOIR: I can tell you the biggest difference in two words: We decided to make the film much more Indian. In Godden's novel, which is marvelous, India penetrates the walls of the house, though you never go there. We decided to break down the walls. The part of the Indian half-caste didn't exist in the novel, either; it's an invention of ours that permitted us to bring more of India into the story.

CAHIERS: This character in a sense symbolizes the main subject of the film, that is, the relationship between two civilizations.

RENOIR: Absolutely. I symbolize the theme in this character; it exists in the novel, but in a completely different manner. That is, it exists through the thousand little relationships that Harriet, the heroine of the film and the novel, has, and through the different servants in the house, through the people who come to the house, and through many short conversations, but not through a specific fact like that of being a half-caste. India penetrates the walls of the house by means of a thousand minor details and by means of Harriet. But Harriet, like Rumer Godden in real life (because Harriet is Rumer Godden; it's an autobiography, and this shows up in the film), Harriet is very influenced by India, and Rumer is very influenced by India. Her last book is the story of a voyage she took during the last war in Kashmir, and it is fantastic. She has very deep roots in the country. She lives in England now, but I wouldn't be surprised if she were to return to India.

Death and resurrection

CAHIERS: Which brings us to a question about another aspect of the film, Westerners' understanding of Indian religion and philosophy.

RENOIR: That also is in the novel and in other novels by Rumer. It is especially apparent in a magnificent novel called *Breakfast with the Nikolides*. The Nikolides are Greek neighbors – there are many Greeks in the jute industry in Calcutta – and there is a character in the novel who is very influenced by Hindu philosophy. Harriet is almost the only person in *The River* who is influenced by it. Now in real life, the Westerners can be divided into two categories: those who consider anything Hindu, Indian, or Muslim to be extremely inferior, not even worth thinking about, and who manage, while in India, to reconstruct a purely English, or purely French, or purely Greek life, although the Greeks mix in much more easily. On the other hand, there are those who allow themselves to be absorbed, and they are also very numerous. In the film, the English family is neither one nor the other, which also is possible. They obviously remain completely English, but at the same time they know that the Hindu civilization exists, which is the position of many Englishmen.

CAHIERS: It is, in a sense, a kind of Western meditation on Asia?

RENOIR: Exactly, and it would have been very difficult to do anything else during my first contact with India; I would have risked going completely astray. I had to see India through the eyes of a Westerner if I didn't want to make some horrible mistakes.

CAHIERS: Is it through this contact with India that you became aware of the theme of "acceptance," which has been appearing more and more clearly in your films?

RENOIR: Not really. This is my own theme, but India could not have helped but develop it. The main idea of the Hindu religion – let's not say religion, because it's not exactly a religion, let's say philosophy or Hindu metaphysics – is that the world is one. We're part of it, we're part of the world just as a tree or your tape recorder is. That doesn't imply an acceptance, as in the Muslim tradition, which is fatalistic. No, it's an empowerment. But nonetheless, you can't go back to what has been done. In other words, for example, there is no remission of sin. For them the remission of sin is just like saying that if you cut off your arm, you can glue it back on. It's obviously very impressive; it's a kind of understanding of the meaning of everything that happens. It's a religion that comprehends the world, but it isn't fatalistic; it's a philosophy.

In any case, I must say that Rumer and I were extremely influenced by Radha. Radha is quite a person, she has a master's degree in Sanskrit, and she reads Sanskrit as easily as she reads English or several Indian languages. She's a very educated girl, and she comes from a good family, which means a lot in India, where studying is a tradition. It doesn't mean that she is morally or physically superior to people of other castes. Besides, the idea of superiority from caste to caste doesn't exist in India. What does exist is the idea of specialization. The truth is that the Hindu caste system is a bit like a hereditary union: You belong to a certain union, but you belong to it for four thousand years. That's the difference: You can escape it only by death or resurrection, since death and resurrection are quite common. Radha, with her knowledge of her country, her religion, and the West, was therefore an extraordinary associate, with incredible perception and intelligence. I would have loved to do other things with her as an actress. Maybe you noticed this: At the beginning, when she comes home from school with a little European outfit, doesn't she remind you of the very good Russian actresses? She makes me think of a young Nazimova. Yes, you could do wonders with her, only this is a difficult profession, everything takes so long. Getting a new project going takes years, times passes. But filmmaking is not a convenient profession, and circumstances may never allow me to return to India. There is one other problem. Because *The River* worked so well, now everyone is shooting in India. India is full of producers and directors from all countries.

Jean Renoir, Radha Shri Ran, Patricia Walters, and Adrienne Cori during the filming of *The River*.

The forced pauses

CAHIERS: Did you plan the script's structure in detail?

RENOIR: No, we both agreed to leave the structure rather loose during the shooting. I shot it so that I could either create a narration, that is, stay with a booklike tone or else not tell the story and not have any commentary at all. During the little previews, when I saw that the documentary side got good reactions (let's say the poetic side), I decided to go with the seminarrated form, which permitted me to present certain purely poetic parts without having to back them up with dramatic action and dialogue. But the construction of the script was rather loose, rather easy, and allowed for the two solutions. When I shot these poetic passages, I thought I would use them as they were, but I wasn't sure it would work, and if it hadn't worked, I would have had to shorten them enormously and integrate them into the action scenes.

So I shot the film very cautiously, but this caution did not apply to the scenes. I'm never cautious with my scenes. You know that the main system of film production, all over the world, whether in Paris or in Hollywood, is what they call "taking precautions, being covered." It's like in the army, where you have to have an order in writing before sweeping a courtyard, to ensure that it isn't a prank. The way you cover yourself in film is by taking many shots of a scene, so that you can either lengthen it or shorten it. I wasn't any more cautious in this respect in *The River* than I am in other films. Many of my scenes are shot in one single take and must be used as they are; they can't be cut. No, my precaution was having enough material for the editing so that I could use a commented style or a noncommented style for the overall outline of the film.

CAHIERS: There is still another aspect of *The River:* its metaphorical, or symbolic, side, which I am unable to define clearly, but many images, for example, the recurring one in which three boats come together, make one think of a meaning other than their immediate one.

RENOIR: It's obvious that not only I but also most of my collaborators, and especially my Hindu collaborators, had our minds off in that direction and that solutions of this type constantly came to mind, so that often it was intentional. Not that it was planned, but it was intended in the sense that we were attracted by this kind of mental exercise, and we were extremely open to such solutions.

CAHIERS: Thus, the stairway sequence...

RENOIR: That one was entirely intentional, and for a good reason: The sequence is an edited piece, which means I did it at the end, when I was much surer about my principles. Don't forget something that I repeat all the time: You discover the content of a film as you're shooting it. You obviously start with guiding principles that are as firm as possible, but when the subject is worthwhile, each step is a discovery, and this discovery brings others, and so a subject... That's perhaps the main thing about film, which is why certain films have become so important to the history of cinema, to the history of culture and modern civilization. It's that the film medium carries technical obstacles that make it a slow means of expression (you can't shoot a film quickly), and this battle with technical obstacles forces you – more than in any other medium – to discover and to rediscover. You benefit from forced pauses that a writer would be obliged to impose on himself. The halts, the delays, are very good for the quality of a film, and this one was greatly strengthened by them.... To begin with, I had a lucky break: We were supposed to start on a certain date, but the camera blimp, the sound insulation for the cameras, hadn't arrived, so in order to avoid problems for the producer, I had to start filming certain things without sound, and so the camera noise didn't matter. It was a delay, but this delay helped me, because whatever I filmed in this way was purely documentary. It therefore forced me, before starting the film's real scenes, to get more in touch with the country by means of the documentary, and this did me a great deal of good.

One, two, three

CAHIERS: After seeing *The River*, one cannot help being struck by something that also appears in many of your other films, but in a less apparent way: the predominance of the number three.

RENOIR: That's not something I owe to India. I owe it more to my admiration for early films in which the number three was a kind of magic number. I don't know whether you've noticed it, for example, in Mack Sennett's comedies. It's also a very old music-hall and café-concert theory. In Mack Sennett's comedies, the gag generally worked only the third time, and so I guess that film's early directors tended to use this number three. I was brought up on the films from this period, and I still admire them greatly. I obviously must have been influenced by them; they were my film education. But, you know, the slightly ridiculous actors of the great romantic period, at whom everyone laughs today but who carried some weight with the public, believed in the number three. I'll always remember, when my brother was very young and was beginning to think of an acting career, and to get practice in it (it was before he went to the conservatory), he took lessons with an old romantic actor who could no longer take roles, who was crumbling with old age and who, from time to time, came to our house in Montmartre to give lessons to this young man who wanted to pursue a career. I remember the following bit of advice very well: "In the *Tour de*

Nesle you have this line: 'It was the noble head of an old man that the assassin often saw in his dreams, because he assassinated him'; here you count: one, two, three, and you say, 'the villain.' "

CAHIERS: So you use this kind of construction as a springboard, in a sense.

RENOIR: I don't think I used it intentionally, but I saw so many films from the beginning that it probably became almost automatic. Besides, I think we should use every technical and practical means, but we must be sure of them, and apply them instinctively when they're convenient.

CAHIERS: We don't want you to tell us your professional secrets.

RENOIR: I don't have any. That would be very difficult, I couldn't talk about it. No, I think that the only secret – which is very convenient in our profession, as in others, and which helps a great deal – is to try to see and to fill yourself with good things. If you're a playwright, better to read Shakespeare and Molière than to read... an inferior writer. In film, it's the same thing, and I was very lucky to start loving films and to want to make them at a time when they were really good. One can honestly say that the bad films were the exceptions. This was because it was a primitive period and the primitives have an easier time doing good work than do people who have the advantage of better technology.

Classical Italy

CAHIERS: *The Golden Coach* was also an old project.

RENOIR: Yes, but the *The Golden Coach* that I filmed has nothing to do with this very, very old project. I had thought of it in the days of silent films, and I saw it as a kind of great adventure story. It no longer corresponded to my ideas at that time, and when I was asked to film it (I wasn't the one who had the idea for *The Golden Coach* at the time, it was also one of the producer's old projects), when I went to shoot it – I was, in any case, convinced that it would be shot in France. I didn't know it was an Italian project – I agreed to do it because I was very interested in Magnani. Having seen her in many films, I was convinced – despite her usual appearance and her reputation as more of a romantic, naturalist actress – I was convinced that I might be able to make a move toward classicism. It was my pilot film. An admiration for classical Italy replaced India for me in *The Golden Coach*, the Italy from before Verdi and romanticism.

CAHIERS: Which in the film is expressed by Vivaldi's music.

RENOIR: That's right. My first draft was without Vivaldi; I owe Vivaldi to a friend.... You know, when you work in a country, you have to allow yourself to be absorbed by the country, or else you have no chance of doing something correctly; and the character who played the role in *The Golden Coach* that Radha played in India was a director, my assistant for the film, whose name is Giulio Macchi. Macchi is not only very intelligent, he is also a very cultivated man, and he's the one who pushed me to Vivaldi. I hadn't begun the shooting script yet, nor the treatment, and I only had some vague ideas as to how I wanted to handle it. I bought all the Vivaldi records I could find. There was a composer at the Panaria Company who generally took care of the music in the company's films, and I asked him to help me get to know Vivaldi better. You know, Vivaldi is still unknown, his manuscripts are being discovered every day. It's incredible what he did. Just played on the piano, this music made me hear things I had never known, and Vivaldi's influence obviously had a tremendous influence on the writing of the final shooting script.

CAHIERS: But in what way did Vivaldi's music influence you?

RENOIR: It influenced the entire style of the film, a side that isn't drama, that isn't farce, that isn't burlesque. It's a sort of irony that I tried to combine with the light spiritedness one finds, for example, in Goldoni.

CAHIERS: That's almost what you had looked for in *The Rules of the Game*, but I suppose in a very different manner, since many admirers of that film were disturbed by *The Golden Coach*.

RENOIR: Luckily, we are constantly discovering things in life, and I think that little by little, as I grow older, I rediscover things that I unconsciously knew all along.

The Medicis brought forks

CAHIERS: Because of Italy . . .

RENOIR: What happened in Italy is extremely important. Italy, in my mind, is perhaps first and foremost the active symbol of a particular civilization. I told you of my interest in, my love for India. Nonetheless, I remain a member of a particular community. Italy happens to have transmitted the elements of the civilization to which we belong. You can go anywhere, to any world capital, but you will notice that although London, for example, is essentially an English city, most of its monuments were built by Italian architects. The Italians influenced our entire civilization. If we eat with forks, it's because the Medicis brought them to France; if our chairs are a certain shape, it's because we imitated the Florentines at a certain period.

That said, I don't think that Italians are important as Italians per se. Rather, I think they are important because of their geographical placement (their country was the center of the Roman Empire, which brought together all the elements of our civilization). They could gather together all the different parts of this civilization and then spread them around.

Therefore, the more time that passes, the more I become convinced of Italy's importance to the history of our civilization's development, and the more I want to assimilate the Italian spirit in order to do things in this vein. In our profession, especially in theater, they were often our masters: Molière was very influenced by Italian comedy; Marivaux started by writing for the Italians; and all our theater, up until romanticism in which the German influence became predominant, all our classical theater was influenced by Italy. So that's the reason for my attraction to Italy. It's because I accept what I consider to be a fact. Whether we like it or not, we belong to a civilization that started in Greece, continued through Rome, spread throughout the West by way of the Christian revolution, or, that is, by way of the Jewish influence.

CAHIERS: And at first, you wanted to make a "civilized" film.

RENOIR: Yes, I wanted to make a civilized film. Thank you for thinking of that; I wouldn't have thought of it myself, but you've put your finger on it.... We have many ideas in our minds, but we don't know how to find the words to express them; and it's true, this desire for civilization was the driving force that pushed me to make *The Golden Coach*.

CAHIERS: That explains the relief of each detail, and that an article of clothing, or the design on a chair, can have the same importance to the whole as does each of the plot's shifts in the action.

RENOIR: Yes, that's true. I think that if one wants to create a classical work, one must do that. The idea of artificially attracting the audience's attention to certain elements, to a star, for example, is a purely romantic idea. Even in painting, in drawings, modern people are used to romantic simplification and get lost when they see classical works such as tapestries; they find them a bit busy. They aren't actually busy, but classicism contains an idea of evenness that no longer exists in romanticism.

CAHIERS: Despite all the prefaces, in which the romantics proclaimed almost the opposite of what they did.

RENOIR: As usual, that's why one must avoid having very precise theories, because it seems that fate maliciously enjoys contradicting you, leading you to goals that are the exact opposite of what you intended. This tremendous contradiction is rather strange. It is, in fact, expressed very clearly in the writings of every religion, notably in the Christian religion. Proverbs like The first will be the last, or the parables on wealth – The poor will be rich, Little children are the most intelligent – aren't paradoxical, they're the truth. This world is made up of contradictions, often comical contradictions. The fact that the powerful will fall, for example. I've witnessed that four or five times during my life, which hasn't been relatively very long.

The box game

CAHIERS: There is a musicality pervading *The Golden Coach:* The scroll of the violins, for example, seems to be present in all the spirals of the decor, and even in certain details of the clothing.

RENOIR: I will repeat the same thing about *The Golden Coach* that I said about *The River:* I think we try to perfect ourselves, we try to learn, we try to work constantly, we discover things at each stage in a career. But the discoveries and the little we've learned are a bit like a battery, and we are not necessarily conscious of the electricity released from it. So we try to keep all of this inside ourselves, and we use it, hoping that it will come when we need it. It doesn't always come when we need it, however; that's the trauma of creation. Often, all that we've accumulated, all that we've tried to learn, comes too late or too early and not at the moment we need it. On the other hand, if we proceed in too orderly a fashion, that is, with notes, cards, with filed memories, and if we try to apply them mechanically and arbitrarily, I think we become removed from life. One must be very wary of knowledge and theories. One has to have them, but it is best to tackle each subject as if we knew nothing, as if we were completely new to it, and as if the subject were unexplored. If we don't approach a subject with a certain degree of freshness, then we're not alive, we're dead. You also have to have a good time while you make films. It's very important. I had a good time while making *The Golden Coach*. It was very strenuous, it was very hard, but I had a great time.

CAHIERS: Doing what, exactly?

RENOIR: Well, constantly discovering a classical Italian spirit in modern Italians. I had fun dealing with the Italians, whom I found to be exceptional people, people who have maintained a classical freshness, I might say, particularly in their way of approaching life's problems with a kind of simplicity, a very direct side, although it's hidden beneath superficial complications. But these complications are only superficial. When it comes to feelings, their feelings are very straightforward, very simple.

CAHIERS: Which is a type of classicism . . .

RENOIR: It also is classicism, like a piece of lace, whose design – which is really quite distinct – we decipher little by little. There is an American critic who doesn't like my films. He showers me with praise, but he makes one very interesting criticism. This is what he says: "It's a little like those boxes that you open, and there is another box, and you open it, and there is another box." Note that this critic made me very happy by saying this. He considers it to be a defect, however, that a film shouldn't be made in this way, but personally I find this box game rather interesting.

CAHIERS: There is one question we would like to ask you about each film: What role does improvisation play? Isn't the structure, which seems subtle and complex, already decided in the script?

RENOIR: Oh yes, the outline is planned. It's the dialogues that are improvised. Or if you like, the scenes and their sequence have been decided in advance, but the way of arriving at the final goal, which is the last shot of a scene, sometimes changes. It takes place on the same set, with the same characters, but often the words or the characters' reactions are different.

CAHIERS: In the morning, I believe, you rehearse the scenes that are to be shot that afternoon. You decide then on the placement and the shooting, according to the acting?

RENOIR: Yes, that's right. The so-called French system, which is to start working at noon, is excellent, in my opinion, for the film's quality. First because the actors, the technicians, and the workers like it better; they come to work well rested; they spend the morning at home, with their families; and they eat dinner a bit later, but also at home with their families. From this point of view, it's very good. And it allows the director to spend the morning on the set, or in any case to concentrate on certain problems before getting caught up in the whirlwind of shooting.

CAHIERS: And that's how you did *The Golden Coach*?

RENOIR: Yes, but I also do that for all my films.

CAHIERS: You rehearse the actors first, then, without worrying about the camera?

RENOIR: Oh, I do more than that, you know. I really believe in one method of rehearsal: It's first to ask the actors to recite their lines without acting them out, by allowing them to think, shall we say, only after several readings, so that when they're ready to try out certain theories according to which they will have certain reactions to the lines, they'll have these reactions to lines they know, not to lines that they don't yet understand, because you understand a line only after repeating it several times. And I even think that the method of acting must be discovered by the actors, and when they've discovered it, I ask them to temper it, not to use it right away, but to search, to advance cautiously, and especially not to add gestures until the end, so that they completely understand the meaning of the scene before they move an

The Golden Coach.

inch, grab a pencil, or light a cigarette. I don't ask them to try to act naturally, but to act in such a way that the discovery of exterior elements comes after the discovery of interior elements, and not vice versa.

In any case, I am extremely opposed to the method used by many directors, which consists of saying: "Look at me, I'll act out the scene for you. Now, do as I do." I don't think this is a very good method, because the director doesn't act out the scene, the actor does. The actor has to discover the scene himself and has to bring his own personality to it, and not the director's.

CAHIERS: In this film, you were looking for a dramatic atmosphere that would be that of both film and the theater?

RENOIR: Yes, because the period and the subject were so theatrical that it seemed to me the best way of expressing the period and portraying the subject was to subordinate my style to a theatrical style.

The Rules of the Game.

CAHIERS: That's why *The Golden Coach* is structured like a three-act play?

RENOIR: Yes, that's right.... To create this intended confusion between theater and life, I asked my actors, especially those who played real-life roles, to act with a little bit of exaggeration, so as to give life to this theatrical side and to allow me to create the confusion.

CAHIERS: So there is no fourth dimension, everything happens facing front?

RENOIR: Yes. Note that at first, I gave certain sets a fourth side, but little by little I gave that up, and I shot the film almost entirely as if I were on stage, with the camera in the place of the audience. Sometimes I used the fourth side, but not in the same scene. Each scene was conceived of as seen from one side. Moreover, I must say that as time goes by, I'm starting to use this method in all my films. In *The Rules of the Game*, it's already extremely clear: There is no fourth side.

CAHIERS: But in *The Rules of the Game*, the camera constantly pivoted whereas it seems that more and more, you direct with still shots and panning shots. Thus in *The Woman on the Beach* . . .

RENOIR: Yes, but *The Woman on the Beach*, for the reasons I gave you, is a film in which the fourth side plays an important role. It's a film that has reaction shots. Theoretically, *The Golden Coach* has no reaction shots. Those that it does have are simply to get close to the actors once in a while so that the audience can understand what's going on in their heads. But it's simply a practical necessity, not a style. The style consists of placing the camera in front of the scene and shooting it.

The adjective *modern*

CAHIERS: You've talked to us about classicism, but another striking thing in *The Golden Coach* is its modern character. Aren't you looking for a certain modernism through this classicism?

RENOIR: Yes, that's obviously true, but if the results I got can be called modern, I think, once again, that it can't be done deliberately. I believe a great deal in teachers, in school, in examples. I told you that. I think that seeing films one admires, good films, helps enormously. I'm very disciplined in my way of working, and I'm convinced that if you start by saying "I'm going to destroy everything, I'm going to be modern," then you won't be modern. You can be modern, and you must want to be so, because you must contribute something, but you can be modern only by humbly following your predecessors. Now, in spite of yourself, if you're good at that, you'll be modern without even trying.

CAHIERS: So, for example, you try to achieve a juxtaposition of elements rather than a connection?

RENOIR: Yes, because it's easier for me. You know, in this profession I have almost always been guided by practicality, by convenience. After all, you're trying to tell a story, and you're looking for the most practical ways of doing it.

CAHIERS: For you it's a springboard, not an end.

RENOIR: It's not an end. No, absolutely not, but it's a means.

CAHIERS: And it's the simplest, therefore the most efficient?

RENOIR: I think so. . . . Of course, each time, after having rehearsed, I find myself faced with the problem of shooting a scene. For example, I never start with an idea of the camera angle, I start with the scene. I rehearse it, and then, with the help of the cameraman, we decide on the angle. We say, "Well, this scene could be shot like this." There is another thing I never do. I never divide up a scene into action and reaction shots, start with a master shot, and then move to closer shots, and then, in the editing, use all of them. It seems to me that each piece of a scene has one angle and not two. In fact, the cutting of my films, except in special cases like *The River*, is extremely simple. It consists of merely putting pieces back to back that were shot back to back.

CAHIERS: You shoot chronologically?

RENOIR: The scenes, in any case, yes.

CAHIERS: And the film? Wasn't *The Rules of the Game* shot...

RENOIR: Yes, almost chronologically. You can't do it completely because there are location shots and also the matter of contracts with the actors, people who are free or not free. But in any case, I like to shoot chronologically as much as possible.

CAHIERS: And *The Golden Coach*?

RENOIR: It was shot almost chronologically, but not entirely.

Red, white, and blue

CAHIERS: There still is one question we'd like to ask you, the question of color: What, in your opinion, is the best way to use color?

RENOIR: First of all, it seems to me that color is not important. Certain subjects do have to be in color, and others are better in black and white. But in the end, I think here again, as in everything, that technology is at the service of the story. The goal is to tell a story. If it helps to tell it in color, let's tell it in color. Now, how should this color be used? I think it should be used without much thought to technology. At this point, all the different systems are very good. Technicolor in London is exceptionally good, but that is due mostly to the quality of their laboratories. They have old crews that have been working on color together for years. Here again, it's not the machine or the invention that creates the technical superiority, it's the quality of the manpower.

Therefore, you have to admit that we have a good color system, and if we do have a good system, I think that the only way to proceed is by trying to see things clearly. One thing that has happened over the past fifty years is that people have lost the use of their senses. This is due to what we call progress. Note that it's normal for them to have lost the use of their senses: We turn a button and we have light, we push another button, and we have a flame on a gas range. Our contact with nature takes place through so many intermediaries that we have almost completely forgotten how to feel natural things directly. We can therefore say that people don't see very much now. For example, everyone thinks that the French flag is red, white, and blue, but the French flag is no longer red, white, and blue. I don't know why, but the blue is violet, probably because the manufacturers found that making true-blue material was too expensive. The blue is just about the color of your jacket, it's not blue at all, it is nowhere near blue. Yet everyone is convinced that it's blue. So when you photograph a French flag and you see a kind of violet on the screen, everyone is surprised. It's simply because they haven't looked.

Therefore I think that the way to use color is first of all to open your eyes and look. It's easy to see if things correspond to what you want on the screen. In other words, there is practically no translation of the color onto the screen; there is photography. You simply have to place what you want on the screen in front of the camera, and that's it.

CAHIERS: You are aware, however, that there are many critical theories of color, one more clever than the next, "When painters get involved . . . ," and so on.

RENOIR: I'm convinced that if a painter, or any gifted artist, decides to make color films, he will do a very good job but will not use his knowledge as a painter to obtain good results in Technicolor. He will surely be helped along by the fact that his profession gave him an educated eye, which is indispensable. It's in this way that painters could perhaps help in color films: They would bring with them the collaboration of someone who has received a visual education. It's not by applying their knowledge as painters but by applying the exercises they've done with their eyes when learning to paint.

CAHIERS: You don't believe in chemical or optical treatments of color?

RENOIR: Absolutely not, I'm absolutely against that. It exists of course, and it gives good results sometimes, only right now I'm talking about my own way of working, and personally, I'm too egotistical to rely on a chemist for my film's final results. I prefer to have confidence in my eyes and in the cameraman's eyes, rather than in some chemical solution. It seems more fitting and, once again, more practical.

CAHIERS: You prefer to stick to the idea of fidelity?

RENOIR: That's right. Note that there are many special effects in black and white, more than in color. Contrasts, for example, can give unexpected results. There's an element of surprise in black and white that you don't have in color. Black and white also gives the director and the cameraman an infinite number of possibilities for special effects. Suppose you have an actor who can't play a scene well. You have to admit he's a little weak in expressing certain emotions. So you use some unrealistic lighting, with exaggerated lights. On one side you have absolute blackness, and on the other you hide half of his face. He emerges from a kind of vague shadow, and suddenly he becomes very talented, and the scene can be very good. So I think that with color, you have to abandon these special effects; it's a matter of being more and more honest. That's all.

CAHIERS: You seek purer colors?

RENOIR: It's a matter of taste. I like simple colors. In Bengal, in India, nature is divided into fewer colors. Compare a tree on the avenue Frochot with a tropical tree: The second has fewer greens, only two or three, and this works well in color films. Take this room, for example: It wouldn't be bad in color. There's one thing that wouldn't work, the brown tone of the chimney and the table; but the gray of the door and the walls, the white curtains, all that would be very easy to photograph in color. I think that this chair, on the other hand, would be horrible, it would be abominable. But in fact, it's abominable in real life, too. In the end, it's all very simple, it's a matter of putting things that you like in front of the camera.

CAHIERS: You like to arrange foregrounds full of lively colors in front of rather neutral backgrounds?

RENOIR: Yes, but I think that one could do the opposite. For example, one could do the opposite with the greens in nature. Use *powerful* backgrounds. I do have a few of them in *The River*, in fact. I shot in a banana field with a small lake just because of the green, which made a wildly powerful background.

CAHIERS: But for the interiors you kept very soft tones.

RENOIR: Yes, which is how things are there. The interiors are often shadowy and soft. Although in *The River*, I am far from conveying the impression of the colors of Bengal, far from it, especially those of the houses.

CAHIERS: And you don't give any thought to the rules of relationships among colors?

RENOIR: No, I'm convinced that our profession is that of a photographer. If we arrive at a set saying, "I want to be Rubens or Matisse," I am sure that we will wind up making big mistakes. No, we're photographers, nothing more, nothing less. I think that the concerns with plasticity have nothing to do with our profession. I don't think that the dresses in *The River*, for example, have any pictorial value. I think that they have a value on the screen, a photographic value, or, rather, a film value, because it's photography... no, it's cinematography; it's a category in itself.

CAHIERS: And color, a realist method, necessarily limits the filmmaker to realism.

RENOIR: I'm convinced of it. We live in a period in which we all are more or less intellectual before we are sensual, and our beliefs or our choices are decided for intellectual reasons. For example, it's the Dubonnet ad opposite the café where you drink your aperitif that makes you instinctively ask the waiter for "A Dubonnet!" Our senses have nothing to do with it, it's a mechanism of the mind and not of the palate. It's the same in everything, and it's extremely dangerous. I think that one of the artist's roles is to try to recreate the direct contact between man and nature.

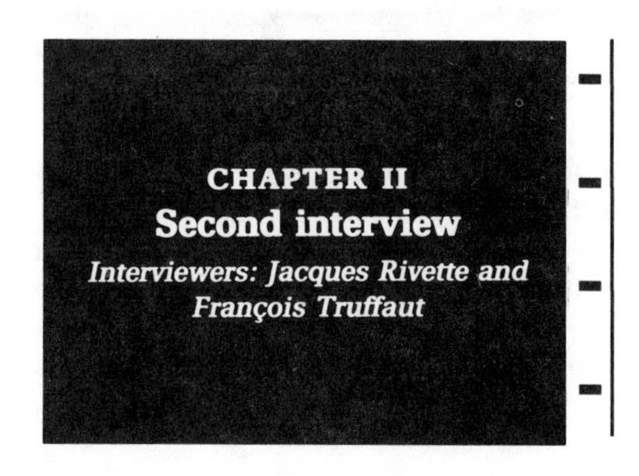

A temporary craft

CAHIERS: We'd like to begin by asking you about your older films. We know that you had the chance to see several of them again when you showed them to your actors, during the rehearsals for *Orvet*. What was your impression of them?

RENOIR: Well, it's very nice to see old films again, because there is no longer any debate about them. They've been reviewed; there's nothing more to win or to lose, and no matter how one tries to protect oneself, one must admit to being extremely sensitive – in any case, I am – to public opinion, to the opinion of audiences especially, and to the opinion of the critics. One is very vulnerable, and so it's quite nice to see films that one has forgotten a little. You see them as if they were new, as if you had just finished them, but without the horrible anguish of knowing that they're going to be judged.

CAHIERS: You can still feel the anguish of discovering changes in them. For example, the close-up of Simone Simon dead disappeared from *The Human Beast* (*La Bête humaine*).

RENOIR: Yes, then it's very upsetting. Once again, you become aware – I noticed it each time I saw screenings of my earlier films – how fragile our craft is. When I began in film, I considered that one of the ways in which films were better than the theater was that they were tangible and they lasted, as a painting or a statue lasts, whether good or bad. I'm not talking about quality, only about duration. But in the end, this isn't true, they don't last.

Now I'm sure of it: Film is also an ephemeral craft, because despite the enormous and devoted efforts of various film archives, prints do disappear.

For example, I recently was able to reconstruct *Grand Illusion* (*La Grande Illusion*) to what it was when I shot it, with the help of a few duplicates found here and there. We now have a very good copy, the complete film, but it took an enormous amount of work, and in any case, the complete negative itself has disappeared.

But it doesn't matter. Today, we make excellent duplicates, but it's a small miracle that we were able to bring everything together, and we could just as easily have failed. In America, for example, I noticed that the Museum of Modern Art has an extremely cut-up copy, rearranged for the needs of the film business, and that's all. When that one wears out, nothing will be left. Not even a duplicate.

Paper and marble

The truth is that a film is a very temporary thing. Seeing my old films again led me to revise this idea about the permanence of our profession, of our art, to reconsider its comparison to the plastic arts. It isn't as temporary as journalism, but it's less lasting and less solid than, say, a book.

CAHIERS: A painting fades too: The colors change with time, and a painter has to anticipate that.

RENOIR: Yes, but he does anticipate it, whereas the filmmaker doesn't. We imagine that the film will always be the same as when we release it, as it is right after its final editing. Note that technically this is right. A film in Technicolor doesn't change. You can make Technicolor copies to last for centuries, and theoretically they will always be the same. But laboratories disappear. There are always events, like wars, that cause many things to disappear, that destroy lives, and also, much less importantly, films.

Now I've even gotten to the point of asking myself – for several months now – if all human work isn't temporary, even a painting, even a statue, even a piece of architecture, even the Parthenon. No matter how solid the Parthenon is, relatively little is left of it, and we have no idea of what it was like when it was first constructed. And even what is left is going to disappear. We may manage, by putting cement into the columns, to hold it up for one hundred years, two hundred years, say five hundred years, say one thousand years. But in the end, the day will come when the Parthenon no longer exists. I wonder whether it wouldn't be a more honest approach to what we call a work of art to bear in mind that this work of art is temporary and will disappear and that the truth is, all things being relative, there isn't much difference between a work of architecture built in solid marble and a newspaper article printed on paper that we throw out the next day. I'm even at the point of wondering whether the only excuse for a work of art isn't the good it can do mankind. This good doesn't mean the exposition of theories – you know my fear of messages – but a small contribution to what the work of each man should be, which is man's culture: the betterment of man, physically or morally, or, most of all, philosophically.

CAHIERS: When the Parthenon is completely destroyed, the memory of it will still remain. The idea of the Parthenon will survive, like that of Phidias, for example, none of whose sculptures remains.

RENOIR: Absolutely. That's why I ask myself if the idea that remains of a work isn't more important than the work itself, and if, in turn, the importance of this idea isn't based on the good that the idea was able to do for people. This good is absolutely undefinable, and I would not attempt to classify it. I refuse to say, "This is good and this is bad." But there is a good and a bad just the same, no doubt about it. There is, in any case, a philosophical plane. Ever since the world has been the world, there has been a kind of attempt, an obvious attempt, to escape from matter and to approach the spiritual, and I believe that every work of art that brings us one tiny step closer to this spirituality is worthwhile.

CAHIERS: Yes, because even when the work of art is destroyed, the step has been taken.

RENOIR: The step has been taken. And after that, we take steps backward. We have to start again: that's the story of the world.

A liter of wine

CAHIERS: In reading the interview in *Le Monde*, we were struck by the seemingly pessimistic tone of your comments on the future of Western civilization. We thought of what you wrote five or six years ago, at the time of *The River*. You were convinced that we were entering a better age, an age of goodwill.

RENOIR: I still believe in goodwill, I believe in it absolutely, but I wonder whether this goodwill will be enough to stop the damage done to the human spirit by material progress. And since *The River*, material progress has taken a giant step.

For example, I think that peoples like those of India will have a hard time assimilating progress, which they do not reject – on the contrary, they seem to cry out for it – and will risk destroying their civilization, which is based on principles, emotions, and sensations that are absolutely opposed to the principles and sensations that go with mechanical, physical, or chemical progress.

I think we're getting back, once again, to the never-ending story of the spirit and matter, and it seems that some clever spirit wants to destroy all attempts made by man to rid himself of matter. Because in principle, progress should free us from matter, since it frees us from so many material needs. It frees us from the need to make a fire in the morning or to have someone else make it. Today we turn a knob and we have an electric heater that warms us very well. There seems to be some kind of law that says that each step that removes us from this matter will nonetheless bring us closer to it in a roundabout way and bring us even closer to it than we were at the start.

In my opinion, the first problem – the most important problem in our world – is the problem of dissemination, and it's the conception of this dissemination that may lead to catastrophe. We're at the point of wondering whether the idea of the masses – which was our religion – of universal suffrage, whether in art or in politics, if this idea of the masses shouldn't be revised or at least used in another way. The way it's used now, the influence of the masses leads to nothing but the scattering of material. For example, think of a liter of wine: It's certainly sufficient when shared by three or four people. But if we want this same liter of wine to be shared by one thousand people, we have to put water in it, and then it's useless. We have to wonder whether something like this doesn't happen in the process of dissemination.

And at the same time, the world is in the process of congregating around little cliques of specialists. It now is obvious that nuclear physics – which is big news – is in the hands of a small number of people, and that even if this small clique were to tell what it knows, people wouldn't listen and wouldn't understand. We may, therefore, return to Egyptian esotericism, which in any case didn't do so badly, as Egypt did last for five or six thousand years and covered the banks of the Nile with quite a few masterpieces.

CAHIERS: Or the civilization of the Middle Ages . . .

RENOIR: Which was an esoteric civilization. In any case, when I do allow myself to sound a bit pessimistic, I'm referring especially to the civilization to which I belong, which is the civilization of the Renaissance. A few hundred years ago we destroyed the Middle Ages, and we may have been wrong; the Middle Ages was a good period. But in fact, we weren't wrong, given that nothing is ever destroyed. Things destroy themselves; the elements of destruction are within individuals and groups of individuals.

We are told that during the French Revolution, the people destroyed the monarchy in 1789. It isn't true, the monarchy destroyed itself, all by itself, because it contained all the elements of destruction within it.

The same thing must have happened with the Middle Ages. The Middle Ages was replaced by the state of affairs in which we live and in which I was raised. A state of affairs that consists of dividing the world into not-too-large groups and into different languages, and of giving each of these groups an opportunity for a kind of artistic, literary, musical, human expression that is rather exciting.

In other words, the type of civilization that produced Mozart, or that produced my father, seems to me to be in danger, and my pessimism refers to these observations.

CAHIERS: And the other pole, one might say, that of goodwill, is beyond . . .

RENOIR: The pole of goodwill is outside this observation, because I am convinced that men are going to find a way after all. What are we seeing right now? A new attempt to construct the Tower of Babel. My God, it must not have been too bad during the days of the Tower of Babel, it must have been great: Everyone spoke the same language, and everyone got along. Maybe we are going to see that, but before we manage to lay the first stone of this Tower of Babel, I fear that we are going to have some problems. I'm not alone, in any case, we all believe this.

Nature changes

CAHIERS: Let's go back to the past. Before the war, you wrote a now-well-known article in which you said that you considered *Nana* to have been your first film. Do you still feel the same way?

RENOIR: Yes, I still feel the same way. *Nana* was the first film in which I discovered that one doesn't copy nature but must reconstruct it, that every film, every work that aims to be artistic must be a creation, whether good or bad. I discovered that it was better to invent something, to create something bad, than merely to copy nature, no matter how well one may do so.

CAHIERS: There's a world of difference between *La Fille de l'eau* and *Nana*, but one cannot say that *La Fille de l'eau* was a realist or naturalist film. You were already seeking something else.

RENOIR: Absolutely. But it was when I looked at this first work, once it was finished, that I seemed to be able to learn something. It seemed to me that the parts in which I did the best work were precisely those in which I got away from directly copying nature. By nature, I don't mean just the trees and the roads. I mean the human beings and I mean everything. I mean the world.

One thing that has been a convenient source of inspiration for the French over the past one hundred and fifty years is what we have agreed to call realism. But this realism is not realism at all. It is simply another way of translating nature.

I am absolutely convinced that the way in which a writer like Zola, like Maupassant, translated what he saw around him was just as di-

Catherine Hessling, Pierre Champagne, and Pierre Philippe in *Nana*.

gested, just as composed, as it was for a writer like Marivaux. And then, nature changes, because nature in a civilized country is created by people. For example, the hills of Bourgogne look completely different from the way they did when I was a child. It's simply because the vines were planted so that they could be worked using a little mechanical plow: They're very straight, with metal wires, instead of disorganized sticks. The landscape has changed completely. In the same way, new methods of planting trees in the forests have been adopted. One could say that the natural side of France has changed considerably since Louis-Philippe, because of theories of improving the land. For example, there is one tree that is very common in France now but that

Catherine Hessling in *Charleston* (photo by "Avant-scène").

didn't exist at all then, or almost not at all. It's the evergreen, especially the pine. Louis-Philippe planted pines in the Landes and in the forest of Fontainebleau, which were sandy deserts. So a country's appearance does change considerably. That's why what remains of an artist isn't his copy of nature, because this nature changes, it's temporary. What is eternal is his way of absorbing nature, and as we said at the beginning of our conversation, it's what he can bring to men, thereby serving man with his copy or, rather, with his reconstruction of nature.

The truth is that I often like to use paradoxes. I like to do it because people complain and can't understand the paradox. They may be right.

I therefore like to claim that all great art is abstract, that Cézanne, Renoir, or Raphaël are abstract painters, and so they can't be judged by the resemblance of their paintings to their models.

I believe, on the other hand, that we would be wrong to say that all great art is subjective. It's dangerous, as I've said before, for an artist to think that his art is purely subjective. The great artists were absolutely convinced that they were objective and were mere copiers of nature, but they were so powerful that in spite of themselves, they created their own portraits, and not that of a tree.

CAHIERS: Whereas painters who want to be abstract from the start may violate the spirit of art?

RENOIR: Yes, they often end up with something a bit dry and end up not showing themselves at all, because in trying to show themselves, they start by hiding from themselves, they start by creating an idea about themselves. An exact portrait can be done only unconsciously. It's like photography. If someone says to you, "I'm going to take your picture," you immediately freeze up. You make a funny face and so the photograph looks nothing like you. But if you don't know that you're being photographed, the photo is often good and looks like you.

The love of contrasts

CAHIERS: *Nana* was a commercial failure?

RENOIR: *Nana* was a complete failure commercially. After *Nana,* I did a few extremely profitable films, and I must admit that I haven't seen them again. They've completely disappeared.

CAHIERS: *Marquitta* disappeared. We were able to see *Le Bled* and *Le Tournoi,* the latter in what is apparently an incomplete copy. We had the impression that you were mostly interested in technical problems.

RENOIR: Oh yes, I remember. At the time of *Le Tournoi,* I believed in camera positions, in camera movements. For the banquet scene I had an instrument constructed that really surprised my friends in the studio, all the producers, all the technicians. It was a kind of table, a platform with legs on wheels. The camera was suspended below, just low enough to be at the level of the plates or the candles on the table. But on the sides, the platform lifted up so that you could reach above the guests' heads, high enough so that the women's hairdos wouldn't be cut off. I used a similar apparatus for *The Lower Depths* (*Les Bas-Fonds*).

There were also many technical difficulties in *Le Bled,* which we weren't able to resolve because we were in Algeria. It took a long time to shoot the film. And I did a great deal of work. We had to construct

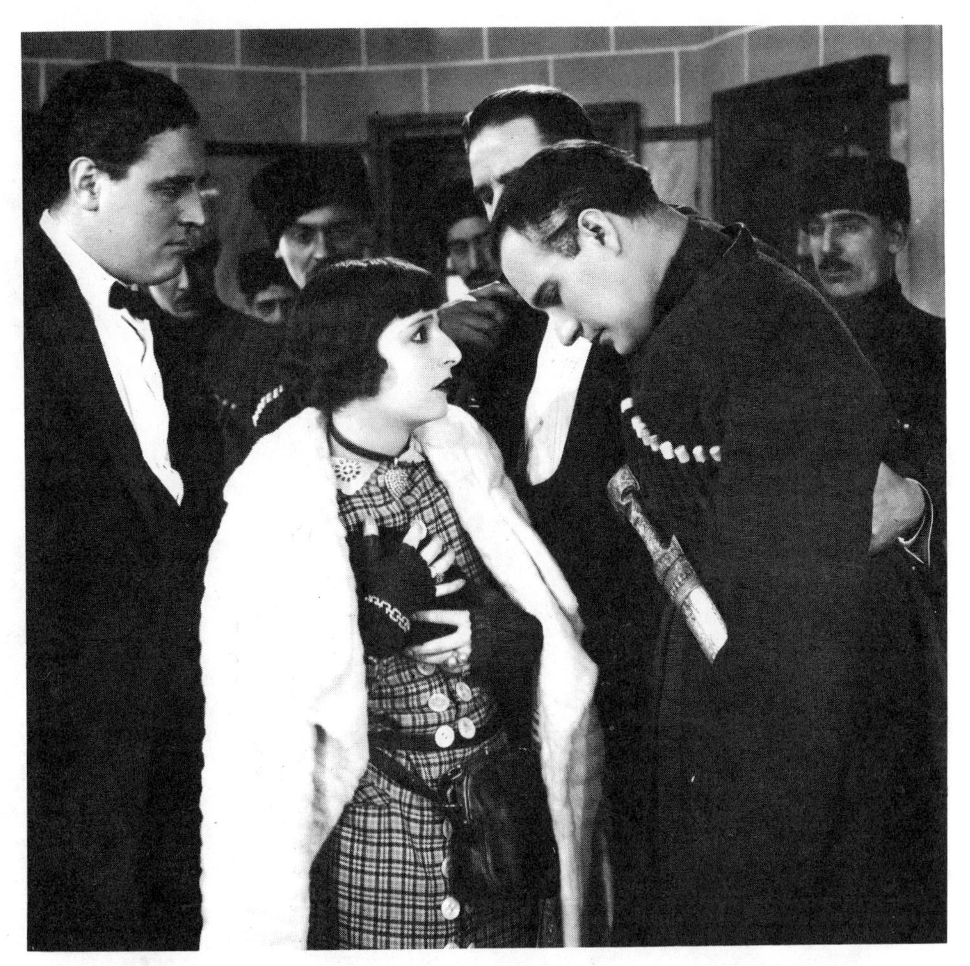

Pierre Philippe, Marie-Louise Iribe, and Pierre Champagne in *Marquitta* (photo by "Avant-scène").

a dolly track through the vineyard using just boards, and it was extremely well done.

It gave me a chance to get to know the people who did the work. They were Arabs, directed by a kind of foreman who I believe was an important religious character in his village. They were a charming team of splendid people.

CAHIERS: *Tire au flanc* is very poorly treated in the film histories. It's presented as one of the few films you did just for money. So, we were surprised to see a very high quality film, a disorderly film...

RENOIR: *Tire au flanc* was done after *Le Tournoi*. When I made *Tire au flanc* I was a bit more in control, I had started to understand where I

Le Tournoi (photo by "Avant-scène").

was going. I didn't understand it very well, because one never really knows – even now, I don't know – but I thought I had some sort of direction. I was beginning to understand that I could express certain sides of my character without shocking the audiences too much.

I like paradoxes, and I knew that I could let myself go with my love of paradox. I also knew that I could let myself go with my love of contrasts and not think I had to have elegant and harmonious connections all the time.

CAHIERS: It's true, it's very extreme: a little too sad, a little too joyful. Was *Tire au flanc* your idea, or was it suggested to you?

RENOIR: I don't really remember any more. I know that we were a group of friends, all determined to work together. Braunberger was in the group. We chose the title *Tire au flanc* (trans.: The Shirker) because it gave us a chance to do something interesting and also because the title, which was very well known, would make it easy to sell.

Besides, that's the case with all films. It's wrong to think that films are decided for purely artistic reasons. It is, after all, a business. It has to sell, and so other considerations come into play.

I think it's wrong to get involved with a project that one isn't attracted to. But it's equally wrong to want to make a film when it won't be successful. Some people have to see it, or else why make it?

CAHIERS: Apparently it was a very improvised production.

RENOIR: Oh, more than improvised!... One big reason for doing *Tire au flanc* was my admiration for a dancer named Pomiès. He wasn't just an interesting dancer, he was a wonderful person, an ascetic, a true altruist. Yes, Pomiès was a fascinating man, and it's partly because of him that I did *Tire au flanc*.

CAHIERS: There was Michel Simon as well.

RENOIR: Michel Simon, of course! Michel Simon is an actor whom I more than admire. He seems to personify theater or film; he's an incredible character. He's an unbelievably gifted man.

But you know, I was lucky in life. What I've said about Michel Simon, I could also say about Jean Gabin, for example. In France we have a few people like that, who were invented solely to allow us to make great films.

I adore Andersen

CAHIERS: You did another important film during your silent period: *The Little Match Girl* (*La Petite Marchande d'allumettes*).

RENOIR: I did it, we did it at the Vieux-Colombier, Jean Tedesco and I. We made our own electrical current. We bought the motor of a Farman automobile that had been in an accident, and we cooled it with tap water. And we made our own lights or, rather, our light holders, our reflectors. I must mention that there were people who helped us a great deal to do this, the people from the Philips company. They were interested in it, because at that time, no matter where you went in the world, films were made with orthochromatic film, whereas *The Little Match Girl* was made with panchromatic film. We only used it for the outdoor shots, because panchromatic film requires a certain type of color spectrum. Now, the arc lamps didn't give us this kind of color spectrum, nor did the mercury arcs often used in studios. The idea of using incandescent lights hadn't been thought up yet.

Michel Simon in *Tire au flanc.*

I even shot *Le Bled* and *Le Tournoi* with this device we made at the Vieux-Colombier, which consisted essentially of a kind of wooden frame. Three pieces of wood, one on the bottom, one on each side, and each between one and a half and two and a half meters long, a weight on the bottom to keep it upright, and behind these three posts was just some white sheet metal we'd bought, which created a reflector. We cut it with metal shears and nailed it on.

With Philips's direction, we made the resistance dimmers ourselves, with metal that we rolled around a stick like a corkscrew. And then we tested it. I was lucky enough to have as an associate someone who had been one of the first people to work in a laboratory, in Hollywood, at the very beginning. His name was Raleigh, like Sir Walter Raleigh who imported tobacco to England. He's dead now. He was a good friend, and I miss him very much.

Raleigh lived in Paris. He had some savings and a small house in Neuilly and was a very old gentleman. He lived in Paris because he thought the French perspective on women was better, more logical. He didn't like the Anglo-Saxon perspective. That's why he was in Paris.

We created a laboratory in his kitchen. We put up black curtains, and so on. We made some wooden tanks – it was very easy, by the way – and that is how we developed all of *The Little Match Girl* in Raleigh's kitchen.

And then we did the first printing with an old camera. The copies were really good. Only after that did we give the film to a laboratory. The sets were also painted on location.

That was my only attempt at a small-scale production, with a group of technicians who had fun with it. We were very enthusiastic and very happy.

CAHIERS: That must have been a lot of fun.

RENOIR: Oh, it was marvelous, it was exciting, and it was all the more exciting because the results were beautiful! The photography was new; we had gray tones that didn't exist in orthochromatic film, and we were very happy with it.

CAHIERS: But you didn't choose the subject of *The Little Match Girl* just because it allowed you to do this experiment...

RENOIR: We chose it for two reasons. The first is that I like [Hans Christian] Andersen very much, and that even now, if I could, I would like to shoot some Andersen fairy tales. I don't do it, though, because the people who are involved with the commercial end of films wouldn't approve of the way I'd want to shoot them.

But aside from that, if I could shoot stories like "The Four Winds," for example.... Do you remember "The Four Winds"? You know, the witch who lives in a mountain cave. Her sons are the four winds: the wind of the West, the wind of the North, the wind of the South... and they come home carrying perfumes from all the countries they've passed through. And the mother is very strict, she scolds them, she beats them when they've been bad. It's marvelous.

I adore Andersen. And then the second reason is that a film with special effects can be done in a very small studio. With special effects, toys, blown-up characters, you can manage to make a film in a very

Catherine Hessling in *The Little Match Girl*.

small space that claims to be more than it really is, and it was the possibility of special effects that attracted us to the project.

Now it's easier, because laboratory processes and the quality of mattes let you add anything you want onto the same piece of film, whereas at that time, you had to shoot it directly. We had to have a mask and to know exactly what we would put on the other side of it, on the hidden side.

CAHIERS: But at the same time, what we get in laboratories today has less clarity than what we got in the past.

RENOIR: That's true. It's very strange. That's what we were talking about at the beginning of our interview, isn't it? Technical progress kills a kind of human quality in us. It's very strange.

You spoke about my pessimism a little while ago, and I tried to answer you. But I forgot one comparison: the comparison with film. We can definitely say that technical progress has not improved films. I don't know whether it's done any harm, but in any case it hasn't improved them. I don't think we can say that *Around the World in 80 Days* is better than *Shoulder Arms*, for example. I don't think so.

Playing with toys

CAHIERS: *The Little Match Girl* was your only experiment with special effects?

RENOIR: No, I began my career in film because of my love of special effects. In the beginning, I had no intention of writing, of being a writer, of inventing stories. My ambition was to create special effects, and I did quite a few, right from the start.

CAHIERS: In *La Fille de l'eau*?

RENOIR: I did some in *La Fille de l'eau*. In *Marquitta*, for example, I had the idea – it's funny, there always are several people who have the same idea at the same time. In Germany at that time, Schufftan, I think, had the same idea, but I didn't know it, and he didn't know that I had the idea either – the idea of showing a corner of one of the outer boulevards, the ones that follow the line of the old fortification, with the town. We did it with mirrors, the backs of which we scraped to leave enough room for the characters, and then the set, which was a miniature, reflected in the mirror.

I always had lots of fun with these things. It's very exciting. The only thing is, it doesn't go beyond playing with toys. And when you progress in a profession – if by chance you do progress – you become more ambitious, and the game-playing side of the profession becomes less enthralling.

CAHIERS: Would making a film based mainly on special effects still interest you?

RENOIR: Oh, yes! Very, very much! I have a friend and an associate, by the way, who made it his profession: Lourié. He did a film showing a big sea serpent eating up New York. And now he is going to do an-

Catherine Hessling and Pierre Champagne in *La Fille de l'eau.*

other sea serpent, unless it's a bird, which is going to eat up London, I think.

The fun you have in doing a film, in building something out of small pieces, pieces that are easily available, is thrilling. The fun of filming a matchbox and of presenting it as a skyscraper . . . ! It's one of the most fun parts of the profession.

Take Man Ray: There's someone who has a marvelous understanding of all that and whom I admire very much. What Man Ray can do photographically is unbelievable! Oh, yes, I love all that!

Another thing that still excites me when I do color films is cheating nature. In *The River*, for example, Lourié and I spent a fortune painting Bengal's trees green! We walked around with big cans of paint and changed the green completely!

CAHIERS: Even in *Eléna et les hommes* (*Paris Does Strange Things*), aren't there special effect shots – the sunset over the army drill?

RENOIR: Yes, of course.

CAHIERS: It's so beautiful that you don't want to believe it's not real. You say to yourself, "It's too good to be true."

RENOIR: It's put together well, and beforehand, Claude and I had fun, crazy fun, using lights that were really red! Without blinking an eye, we lit red lamps in the studio. Everyone around us said, "That's crazy!" That's right, it was crazy! So? We're hoping that the film will also be a bit crazy.

CAHIERS: It's the same thing in Ophuls's *Lola Montès*.

RENOIR: I haven't seen it yet. I was hoping to see it in America.

CAHIERS: But the American version will probably be awful.

RENOIR: They'll do what they did with *Eléna*, which they really massacred. They reedited it. They even shot a beginning and an end with Mel Ferrer. I don't even know what he says. I haven't wanted to see the film. The whole thing makes me sick, it was such a shock! I think they did it because they thought the audiences wouldn't understand it otherwise. I think what they did was an explanatory beginning and ending. The film came out in America right when Ingrid Bergman had just gotten an Academy Award for *Anastasia*. According to the publicity agents, people expected her to do very sentimental stories. And since *Eléna* wasn't sentimental, they tried to change it, to apologize for it. But as far as I'm concerned, I'm not interested in sentimental stories.

The age of Hoff

This thing with *Eléna* in America made me so sad that I couldn't go to a movie theater and look at a screen for six months. It made me absolutely sick, really.

CAHIERS: America does strange things.

RENOIR: It's not America, though, it's the production world. It's the film industry. You can't really accuse anyone. In *Le Grand Couteau*, for example, I find Hoff, the [character who is the] producer, to be very nice. He defends his perspective, but he defends it very well. When he says,

Rehearsal for *Le Grand Couteau* (*The Big Knife*): Daniel Gélin and Jean Renoir.

"I built this studio with my own hands," it's true: He built it with his own hands, and it's probably a beautiful studio that makes very honorable films. I'm convinced of that.

But that's the way it is. There are particular circumstances: Suddenly someone says, "Oh, excuse me, this is a farce, a French-style satire. Maybe we should explain it a little." So to explain it, they add a shot. Then they start the destruction, and it doesn't stop. I know how that works. I wasn't there, but I know that *Eléna* was entirely destroyed, and it's a pity, because it could have been a great success in America. It's the fault of human blunder.

Let's admit it, the age of Hoff is gone. People are no longer passionate. Suppose a man like Thalberg had presented *Eléna*. Either he would have completely destroyed it, that is, thrown it in the wastebasket, or he would have been of the same opinion, would have asked to add things in the same vein. But today, we have a tendency to thin things out, to create a product with a mediocre flavor. We tend toward bland cuisine.

At the beginning, you consider only advertising. You have to be able to say, "Our subject is scandalous." That allows you to find money and to attract audiences. But then, you're afraid. There's a kind of panic, a panic for which no one's to blame. It's the fault of the times. Currently there is a lack of artistic audacity. The public is also responsible, because film is the result of the collaboration of many people, including the public.... You can see that you weren't exaggerating when you thought you sensed a kind of pessimism in my interview with *Le Monde!* That interview's pessimism may merely be the final aftertaste of my unpleasant experience with *Eléna*. We're not made of steel. We're made of flesh and bones and nerves, and we can be influenced, and seeing a film that I liked very much, which I worked on a great deal and shot under horrible physical and even moral circumstances, because I was very difficult... After having gone through so much trouble, to see that the English version was destroyed didn't make me optimistic. They wanted to categorize *Eléna*, and once you say the word *category*, you're talking about mechanization. Before I knew that they had played with the film and that the American critics wouldn't like it, some people, professors, told me, "Oh, you know, it's a farce, and if it isn't reviewed by people who know something about farce, it will probably get bad reviews, because very few people are imaginative enough to accept an actor's changing roles." Yet we're going to have to get used to living with mechanization, or else we won't live. We have to stop at red lights when we're in a car, or else we'll get hit. Red lights are awful. For me, red lights symbolize the side of our modern civilization that I don't like. A red light appears and we stop! For me, it's insulting. Yet we have to accept it because if we were to go through the red light, we would probably be killed. That's what we have to consider. People like me, who were born at a time when a certain lack of physical discipline was still permissible, probably find this to be a difficult change.... But let's go on to something else.

We talk too much

CAHIERS: We're up to the beginning of the talkies.

RENOIR: The talkies arrived during *The Little Match Girl*, which didn't help its release. *The Little Match Girl* had no luck.

The company that released *The Little Match Girl* tried to do a kind of musical score, which still exists. But audiences wanted speech; they wanted the actors to open their mouths and words to come out. So *The Little Match Girl*'s flight was checked by the arrival of the talkies.

CAHIERS: Your first talkie was *On purge bébé*.

RENOIR: Yes, there was a man in that who was great. It was Fernandel. No one from the studio wanted him. He never forgot that, and every

Fernandel, Marguerite Pierry, and Olga Valery in *On purge bébé* (photo by "Avant-scène").

time he sees me, he shakes my hand and says, "You gave me my first break."

CAHIERS: You shot this film very quickly.

RENOIR: Yes. But I shot it for one reason: I wanted to do *La Chienne*, which required a particular budget. The last films I had shot, like *Le*

Bled and *Le Tournoi dans la cité*, took a long time to shoot. I therefore had to prove how fast I could work to the Braunberger–Richebé studio. . . . It's taken from a play by Feydeau, an excellent comedy. I must have written the script in a week. I shot it in less than one week, in four or six days. I edited it in one week. At the end of the third week, it came out at the Aubert Palace! And at the end of the fourth week, it was already making a profit!

CAHIERS: That's no longer possible.

RENOIR: No, and it's too bad. First, we talk too much; we examine a project's value for months, for years sometimes. So all the inspiration vanishes, the kind of spontaneity that allows you to do things like that.

I liked *On purge bébé*. Of course, because it was shot so quickly, it might not have had enough close-ups or varied shots. At times I would have liked to use the camera more, but I had to limit myself in order to do my thirty or forty shots a day. But it was fine. I was happy! And then, the best part was that it was a great experiment with actors, it was very well acted.

CAHIERS: And was the sound also an experiment?

RENOIR: Yes, the sound as well, of course. I've told the story a thousand times about the experiment with flushing the toilet, which earned me the reputation of a great artist overnight! The idea of taking the microphone, of going to the place in question, and of pulling the chain. . . . It seemed like a daring kind of innovation. Note that it was much more difficult than everyone thought, because there was no mixing then. You had to have a second microphone, a signal light, to have studied the density of the sound of the toilet beforehand, so that the mixing could be done during the shooting. It's true!

And then there was the music, which was recorded in the studio during the acting. At the time of *La Chienne*, there was no mixing either. I had some minor difficulties with the editing, which explains the mistakes in the sound during the song. The sound that was recorded in the room was used during the scene downstairs, in the street, although I had recorded the sound in the street full of automobiles honking, wonderful noises, but it was lost.

A slight lag

CAHIERS: The success of *On purge bébé* allowed you to shoot *La Chienne* with great freedom?

RENOIR: Total freedom.

CAHIERS: It was later that things turned sour?

RENOIR: Yes. *La Chienne* had a hard time being released. People didn't want it. That's what was difficult. The first showings in Nancy were disastrous. I think the people in the theater were destroying the seats. The film lasted two days. The studio had decided to try it out in Nancy before going to Paris, and the person who saved me there, really saved me, was Siritzky, a theater owner who had quite a few movie theaters, two of which were in Biarritz (it was only later that he owned the Marivaux and the Max Linder, where he released *The Lower Depths* [*Les Bas-Fonds*]).

He was a man whom I admired a great deal, and for a reason that had nothing to do with movies. It was because he had been a marine in the Turkish marines. It seemed to me that to have been in the Turkish marines was something extraordinary. He was very strong. He knew how to do tricks with a blacksmith's hammer on an anvil, and he absolutely saved me by taking *La Chienne*, which no one wanted, in his Biarritz cinema, and by doing a very clever advertisement which stated: "Please don't come see this film, it's awful!" And everyone went to see the film. For the first time in the history of his theater, he kept a film for three weeks, I think, instead of four days, and the word got out in Paris. So Jacque Haïk, the owner of the Colisée, made an appointment to see me. He said, "Listen, Jean Renoir, if it's OK with your producers, I'll take your film." So that's how it got off to a start, and a good start. It was even a big success.

CAHIERS: How did it happen then, that after *La Chienne* you had a rather difficult period?

RENOIR: I've always had difficult periods in my life. It never changes, for the simple reason that . . . no, after all, it's not so simple as all that. I think the real reason is that the films I produce, that I shoot, are never shot at the exact moment they should be. There is always a slight lag between my work and public opinion. People realize this and say, "We can't order any more films from this guy, because he might do something very good, but it won't go over well." That's all, and because *La Chienne* had trouble being launched, having been successful only after several months of difficulties, of negotiations, of struggle, it didn't encourage the producers to give me other films.

There is another reason. René Clair gave this reason, and I strongly agree with it, because René Clair is a marvelous analyst of film conditions in our society.

René Clair claims that the industry never forgives a director his financial success. Yes, he claims that the only way to get good films, with a good budget and a good salary, is to have total failures, total financial failures. Then people rush to you and cover you with gold; they're enchanted, they love it!

So, the experience with *Eléna* did me considerable good. This bad American experience hit me hard, but on the other hand, in America, people know that some of the mistakes that were made in the presentation were not my fault, and since then, I have felt a sort of wave of commercial sympathy heading in my direction, which I may not know how to benefit from, but which is apparent. Right now, if I knew myself what I wanted, it would be easy for me to shoot films.

Lucullus' kitchen

CAHIERS: Was *La Chienne* a very important film for you?

RENOIR: I wanted to do this film for the same reason that pushed me to do many other films. It was because of my admiration for Michel Simon. I thought that he would be phenomenal in the character of Legrand. I saw the film again not too long ago. I have a 16mm copy that I lent to some friends.

CAHIERS: This film marked a turning point for you.

RENOIR: Yes and no. The truth is that I had dreamed about this kind of story for a long time. I hadn't been able to bring it to the screen, but I'm sure that there are things even in *Nana* that led to *La Chienne*. We have old pet subjects like that, hidden loves of certain forms of expression and even of physical forms.

As for Michel Simon, I had dreamed of seeing him on the stage with certain expressions, with his mouth pinched in a certain way. I had dreamed of seeing him with this sort of mask that is as thrilling as a mask from an ancient tragedy. And I was able to realize my dream.

Excuse me for jumping to another subject, but I just read an article about the dress rehearsal of the *Le Grande Couteau*, in which a writer says he saw a spectator who should be invited to all the dress rehearsals because he was having a great time, and it was me. But this journalist, who was nice enough to talk about me in this way, doesn't know something: I always have a good time. If I didn't have fun, I wouldn't be in this profession.

Obviously, for me, seeing actors as I've dreamed of seeing them, seeing them act the way they've acted in my imagination, is divine, it's simply paradise. I don't see why I wouldn't like this kind of spectacle!

I could cite a quotation from this writer, certainly an apocryphal one, by a Roman general whom I admire more than all the others because he brought cherry trees to Europe. It's Lucullus, "Lucullus dines at Lucullus'." I don't see why Lucullus should like the food at Lucullus'! There's no reason for it.

It isn't because I think that Lucullus' cooking is better, not at all. It's simply because it's wonderful to do your own cooking and to eat

Michel Simon in *La Chienne.*

your meal with a few friends afterward. It's the best thing in life, even if we know that the chef at the restaurant next door would do a better job. In all honesty, it's fun to cook, no doubt about it.

To get back to *La Chienne,* what happens with great actors, and consequently with Michel Simon, is that they unmask you, bring dreams that you've had, but haven't expressed, to light.

The truth is that this is the eternal mystery of creation. A time comes when you are no longer responsible for your creation, when it escapes you, and yet it still corresponds to the dream you've had and allows you to discover it.

That's why I'm so wary of scripts that are too rigid, because it seems to me that in producing this dream, they risk eliminating whatever was beyond the conscious part, and this unconscious part is, after all, what creates the surprise and the fun of the profession.

Conversely, we often let ourselves admire certain utterances that don't deserve this admiration. I'm not talking about Michel Simon but about less important actors, less extraordinary ones. I have often let myself be drawn to solutions that weren't good, simply because of a kind of temporary and illusory admiration.

In a fairyland

CAHIERS: We recently saw *La Nuit du carrefour* again. The striking thing is that this is an imaginary adventure film. You never try to produce terror but, rather, a kind of disorientation, and at the same time it's incredibly realistic.

RENOIR: The fairylike quality came despite me, and simply because an intersection thirty kilometers outside Paris on a road going north is an enchanted place. When you drive around at night on the roads outside Paris, you're in a fairyland. In the end, reality is always fairylike. In order to avoid making reality seem fairylike, certain writers go to a great deal of trouble to present it in a truly strange light. But if we leave it as it is, it's fairylike.

CAHIERS: This is true of all your prewar films; it's true of *Toni*, of *The Lower Depths*, of *Monsieur Lange*.

RENOIR: This comes solely from my desire to try to see reality. I love reality, and I'm happy to love it because it brings me infinite joy. But it happens that many people hate it, and most human beings, whether or not they make films, whether they're workers, store owners, or dramatists, create a kind of veil between reality and themselves. And in order to create this veil more easily, they use elements provided by society: the people around them, conversations in the street, newspapers, theatrical productions. This veil is extremely monotonous, because it becomes the same for everyone. And so when someone pierces through it and shows the reality behind it, people say, "Oh, no! That's not true! That's not the way it is!" But it is the truth.

After all, the reality is in being enchanted. It demands great patience, work, and good faith to find it. I'm convinced, in any case, that it isn't a question of talent or gifts, just of good faith. If you want to find reality, you'll find it. You just have to eliminate whatever seems to you to have been created by the habits of your times, to eliminate

Pierre Renoir in *La Nuit du carrefour.*

these habits first, but to take back later the ones that seem to conform with reality. The reality of daily events, of romantic adventures, is absolutely twisted, deformed, as if they were seen in a funhouse mirror. I even think that the reality of romantic adventures is the one that is the most deformed, even more than that of films, novels, or newspapers. It's insane how lovers who fight can suddenly see facts and the world through a distorted glass and lose all sense of reality. It's the romantic tradition. We have to deal with a hundred and fifty years of romantic tradition, concerning love, women, the way to approach women, what we call emotions. Despite its lace covering, the reality of love seems much truer to me in Marivaux, and up until the end of the eighteenth century, even in the revolutionary works. It must have changed during the Empire. It might have been Germany's influence.

Anyway, because romantic adventures are often used as a basis for literature and because these romantic adventures are very distorted, we wind up with a literature and films that are rather distorted.

CAHIERS: It is, therefore, once again, a question of trying to see things as they are.

RENOIR: I think that is the work of every – I won't use the pretentious word *creator* – of every living being. If we live simply and make our living in any profession – say as an employee in a business – we can still try to break through the kinds of veils that surround us and to see things as they are, since they're so beautiful, so enchanting. People say, "If only film brought us more enchantment and put us in a pleasant dream!" But instead, it's reality that's the pleasant dream.

Literary, theatrical, or film masterpieces occasionally produce a quality film that is also a fairytale, an illusion, but this illusion has the advantage of bringing you closer to reality, or maybe of being a higher-quality illusion. Maybe... In any case, I spend my time writing stories in which the mixture of theatrical and real-life enchantment form the basis of the intrigue. Even now, my last play is more or less about that. It takes place in Paris during the war, during the occupation. There are Germans, the Gestapo, unhappy people; there's a bit of everything, but in the play it is very much a question of illusion and reality. Sometimes when you're shooting a scene for a film and you've found an expression very close to reality, everyone on the set decides this isn't right. They say, "It isn't natural." On the other hand, you do have to maintain a certain degree of caution so as not to shock the public. Too much caution is also very bad.

It's rustic

This business of a "veil" that we're talking about is only one way to explain the mystery of our profession. We could explain it in a hundred other ways. I do believe, however, that it is an important thing. A certain school, say Hollywood at the beginning, from around 1918 to 1920 up until around 1925, finds a certain reality and surprises people by presenting a vision of America that, even in bad films, is a very accurate vision. People at that time who saw American films had a certain impression of America that was fairly correct. In order to present this idea, the actors copied the everyday gestures of the people and reproduced them with a certain innocence. I'll give you an example: The French *théâtre du boulevard*, which existed before American film, took certain so-called natural stances, which Antoine had discovered and introduced as a reaction against romantic theater. But the truth is that these stances became as fixed as the romantic stances they had replaced. When I shot *Madame Bovary*, I was lucky enough to find a rather elderly opera director, and a company of singers who were familiar with the manner of singing from before Antoine's revolution, before *verism*, before realism. I have a small piece from *Lucia de Lammermoor* in *Madame Bovary*, which is sung as it had originally been sung. The actors face the audience, avoid looking at one another, and the declaration of love to the young woman is not made facing the woman but facing the audience. When he gets on his knees, he goes only three-quarters of the way. People found that hilarious. They said, "My God, how poorly they acted then, how unnatural they were!" Antoine substituted this manner of acting for people who spoke directly to one another. In both costumes and sets, he introduced a kind of copy of reality.

But in twenty years, this copy also became conventional. When I started in film, we were used to this convention, and I will always remember the conversation I had with some carpenters and set painters during the first film I was involved in. I was explaining that for the set, we needed a common room on a farm in southern France, and because in southern France there are many stone walls, covered irregularly with mortar, it would be a good idea to give an irregular look to the walls and to whitewash them. They listened to me with a kind of impatience and found my explanations unnecessary, because this kind of set was already known and pigeonholed. They kept saying to me, "But Monsieur Renoir, we know what it is, it's *rustic*. – Rustic? – The rustic style has irregular walls and exposed beams. – But there you have it, I don't want exposed beams. – Oh, excuse us! The rustic style has exposed beams."

The same thing happened with the makeup and the acting; little by little this American acting that had been so natural became false. It was catalogued and categorized. The man who sits on the arm of an armchair instead of sitting in the armchair – it's very nice when he sits there without thinking about it. But as soon as he *must* sit on the arm of the armchair, it becomes as false a convention as d'Artagnan's sword.

And this probably happened with Italian neorealism, which now produces works that are as false as Francesca Bertini's acting was. The truth is that this "veil" constantly returns. A kind of opaque cloud forms between our eyes and reality again and again. . . . It's our own mind that forms it, that accepts it, because it's so convenient. Basically, the problem is that for films to remain lively, each cameraman, each worker, each set painter, each carpenter, each designer, each actor must reinvent everything each time. But it's very tiring. It's so much easier to pull out a little file and say, "*rustic*!" And we go with the rustic, and we're set.

CAHIERS: The only consolation is that works that discover something do not go out of style as much as do those that copy other people's ideas. Griffith, for example, remains.

RENOIR: I would even say that Griffith's most beautiful pieces are more important today than when he made them. Unfortunately, making films is an expensive profession, and you can't do it if the films don't make a profit. My word, this is quite a problem. But on the other hand, even if you have a chance to work outside the normal channels, it also seems to me to be a problem. I think one must work normally, with the idea that the film will be shown to the public, will please them, and will make a profit. Too bad if it doesn't. But you have to start with the very progressive idea of making a popular work. The very nature of motion pictures makes this necessary, because they are expensive and are based on the idea of dissemination, that they will be shown on thousands of screens. They therefore have to please in thousands of different places. What is happening now is that there may be room for a motion picture industry whose products – instead of being reproduced nationally on hundreds of screens in the same country – are reproduced internationally on somewhat more specialized screens. There may be a way of deciding on the requisite number of theaters and screens from all the countries in the world, instead of in just one country. That, in my opinion, is the great phenomenon of our times.

An easy scenario to write

CAHIERS: *Madame Bovary* is somewhat similar to *Tire au flanc*. We don't know why, but these films have the reputation of being purely commissioned works.

RENOIR: I saw *Madame Bovary* again. That is, I saw a part of it again, not too long ago, maybe two or three years ago, at the Cinémathèque, I believe. There is one person in it whom I admire enormously: it's my brother Pierre, I found him . . . ah! really very handsome. And Valentine Tessier is simply delicious, she's adorable, she has a way of walking, of twirling her skirt, of entering, of leaving, a type of security. . . .

I can tell you that the reason – there are always many reasons for doing films – the main reason for this film, what attracted me, is that it was an experiment with theater people. Valentine and my brother were essentially theater people, and along with them we had a group composed of many other theater people. Max Dearly was above all a man of the theater. And I was very happy to do a film, to write a script for theater people, with dialogues that seemed as if they had to be spoken by theater people. Basically, this experiment is somewhat like what I'm doing now on the stage, only it was on the screen. You know, the joy of having certain phrases that you know must be spoken by lips accustomed to speaking words.... It's a great pleasure.

CAHIERS: The film you shot was much longer than the one we see today.

RENOIR: Oh, yes! It was very long, and it was much better. To tell the truth, there again a film was destroyed by being cut. It wasn't the producers, who fought as much as they could, but the distributors, who didn't dare release a film that lasted over three hours. It just wasn't done. It was a period when double features seemed to be the answer to the movie crisis, because there was a movie crisis, just like the one now. The distributors said, "No, we like this film, but we can't do it, it's not possible... it has to be cut." So I cut it. But oddly enough, once it was cut the film seemed much longer – yes, intellectually – than before it was cut; it went on and on.

You know, in its present state, I find the film to be a little boring. But when it lasted three hours, it wasn't boring at all. I showed it before it was cut. I had maybe five or six showings of it in a screening room at the Billancourt studio, which holds fifty people, and they all were delighted. Bert Brecht saw it, for example, and he was absolutely enchanted by it.

Unfortunately, I'm sure that the full version disappeared as soon as it was cut, when we made cuts in the print and then in the negative, and that the trims were thrown out and burned.

CAHIERS: There is a greater richness in *Madame Bovary* than in all your earlier films.

RENOIR: The more work I did, the more I learned to develop scenes to their fullest. I don't think that it's the only method for making films that start at the beginning and end at the end and that are like one enormous scene. But personally, I prefer a working method that thinks of each scene as a separate little film. That's what Chaplin does, by the way, and God knows it worked well for him.

CAHIERS: In your case, that might be what disorients the audience.

RENOIR: I think that it's very disorienting and that it can't be used for a film whose action is very engaging; people get upset with you. I think that it's – you can't say it's a fault or a quality – let's say it's a characteristic that must have hurt me quite often.

CAHIERS: It's your taste for changing the tone.

RENOIR: Yes. I'm most attracted to the idea of constructing a film from small, complete pieces. The only problem is that this often works against me because of another of my obsessions, of slightly neglecting the importance of the story line. I'm obsessed with the idea that in reality, the story isn't very important. Now, if you have a strong enough story... Take, for example, *Grand Illusion*, which has the type of script that's easy to write. Because it's easy, it's strong enough to hold the audience's attention. It's the story of people who want to escape: Will they or won't they succeed?

It's quite convenient to have this sort of thing, and in the film you can allow yourself as many little sketches as you like, many little side scenes as varied and as different as you like. You can suddenly stop in the middle and have a discussion, for example, on the meaning of Jewish generosity. That's one scene that was never cut from the film, even by those most prone to cut, and no one ever realized that it had nothing to do with the film. It seemed to me simply that a discussion of this type would be interesting.

The ride in the handcart

CAHIERS: And right afterward, you had the ordeal with *Toni*.

RENOIR: I just saw *Toni* again. I saw it with its producer, Pierre Gaut, who is a good friend of mine and who played an important role in the shooting. After all, the producer of *Toni* had to be convinced that it was worth making a film outdoors and without any stars, with events that, because they were taken from a true story, were necessarily somewhat brutal. At the time, corpses weren't accepted in films, or else they had to be rather noble corpses. The death had to have taken place before the revolution, and there had to have been a duel. A gentleman killed in a duel without too much blood was acceptable. But a gory murder like the one in *Toni* was not acceptable to the usual distribution channels. So it was very difficult to release the film. Unfortunately, I lost the shots dealing with this murder, for example, the ride in the handcart, the laundry cart in which the corpse was hidden, and the corpse's ride in the cart, with the singing Corsican coal workers who were passing by and who jokingly decided to follow along and sing. It was a good scene, I think, but we had to cut it and it disappeared. Yes, it's too bad.

CAHIERS: Was it a project that you'd had in mind for a long time?

RENOIR: Yes. I have a friend whose name is Jacques Mortier and who at the time was the commissioner of police in Martigues. He writes quite well (he wrote a detective novel, *Le Singe vert*), but in this case, it wasn't a matter of writing a novel. He simply gathered and related the facts about a real murder, a story of jealousy among the foreigners living in Martigues. Together, we decided from these facts that it would be interesting to make them into a film in which the drama, if I

Toni.

may say, would not be dramatic but would happen naturally, like an everyday occurrence. We talked about it a long time ago. Although the story in the film has been changed enough so that the surviving relatives wouldn't recognize it, it is fundamentally true (the inhabitants, the location, and the main characters all are the same). It took place about a dozen years before I shot *Toni*.

CAHIERS: The script is signed by Jean Renoir and Karl Einstein.

RENOIR: Karl Einstein was a friend of mine and of Pierre Gaut. He had a very wide-ranging mind. It seems to me that having people who are not involved in film but who have expertise in their own fields contribute to films can sometimes enrich a film, give it a certain nobility, as Koch did in most of my prewar films. Karl Einstein wrote about art; in fact, he wrote some of the best books on abstract painting.

It has to be Minou Drouet

CAHIERS: It's our opinion that *Toni* got a cold reception because it came right after *Angèle*.

RENOIR: Definitely. I don't think that the audiences were ready for this kind of story. Even if *Angèle* hadn't been made, I'm convinced that *Toni* would not have been accepted, not easily, at least. People hate to have their expectations upset, and at that time the film was strange, unexpected. And it seemed brutal to people, whereas when I saw it the other day, it seemed extremely sweet, extremely gentle.

CAHIERS: What's striking is how nice the bad guys are, "Le rôti sans la sauce."

RENOIR: Dalban, yes, of course. And Andrex, he's charming, he's marvelous. I just saw Andrex and Blavette again on a television program. I was very happy to see them. They've matured, and I think that this will be a good thing. I feel that it's very difficult to find older actors in France right now, whereas we're swarming with young boys, all as handsome as Adonis, and young girls, all equipped with extraordinary charms. But there aren't many fifty-year-olds.

Audiences weren't ready, that's why *Toni* wasn't a hit at the time. It was as welcome as a hair in a bowl of soup. People are like Panurge's sheep. They follow one another, and each does what the others are doing. For example, right now, a few very good directors have discovered youth, and everyone is discovering youth, and only films on youth are being made. If a young girl over sixteen is raped, no one's interested. And even at sixteen, not too many people are interested. It has to be Minou Drouet who is raped, and then it becomes very interesting.... But things will change. Soon, once again, no one will be interested in that. Very young girls can be raped by the dozen, lined up, gang-raped, no one will watch. They'll only want the interesting "problems" of very old ladies, change-of-life stories.

CAHIERS: Nineteen thirty-five is the year of *The Crime of Monsieur Lange* (*Le Crime de Monsieur Lange*).

RENOIR: You mustn't forget Jacques Prévert's contribution to *The Crime of Monsieur Lange*, which was important. We worked together. I asked him to come to the set with me. He came every day, and I constantly said to him, "Well, old man, here we have to improvise," and the film

Florelle and René Lefèvre in *The Crime of Monsieur Lange.*

was improvised, as were all my films, but with Prévert's constant cooperation.

CAHIERS: You get the impression that there is a continuous conversation between the two of you, that one of you finishes the other's sentence.

RENOIR: Absolutely! I'm sure it would be impossible to trace the origin of ideas in this film, to know whether it was Jacques or I who found this or that. We really found everything together.

CAHIERS: But, for example, the Ranimax pills?

RENOIR: That was all Prévert's idea!

CAHIERS: And Brunius's little dog? I'd think that was yours.

RENOIR: Yes, it was. Brunius's little dog is there only because it was my dog.

CAHIERS: What kind of a reception did *The Crime of Monsieur Lange* get?

RENOIR: A good one. It didn't come easily, but it was good. I don't think *The Crime of Monsieur Lange* was a financial success – that would surprise me – but it was certainly a solid undertaking.

A seductive mistake

CAHIERS: *A Day in the Country* (*Une partie de campagne*) is one of your films about which there are the most conflicting rumors.

RENOIR: I thought it would be interesting to do a short film that would nonetheless be complete, that would have the style of a full-length film, and that would get the production value of a full-length film.

Yet in order to give a short film the kind of care given to a full-length film, we had to find a way to save money, because a short can't bring in a lot of money. We therefore did it with Pierre Braunberger and practically without salaries.

I wrote the script with the shooting locations in mind, because I was very familiar with the Loing region, near Montigny. I thought that part of the Loing could represent what the Seine used to be, close to Paris. Now it's impossible to find spots around Paris without buildings or factories. And most of all, the biggest reason for my choosing these exteriors was that I knew them through and through, I knew what time the light would be hitting a specific group of trees in a particularly pleasing way. I knew even the smallest details of the landscape. I also knew its drawbacks. I knew it might rain there. That's the main inconvenience, but I didn't expect it to rain so much. We had very few sunny days, and we quickly ran over the budget that Braunberger allocated, because the rain held us back longer than we had imagined. So I changed the script once again and adapted it to the rainy season. That's why we had some rain sequences that weren't planned in the original script, and that's why I was able to shoot all the scenes that were planned.

From a technical point of view, I had some extraordinary associates: my nephew Claude, who was head cameraman for the first time, Cartier-Bresson and Visconti as assistants, and Brunius as an actor. The sound was recorded on location. We were determined to do the film without postsynchronizing the dialogue and without sound effects. When the film was finished, I had to go shoot *The Lower Depths* immediately, because the rain had extended the shooting an inordinate amount of time.

Georges Darnous in *A Day in the Country.*

The Lower Depths was therefore delayed fifteen days, during which I had to rewrite the script. Luckily, the late fall weather was good, and we were able to do some outdoor shots without too much trouble! It seemed as if all the rain had fallen on *A Day in the Country.*

I wasn't able to do the editing, because after *The Lower Depths,* I was carried off to the *Grand Illusion,* which I had been trying to do for three years and which all of a sudden became possible. Then, one after another, without a moment's rest, I did *La Marseillaise, The Human Beast* (*La Bête humaine*), and *The Rules of the Game* (*La Règle du jeu*). They all were films that were very dear to me, each and every one, and each time I said, "Goodness, I'll do the editing for *A Day in the Country* later." Then, when the time came, I was in a jam and couldn't do it. And then came the war.

There is also another reason: I thought more scenes were needed, but I was wrong. The scenes were not necessary. And still another reason was that Braunberger was very happy with the results, so happy that he wanted to do a full-length film. He had even asked Prévert to write a script. But it's very difficult, you know, to draw things out, to transform something that was conceived of as a short film into a full-length film. So Prévert made a try, but he didn't like it. And in the end it wasn't shot. In short, all these circumstances, in addition to my preoccupations, brought the film right up to the war.

CAHIERS: So it's not because you were unhappy with it?

RENOIR: Absolutely not. On the contrary, I have always been enchanted with *A Day in the Country*. But on the one hand, Braunberger's reasons for doing a full-length film were very convincing. It was a mistake, but a seductive mistake. And on the other hand, in case we decided to show it as it was, I wanted to work on it seriously, and not in my spare time. And then we were uncertain about the music. Kosma did a musical adaptation afterward, a magnificent adaptation, in fact, but at the time we didn't know what to do.

I don't remember all the extra scenes I had planned, but I had planned an explanation, or a show of feelings, somewhere between the storm and the final return, a scene in which we would have seen Sylvia Bataille in Paris with her husband. But because I had my doubts about it and because I thought we might never be able to shoot it, I shot the last scene so that it could be understood on its own.

I was sure that the scene in Paris was not necessary. It may be the only film I've done (I don't use a lot of footage in my films. . . . I don't usually gobble up film, but some scenes are always dropped) in which nothing was trimmed. Everything is used.

An authentic Russia

CAHIERS: Now we come to *The Lower Depths*.

RENOIR: There are no stories to tell about *The Lower Depths*. Spaak is a wonderful associate, you know, and with him – despite any obsession one may have with improvisation – you start with a framework that even my improvisations couldn't hurt.

Companeez had written an outline before either I or Spaak had arrived on the scene, but we didn't use it.

It's a subject that Kamenka had suggested and that I liked right away. I asked for only one change in the initial project – I'm not talking about the script, which I changed completely, but about the general project – which was that we not try to make Russia look like the real thing. It seemed to me that trying to create the impression of Russia in Paris would be ridiculous, like a carnival.

CAHIERS: It was exactly on this point that the critics were unsure.

RENOIR: Oh, of course! It was always Russia on the banks of the Marne! I think I was right. Russia not on the banks of the Marne would have been even worse. At least this way we weren't pretending to be in Russia. We weren't pretending to be in Paris either. But we had our actors speak a pure twentieth-century French, and it was much better.

CAHIERS: It was also your first film with Jean Gabin.

RENOIR: There you have a true film actor. Gabin is a Film actor with a capital F. I've filmed many people in my life, and I have never met such a cinematic power, he's a cinematic force, it's fantastic, it's incredible. It must come from his great honesty. He's certainly the most honest man I've ever met in my life.... Oh! wait, I know one other honest person, Ingrid Bergman. There's no cunning. And I'm sure that Ingrid's influence on the public – people will say it's her beauty, they'll find a thousand reasons for it – but I'm sure it's her great honesty.

You have to be needled

CAHIERS: We've heard that *Grand Illusion* came about from an exchange of scripts between you and Duvivier. In the beginning, he was supposed to do *Grand Illusion* and you *La Belle Equipe*.

RENOIR: No, this is what happened: I was working with Spaak. We were in the process of writing something or other, *The Lower Depths* probably, and we talked about *La Belle Equipe*. We might even have started to think up the story of *La Belle Equipe* together, I don't remember exactly. In any case, we spoke about it. And then Spaak and I thought we should show the script to Duvivier, because we thought it would be a magnificent story for him! It was right up his alley. Duvivier then changed it himself, digested it, and rewrote the script with Spaak. But there was never any question of my shooting it.

As for *Grand Illusion*, the origin of this film is a story that a friend from the war had told me. His name during the war was Warrant Officer Pinsard and then later, Captain Pinsard, and, when I was shooting *Toni*, General Pinsard. And General Pinsard had really been a war hero, a guy who had escaped seven or eight times. I was eternally grateful to him, because I was in aviation, I took photographs – which meant that I was in a plane that was neither very fast nor well defended – and very often I was attacked by the Germans. The reason I wasn't shot down is that a fighter plane from the adjoining formation always came over and shot down the German, and most of the time it was Pinsard!

So I was shooting *Toni*. Some planes were making a racket above us all the time, and the producer, Pierre Gaut, said, "Let's go see the commander." And who did I find but Pinsard!

We saw each other again, and it reminded me of his escape stories. I said to Pinsard, "Listen, old boy, tell me your escape stories again. Maybe I can make them into a film." So he told me his stories, which I put down on paper and which have nothing in common with the film, but they were a necessary starting point. You do need something to spark your interest at the start, a kind of pinprick; you have to be needled.

The needle in this case was my meeting with Pinsard. So I wrote a script . . . that is, I wrote a story, and when I had digested it a bit, I took it to Spaak, and I said, "Old man, you have to help me. Write a script from this. I think it's a good story." He agreed. He found it to be very good, and he rewrote it with me. And after that, we brought it to the producer who had done *The Lower Depths*, and he didn't think it was any good at all. In the end, we went all over Paris. Luckily Gabin liked the idea, and we were also really good friends. That's how I shot *Grand Illusion*, thanks to Gabin.

Gabin and I went to I don't know how many shady producers, offices, companies. Whether French, Italian, or American, it didn't matter! They all refused, they all said, "Oh, a war story, what a joke, and so on." And then, we were raising many delicate questions, and that's just not done.

Finally, we found a young man who, in my opinion, had great expertise in all of this and helped us tremendously. His name was Albert Kinkéwitch, and he was the assistant, the secretary, the factotum, of a financier named Rollmer, who was thinking about getting into the film business. He may have put money into films here and there, I don't know. Whatever the case was, Kinkéwitch, who was very interested in films but who wasn't involved in them, and Rolmer, who wasn't involved in films either, did *Grand Illusion*, and I'm sure the only reason was that they weren't involved in films. All the professionals were against the story.

All the distribution specialists, the big names in the commercial end of the industry, all adamantly rejected the script. I was able to shoot it only because of Gabin's influence.

CAHIERS: As soon as it came out, it was a big success?

RENOIR: Right from the start, it took off.

CAHIERS: Weren't you also a prisoner during the war?

From the poster for *Grand Illusion* [Jean Gabin and Dita Parlo].

RENOIR: No. I shot this film according to other people's stories, Pinsard's stories, and the stories of many other prisoners whom I interviewed. One great help was that my initial intention in life was to be a cavalry officer, and so consequently, I understood these people's minds and could guess what types of reactions they would have in certain circumstances.

The exterior shots weren't taken in Germany. They were taken in Alsace, in those parts of Alsace that were extremely influenced by the Germans after the war of 1870. For example, the areas and the barracks in which we shot were artillery barracks built by Wilhelm II at Colmar.

The final château is a château built by Wilhelm II. It's the Hoch Königsburg. These buildings are entirely German in influence.

The sides of the scale

CAHIERS: With *La Marseillaise*, you tried to make a film that changed the normal means of production and distribution?

RENOIR: Yes, but in the process, the film became an absolutely normal enterprise and was distributed normally.

CAHIERS: The spirit remains, just the same. We've heard that the system of production was to have the viewers pay for their tickets in advance.

RENOIR: I think there was something like that at one point.

CAHIERS: As far as the budget was concerned, was it the most expensive of your prewar films?

RENOIR: Silent films, like *Le Tournoi* and *Le Bled*, cost even more. The means available at the Société des romans historiques filmés – or, rather, at the Films historiques (Society of Historical Films) – were enormous.

CAHIERS: The film you shot was much longer than the final version?

RENOIR: I was surprised at the length of the script. I saw a 16mm copy that circulates in American universities. I had a drum parade that I was very proud of, but unfortunately it was cut. I'm very sad about that, drums are beautiful.

The truth is, my greatest pleasure in this entire film – one of my greatest memories – was the scenes played by my brother and Madame Delamare. The scenes in the Tuileries were enthralling to write and to shoot. I had the feeling that I was rather close to reality there, that it could have happened like that. When it suddenly gave the impression of being "kitchen" talk, which begins to overwhelm all the important events and people of the world, when you get lost in little things, in tomatoes... In *Toni*, people appear so ordinary that you can have them speak in a poetic language, because the poetry is balanced by their character, their behavior, the way they're dressed. Whereas in a film in which the characters' appearances are far from reality, you have to try to get closer to daily life by means of the dialogue. It's a system of checks and balances. From a technical point of view – I'm not talking about inspiration, or about intrinsic quality – the most important thing is to manage to keep the two sides of the scale at the same level, and when you fall very low, you have to lower the other side right away.

The most difficult thing is that the artistic equilibrium is different for each person, and personally, I have never been able to convince myself that this equilibrium should be derived solely from the story. I spend my time reestablishing the equilibrium in a film, but the idea of reestablishing it only through elements of the "plot" doesn't enter my mind. You can reestablish the equilibrium with an object on a table, with a color – if it's a color film – with a line that means nothing but that has more or less weight than the previous one.

CAHIERS: So that an unbalanced story, to use your term, sparks your interest, in that it compels you.

RENOIR: Yes, it makes me constantly want to insert wedges, as you would under a wobbly table. Unfortunately, I think that this confuses the audience.

Besides, if I were to let myself go, I would start with a set of heroes, and then I would completely forget them. I would move the story on to other people, and then still others.... I've always wondered why a film has to follow the same people.

We're going to have a magnificent child

CAHIERS: We were just wondering whether the promoters of *La Marseillaise* wouldn't have wanted something more schematic.

RENOIR: It's possible. I don't know. In any case, that's the way I did it, and it matches perfectly my feelings and beliefs.

CAHIERS: It's the "balancing act" that you were talking about that must prevent you from ever doing a work of propaganda.

RENOIR: That's right! Obviously. It's really mind-boggling, but we have to admit that each side has good reasons, such convincing reasons! It's terrible, isn't it? I think that my case, which is a serious one, is also the case of many French people and may explain the doubts that our country has right now. These kinds of doubts attack very civilized peoples. And very civilized peoples obviously have trouble defending themselves.

CAHIERS: The feeling one gets from *La Marseillaise* is that the Marseillais and the Royalists have the same ideal and are at odds mostly because of a misunderstanding.

RENOIR: Aside from the misunderstanding, they are separated by something quite obvious, which is essential to the history of the world: by being, or not being in the right place at the right time. It happens that some excellent, unquestionable, and absolutely defensible principles disappear, and even become fatal and disastrous, simply because they aren't right for their times. And it happens that much less refined principles, with much more naive ideas, work admirably: They are in agreement with their times. It's a question of a marriage between human beings, their ideas, their habits, their morals, and the time, and it is an important question in the history of the world. Louis XVI lost because he had nothing more to do at that time. The monarchy had nothing more to do. And we can even say that during revolutions, it's not the revolutionaries who win, but the reactionaries who lose. The two are very different. Even if there hadn't been a revolution, the reactionaries would have lost, would have disappeared on their own.

It's not a question of superiority or inferiority at all. A moment comes in the history of the world when the diplodocus disappears and is replaced by a dinosaur who is happy with a different air density and with the food in the forest, which suits him. And then, the time comes when he also disappears. Just as animal species do, feelings and ideas disappear, whether they are good or bad. It's simply that they can no longer live off their surroundings. I think it's a question of nourishment, even for feelings and ideas.

CAHIERS: The sense of history?

RENOIR: Except that the world is made up in such a way that only people who don't know that they have a feeling for history – who don't even know that they are going to succeed or why they are going to succeed – only those people really succeed in a given direction, let's say, in making a film. There is a kind of law governing humans that also governs trees: The tree that will grow to be enormous doesn't know that it will be enormous. It has no idea. And I think this is an unbending rule. I believe that. You'll tell me that many people who are successful knew that they would be, but personal success doesn't count in history, personal success is just a small thing. Moreover, it's only superficial. Who's to say that the gentleman with thirty film production companies and many cars has succeeded? He may not have succeeded at all! He may be the most unhappy man in the world. More miserable than a hobo.

Simplicity is absolutely essential to creation. Those people who make love while saying: "We're going to have a magnificent child"; well, they won't have a magnificent child, they may not have any child at all that evening. . . . The magnificent child comes by chance, one day after a good laugh, a picnic, fun in the woods, a roll in the hay, then a magnificent child is born!

Indian music

CAHIERS: You did *The Human Beast* and then, right afterward, *La Marseillaise*.

RENOIR: *The Human Beast* is not a subject that I chose. I'm truly happy to have done this film. It proves that it's wrong to think that one must always choose one's subjects. Robert Hakim spoke to me about this one and convinced me that I should do it. I wrote the script in fifteen days. Then I read it to Hakim, who asked me to make some small, unimportant changes. But I didn't choose the subject.

And since I hadn't chosen it (because I'd read *The Human Beast* when I was a kid, but I hadn't reread it in maybe twenty years), my script was rather superficial. One thing happened that had also happened with *The Lower Depths*. While I was shooting, I reworked the script and brought it closer to Zola. I remembered this the other day, on a television program, because Simone Simon had asked me to give her the words she would use in advance. I had no more scripts for *The Human Beast*. I found one at Mary Meerson's, who lent it to me. Unfortunately it was my first draft, and the dialogue she wanted wasn't in it. There was some dialogue that I had written myself and that was very bad, whereas the one I had meant for Simone Simon was almost entirely copied from Zola's text, and it was magnificent. I reinserted it on the day of the shooting. Because I had to work very quickly, I reread a few pages from Zola in the evening, to check that I hadn't skipped anything. And this was all the more important because I had an idea in mind that I have never abandoned – I still believe it – which is that the so-called realist or naturalist side of Zola is not so important and that Zola was first and foremost a poet, a great poet. Consequently, I had to try to find the elements of his style that would permit me to bring this poetry to the screen.

CAHIERS: And yet your film seems more orchestrated than the earlier ones.

RENOIR: You see, I worked the same way on this film that I do on all my films. I arrive on the set in the morning. I read the dialogues. If I can have a few actors with me – that is, I don't often have them – they have to get made up after all, get ready, get dressed. Generally I do it alone with one assistant, two assistants, the script girl, or the cameraman. I imagine the scenes and I partially form them. I don't plan any angles. In my opinion, the angles have to be decided once the actors have rehearsed. Nevertheless, it's only at that moment that I get a general idea of the scene, which becomes a kind of line to follow and to stay close to, so that the actors can be entirely free. In other words, I think that the difference between this method and sticking to the script is similar to the difference between Indian music and Western music since Bach and Vivaldi, since the invention of the tempered scale. In Indian music, there is a general theme, which is four thousand years old, and you must follow it. And then there is a general note given by a string instrument, an instrument that only has one string. Before beginning, everyone comes to an agreement, and the note is repeated constantly, so as to bring the other instruments back to tonal unity. There is a theme and a tone, and aside from that, everyone is free. I think it's a marvelous system, and I try to do a bit of that in motion pictures.

There's my red light

There's one other thing. You know that I'm obsessed with filming stories that come to mind, stories that are based on observations I've made about things around me, about adventures I've lived or my friends have lived, and the truth is I'm not sure whether this isn't a mistake, because it demands a huge amount of work. It requires a lot of time in any case. And I finish by producing very little. When you have a novel like *The Human Beast*, the adaptation is much easier. After all, the greatest writers did it in this way, Shakespeare, all the great writers. The French classical writers copied the Latin classics, which copied the Greek classics. It helps a great deal when you don't have to worry about inventing a story, only about the dramatic construction of an existing story. You can create a much more rigorous structure. With original stories, given one's inescapable self-doubt, you're forced to leave some ambiguity so that you can constantly readjust it. *The Rules of the Game* was a constant balancing act (the balancing act again!). I pushed one side and then the other and then set it upright. "It's going to fall on its face, it's going to fall down." You feel as though you're walking a tightrope, with a big stick and your weight. But it's exciting, I must say. And right now it's very difficult to make films, and when I see successful films (God knows there are many of them!) I'm overwhelmed with admiration. We're dealing with an essentially unstable world, and we ourselves are unstable. Of course I have the right to be pessimistic, to lose some of the kind of confidence that I had when I was shooting *The River*, for example.

I have a friend, a very young friend, who told me something marvelous the other day. In my opinion, this is how things can be filmed. We were talking, as before, about automobile traffic in cities, in Paris, for example, and about the fact that many taxi drivers are irritable at the end of the day. It's a wonder they're not more irritable, because it's awful. They constantly have one foot on the brake; they're in danger of hitting bicyclists, are constantly flirting with homicide or with accidents, or simply with tickets, which are annoying. And the fact that they don't show their irritation even more means that they're polite people who control themselves. And my young friend, who drives a lot in Paris, said to me, "Well, I try – I haven't yet succeeded, but I think I'll get there – I try to think of the traffic obstacles as tranquilizers. For example, there's a red light. You have to stop at the red light. Normally you're impatient, and you say to yourself, 'This red light is endless, it's never going to change, when will it turn green?' But I say to myself, 'What luck! There's my red light!' I take my foot off the pedals, I straighten my legs, I stretch, and I look at the people around me, I try to see what's going on in the street, and when the light turns green, I say to myself, 'How lucky I am! The red light was so short! I'm going to be early and not late.'"

Isn't that great? I wonder whether we shouldn't try to do that in cinema! In fact, it's the continuation of *The River*; it's what Radha, when she explains her problems to the wounded, nervous American, calls "to consent." It's perfectly feasible, once again, that practicing Asian philosophy could help Westerners. In India, the people who really practice this philosophy (it's not really a philosophy, it's simply an attitude toward life) arrive at the following result: If they're very poor, they settle their lives, their home, on a window sill of a large building or a bank, for instance. There they can store the blanket in which they'll sleep (because it gets rather cold at night, and it rains during the monsoon season), and they can cook a bit of food, if they find some. There are many tramways that make a lot of noise, many cries in the street, but they manage to isolate themselves entirely, to think about their own little business with as much intensity as if they were in a house in the country, absolutely alone and surrounded by greenery. Now that's a wonderful solution! It's a system that we must learn, it would be very useful for us.

A slightly pointed nose

CAHIERS: If you don't mind, we're going to skip the period of your life from *The Rules of the Game* to *The Golden Coach* (*La Carrosse d'or*) and go straight to *French Cancan.*

RENOIR: *French Cancan* answered my great desire to make a film in a very French spirit and that would be an easy, convenient contact, a nice bridge between myself and French audiences. I felt that the public was very close to me, but I wanted to make sure.

CAHIERS: Is it also a subject that was suggested to you?

RENOIR: Absolutely. But this time what was suggested had nothing to do with the subject I filmed. Only the title is the same. Whereas with *The Human Beast* there was Zola's novel, here, in what Mr. Deutschmeister suggested, it was merely a question of showing a certain kind of show and keeping the title. He left me the greatest freedom concerning the script, which I wrote as I pleased.

CAHIERS: Did you deliberately repeat many of the themes of *The Golden Coach*, or did they just come to you?

Françoise Arnoul, Maria Félix, and Philippe Clay in *French Cancan*.

RENOIR: I don't think I deliberately used them again. They came to me while I was writing the script. Because the subjects were somewhat similar, I was drawn to the same conclusions.

There was another thing that tempted me enormously in *French*

Cancan. It was the idea of having music in a film, because ever since 1924, I've been obsessed with the idea of filming an opera. And in 1924, it was impossible, because there was no sound. So when I had to write two or three songs for *French Cancan,* it made me very happy. It was a small step toward this old dream. This old dream that still hasn't materialized and probably never will.

CAHIERS: In the beginning, did you envision a final, overwhelming cancan scene?

RENOIR: Yes. But in studying the French cancan with the dancers, I realized that it created a very different effect from the one I had anticipated. One thing, especially, became clear: It's that the cancan had both a poetic and a prosaic side. There's the muscular side, the difficult warming-up period, but that's joined with a kind of extraordinary flight. I think that it's a film that could be shot only in France. I think this kind of innocence, especially among the girls, could only be found in Paris: the open, surprised, unsure-of-oneself side. This television program the other day allowed me to see Claudie again. She's a remarkable character. She could be a very good actress, such a pure Parisian look! She is truly the incarnation of the cancan: very surprised-looking eyes, a slightly pointed nose, and a stubborn forehead pushed back from the rest of her face.

CAHIERS: What struck us was this furious finale that you don't find in the cancan today.

RENOIR: It's become a routine, a kind of Parisian custom. It was furious and extraordinary at that period, and now it's like what we were saying about Antoine's style. Everything becomes old, and the "veil" between reality and convention thickens. The cancan has become a kind of convention, with one leg raised like that because you have to raise a leg, whereas in the beginning, you raised a leg in a movement destined to excite the men in a certain way or to allow for a certain acrobatic gesture.

Thanks to these dancers, I think we rediscovered a little of the way things were. It's the same with everything, with worldly customs, with religions. Things quickly become fixed movements, whose meanings have been lost and even completely forgotten. People no longer know why they shake hands now, it's become a ritual gesture. Rituals replace reality very quickly.

Intimate conversations with Venus

CAHIERS: Right now, your most recent film is *Paris Does Strange Things* (*Eléna et les hommes*). What was your initial idea?

RENOIR: Each film has a reason for being done. Generally, the reason is that a producer asks you to do it and proves to you that it's a good story. You're always happy to shoot a good story. But here, the real reason is that I was dying to do something happy with Ingrid Bergman and had been for a very long time. I wanted to see her laugh, to see her smile on the screen, and to enjoy, first of all for myself – and to have the public enjoy – the kind of sexual abundance that is one of her characteristics. In other words – I did a small record about this, by the way – I was dreaming of Venus and Olympus. But maybe of a Venus revised by Offenbach.

CAHIERS: It might have been just that – her good health – that was shocking.

RENOIR: It's very possible. I don't think that the modern world is ready to have intimate conversations with Venus. Or else, one has to be more clever than I was. You would have to do a film in which Venus reveals herself little by little, and in which you would help the audience discover her. In any case, women are the reason for *Eléna*'s existence, women represented by Ingrid Bergman. I constructed a satire around that, I played with political stories, with stories of generals. I tried to show the futility of human undertakings, including the undertaking we call patriotism, and to have fun juggling ideas that have become the serious ideas of our day. But all that is the gravy. I paid so much attention to the female character that I may have neglected the other questions a bit.

CAHIERS: There is one character that we find intriguing: Mel Ferrer's. According to the broad outline of the script, he's a nice person, but the way the details are treated, we often see him in uncomfortable situations. The audience would like to sympathize with him from the start but can't.

RENOIR: I think that was a mistake on my part. In any case, I was restricted for budgetary reasons during the shooting of this film. I hadn't realized how difficult it was to shoot two versions with people who don't speak English. At the start, we agreed with the producers that the people in the English version would be either English or American. But the producers never found these English or these Americans. We therefore had the lines in English spoken by magnificent French actors, but who didn't understand English. Even though I wasn't born English, I can direct an Englishman, but only if the English actor helps me (just as in French, I need the French actors to help; my manner of directing is not tyrannical, it's a two-way street). But I could not get this help from the French actors, who merely spoke words that they didn't understand, that evoked no feelings, that evoked sounds and meaning, but nothing more. Shooting these two versions was very dif-

The filming of *Paris Does Strange Things:* Jean Renoir and Ingrid Bergman.

ficult, extremely tiring for the actors, for the technicians, and for me. All this meant that little by little, I had to make sacrifices, and I wasn't able to develop all the situations as I could have. I even got to the point that I simplified them in order to present them in simpler language.

CAHIERS: But the film doesn't seem simple.

RENOIR: I just about pulled it off, once again by a balancing act. I'll tell you, I treated the film a little like a silent film. That was my safeguard, my last hope.

CAHIERS: You didn't want this ambiguity then?

RENOIR: I ended up accepting it and using it, because circumstances did not permit otherwise. I'm familiar with this ambiguity, I created it, but if the means had been available, I would rather have created a clearer character.

CAHIERS: We also had the impression that the audience liked Jean Marais's character so much they would have liked an ending in his favor.

RENOIR: I must admit that I searched for a way to have such an ending, but I didn't find one. *Eléna* was a nightmare to shoot, and I managed simply because the actors were wonderful with me. Ingrid was marvelous, she backed me up, comforted me. But trying to do two versions without two entirely different sets of actors is impossible. It's a miracle that I finished *Eléna*. I finished because I know my business, and I used many tricks. This business of contrasts and of equilibrium, for example, God knows that I used it! It was a risky adventure every day, which I got through by using magic tricks, by doing somersaults.

CAHIERS: It's all these somersaults that we find delightful.

RENOIR: Oh, but every day we were in a black hole! The ending alone! I had to improvise the ending in one day, with Juliet Gréco's song, because the song I had planned required words that I could never have had spoken. No, I was in a jam; there was no money left. I constantly had to invent shortcuts. *Eléna* owes its unity entirely to a certain spirit that I maintained throughout the film, by clinging to the main character. That's the glue, the cement that joins it all.

To bring joy to the street

CAHIERS: There are three acts, and what people have the most trouble understanding is that these three acts are treated as if they were three separate plays: the first, a spectacular comedy; the second, a vaudeville satire; and the third we don't know how to define.

RENOIR: A third act of romantic confusion.

CAHIERS: Yes, but with songs. The dramatic conflicts are resolved with song. We find that marvelous.

RENOIR: It was my only solution.

CAHIERS: But you had to be daring to use it.

RENOIR: I also had Juliet Gréco. Why not benefit from her when you're lucky enough to have her? And it was also extremely tempting to write a song whose words would have no meaning – which is a pleasure – or in any case, whose words would have only a general sense, would create a "feeling" but not tell a story.

CAHIERS: The song was also a hit visually. For example, the shot of Gréco among the bohemians. One has the impression of suddenly discovering a Picasso from the blue period.

RENOIR: Yes. I'd thought of that. I hate going back into history. And in my opinion, you can touch history only by making it current.

CAHIERS: Is the conclusion optimistic or pessimistic or in between? On paper, the fact that Ingrid Bergman falls into the arms of Mel Ferrer is a happy ending, but the shot in which she pulls off her daisy and the one of the daisy on the floor are heartbreaking.

RENOIR: That's what I was thinking. I thought that this creature who was made to bring joy to the street, to bring joy to the world, was merely going to end up in the arms of this man, and that her function had ended, that the curtain was going to fall on the marvelous show she had given the world. All these things do not make a film popular. But it's obvious that the ideas that come to you when you're forced to improvise come with a sort of powerful force. It's very sharp, like needles pricking your skin. I don't know whether they are better than the ideas that come in the silence of a workplace. In any case, they're different, and they produce different works.

CAHIERS: You didn't want to do something psychological. The character has a personality that is defined only in relation to the surrounding people.

RENOIR: That's right. We're a part of the world. In essence, it's almost the opposite of the literary, theatrical, and cinematic tendencies of today. Did you see the film by Kazan, *Baby Doll*? It really grabs you, doesn't it? It isn't a psychological film, either. What a beautiful film, wonderfully acted!

If I could marry Leslie...

CAHIERS: In the past few years, you've enjoyed adding purely literary works, and especially theatrical works, to your film activities. You had hardly any direct contact with the theater before the war?

Juliette Gréco and the bohemians in *Paris Does Strange Things*.

RENOIR: No, only a few projects that never came to anything. My first true contact was with *Julius Caesar*. It was a somewhat different experience, given the audience that comes to the Arles Arena. It was thrilling. I'll never forget the people from the city who acted in the play.

CAHIERS: *Orvet* was already written at that time, although perhaps not in its final form?

RENOIR: Yes, *Orvet* had been written. I've changed it since, but it had been written.

CAHIERS: Was that the first play you'd written?

RENOIR: No, I had started to write plays two or three times before. Either they became film scripts, or I never finished them. At one point, I had thought of doing a play using *Monsieur Lange*. I think *Monsieur Lange* would make a very good opera, by the way. It's full of opportunities for interesting songs. The song of the printer, the song of the laundress, the air of the concierge, right in the middle of the garbage cans.

CAHIERS: When did you first write *Orvet*?

RENOIR: I started it in America, halfheartedly. I wrote it while traveling. That year, I returned by ship. Ships are terrific places for writing. That's what I'm going to do to fix up the play I've just finished. I'm going to take a ship, and not a fast one.

CAHIERS: Your meeting Leslie Caron was crucial to *Orvet*?

RENOIR: Yes. This is what happened: I met Leslie Caron for the first time in a train station (I think it was Victoria Station, in London), and she must have been thirteen or fourteen years old, she was very young. I was already preparing *The River*. I almost approached her, thinking that she would have been very good in the part of the young English girl in *The River*, because I thought she was a young English girl, of course. A long time afterward, I met her with her co-actors from the Roland Petit's Ballet. We met and hit it off. What struck me about her was that the shape of her head, her profile, reminded me of some of my father's models. And then when I got to know her, I was able to appreciate her even more. She's an extraordinary girl.

For *Orvet*, I had memories of poacher stories from when I was living in the Fountainebleau forest, memories of a young girl who is, to a certain extent, the character Orvet. I thought it would be marvelous if I could marry Leslie to this character. I asked her to accept, and that's how it happened.

CAHIERS: It was a play right from the start?

RENOIR: Yes. Once the play was written, I tried to make a film from it, but I couldn't. I tried shooting it from every angle, but I couldn't find anything. It's based on a theatrical convention, and the language in which the characters communicate is not film language.

CAHIERS: At one time you planned on making a film from Turgenev's "First Love," which, it was said, would have been called *Les Braconniers* (*The Poachers*). Was that a different project?

RENOIR: That was a different project. I wrote a script with Dudley Nichols, but it was never filmed. It's based on the idea of a house in the

Raymond Bussières and Leslie Caron in *Orvet* (photo by Agence de presse Bernand).

woods, and a girl who lives with people from the forest but who has nothing to do with *Orvet*. It's also a forest idea. There was a supporting character whose name was Orvet, and I asked Dudley Nichols for permission to use the name Orvet for the main character in this play.

The impression of starting from scratch

CAHIERS: You wrote several versions?

RENOIR: The version in which the characters are imaginary is the version that I envisioned. I had written a draft, and I abandoned it. In my next-to-last version, the characters were real, and the male character wasn't a writer. I was afraid it would seem somewhat sordid, and that's why I made it into an imaginary adventure. Moreover, the fact that the imaginary adventure is now so linked to *Orvet* that I can't separate the two is the reason it wouldn't make a good film. I think it's rather difficult to bring a fairyland to film. There's another kind of fairyland in film: That's what we were talking about a little while ago,

Rehearsal for *Julius Caesar:* Paul Meurisse, Jean Renoir, Henri Vidal, and Michèle Morgan.

it's in trying to touch reality, but the fairy-tale kind of fairyland, the Perrault kind, is not up my alley, as far as I'm concerned.

I also changed my play because I was adamant about having an actor whom I admire immensely, Paul Meurisse. My first character was much older. It was really the adventure of a very old man and a little girl.

CAHIERS: The very important idea of Orvet dancing with shoes on came at the last moment?

RENOIR: On the last day of rehearsal.

CAHIERS: During your first theatrical directing, did you feel that you were benefiting from your experience with film directing or that you were starting from scratch?

RENOIR: I felt that I was starting from scratch and was doing a different type of work with *Orvet*. In *Julius Caesar*, on the other hand, I used my film experience a lot. First, every director is used to filming stories out of sequence and needing to have the subject perfectly clear in his mind. I never rehearsed *Julius Caesar* completely. The first complete run-through was the first public performance. And this was for a good reason: Some of the people were from Arles, and they worked all day, so I had to rehearse everything piece by piece and out of order. I think that my experience with doing this in film helped me a lot. It's a practical experience, but it counts a great deal.

Another thing or, rather, let's examine this idea further. In film, you get used to clearly classifying the different parts of a story so that you can shoot them out of order, but also because of a kind of feeling you have for the intensity of the scenes in relation to the place they will occupy in the editing. And then, what was also helpful in *Julius Caesar* was the fact that it wasn't written by me, but by someone named Shakespeare. And let's face it, it's easier that way.

In *Orvet*, on the other hand, my worries were author's worries, and when I worked out a scene with the actors, I wondered – if the scene wasn't what I had hoped – whether the poor results were due to the text or to the situation, and not to the directing. Whereas in *Julius Caesar*, when it wasn't working, I knew it was my fault and not Shakespeare's. I knew that the solution to the problem in *Julius Caesar* was in the staging. But in *Orvet*, I wondered whether it wasn't a problem with the "author."

CAHIERS: That's what was so remarkable about *Orvet*. Usually in the theater, you can easily distinguish between the play and the staging. In this case, it was really impossible to separate one from the other.

RENOIR: Staging plays occupies an important place today, but I think that this is the fault of the playwrights. Many modern playwrights hand the directors somewhat incomplete works and count on the director to finish them, to give them a final meaning. Many plays are written haphazardly.

After twenty years

CAHIERS: We have now arrived at the ritual question about your projects. Right now, you are writing a play and a film?

RENOIR: The film is quite sketchy. I'm in the process of working on it, and each day brings changes. In fact, I have two projects: one is to go back to Simenon after thirty years and to do a film of *Trois Chambres à Manhattan*, to film it on the streets of New York, and to try to blend Leslie Caron and a masculine character who is in love with her into the streets, into New York. It would be in black and white, with many location shots.

As for the other project, I'm in the process of working on it and can

Poster for *Carola*.

speak about it only very generally. I change it every day. It's an attempt to sketch Paris rapidly. I'm back to my idea in *Paris-Province*, but an extremely altered *Paris-Province*. It doesn't take place in a street like the avenue Frochet, but in one like those that you find near the Porte de Châtillon. You know, more of the houses there are made out of wood. You find many artists, plasterers, and set-painting studios. My female character lives in such an area, which is a small world in itself and has trouble adapting to the outside world. It would be a repeat of what's been done a good deal lately: *L'Oeuf* (*The Egg*), for example, which is a remarkable play taken from a novel that I would have liked to film.

It's an extraordinary subject, a preoccupation that I've had for a long time, from way before I read [Felicien Marceau's] *Chair et cuir*. It's a subject that's in Camus's *The Stranger* and that's also in *La Chienne*. It's a horrible drama: "What am I like when I'm outside? How do people see me? Do they accept me?" That's all.

And then, I've worked a great deal on my play [*Carola*], much more than on the film. It's finished now. I think I have three regular acts. It's too long, but I'll shorten it later. If everything goes well, Danielle Darrieux will play the part of the French actress during the occupation. Paul Meurisse will play the part of the German general. It's as honest an examination as possible of the different feelings that run through the mind of each person, whether one is the occupier or the occupied. I wouldn't say it was a sequel to *Grand Illusion*, but twenty years later, it has the same concerns. I show Germans, I show French, I show collaborators, I show Resistance fighters, I show people with no ideas.

The most difficult thing is to find a small setting. Stories that take place in large settings can be seen all the time, but a story that stands up well – that means something and that's in an "egg" – isn't so easy. In this case, I put my story in an egg, because the play lasts three hours, just enough time for the show, including intermissions, from nine to midnight, in an actress's dressing room, in a theater. That's why I'm so pleased.

CHAPTER III
Third interview: My next films
Interviewers: Michel Delahaye and Jean-André Fieschi

CAHIERS: The film that you're working on [*C'est la révolution!*, eventually released as *Le Petit Théâtre de Jean Renoir*] is composed of sketches.

JEAN RENOIR: It's a story composed of separate short stories.

CAHIERS: You haven't done this kind of thing before.

RENOIR: I started, but I didn't finish. I shot *A Day in the Country* (*Une Partie de campagne*) with the idea that the story would be only half or one-third of a film. And then *A Day in the Country* proved to be a bit longer. So this time, I hope that this won't happen to me, I hope that I will be able to contain myself and that all my little stories will be short enough to fit into the film. I have five of them.

CAHIERS: Are they connected to one another?

RENOIR: They're not connected to one another by a plot or by mechanical, technical, or visual means, but simply by a general idea. How can I express this idea? Maybe by quoting a proverb, "The pitcher goes so often to the water, that in the end it is broken." And this general idea can be defined in this way: From time to time, people get fed up, they've had enough of being martyred or bored or bullied or scorned, and so in one way or another, they try to put an end to it. They revolt.

But my revolts are not necessarily grand revolts. They're small revolutions, revolutions in a fishbowl. Yet I also have one that's a great revolution. In short, there are large ones and small ones. It's mixed.

So you see, the stories are connected, but there is no formal link between each one. No link, that is, in the mechanical sense of the word. In any case, I don't foresee any at the moment.

But maybe while working on it, I will realize that it needs a mechanical link, that's possible. . . . Only, up until now, I'm only going over the script, and until I've shot it, I won't know. . . . I won't know because when I shoot, I add a great deal. I add things, I cut things out. In any case, I make changes. I absolutely believe that the true meaning of a film is revealed only during the shooting, and sometimes after the shooting. Not before, anyway. So right now, I know that I have the hope of a sense for this film, the hope that it will mean something, and maybe even something interesting... but I don't know what exactly, since I haven't filmed it. In any case, you do have to start with a certain foundation, since making motion pictures is a profession in which material necessities count a great deal, in which certain technical preparations must be made. I must begin with a script. I have a script, but there are no links among the different stories in it. No visible links, I repeat. The links are only linking ideas.

Each story is a separate entity, with different actors, a different ambience, different locations. Each story exists separately. When you open a book of short stories by Maupassant, for example, the stories are united only by the spirit of the author. It's the same sort of thing here. For now, that's where I stand. Or perhaps a bit further.... As I said, there is a vague general idea, which is that of revolution.

CAHIERS: And what will you put behind this idea?

RENOIR: Revolution.... You see, it's a word that may have disappeared now, but it was an expression that was used frequently in my youth when things seemed unsettled. For example, in the regiment, when the rookies hadn't swept the room, all the older men said, "What's this?... The rookies haven't swept the room? It must be a revolution!"

CAHIERS: And the actors?

RENOIR: I haven't chosen them yet. Because the film hasn't been organized yet, it doesn't exist yet from a practical point of view. All I have is the script, and I asked my old accomplice, Braunberger, to help me get things rolling, but it hasn't been done yet. So given the current state of affairs, the actors I see in the film are only in my dreams and not in reality.

But if you would like to talk about my dreams, I can tell you that I have a sketch, for example, or rather a short tale.... I don't know why, but I don't like the word *sketch*. I may be wrong, but... it's a word that doesn't do anything for me.

CAHIERS: Let's say short story then.

RENOIR: Short story, little tale, anecdote.... In any case, I have one that I would like to see acted by Simone Signoret; I have another that I would like to see acted by Paul Meurisse; I have another that I would like to see acted by Pierre Olaf and Colette Brosset; I have another that I would like to see acted by Robert Dhéry; and I have another that I would like to see acted by Oscar Werner. That's about it, not the casting, but the dreams. The casting dreams.

CAHIERS: What makes you dream of them in particular?

RENOIR: Because it seems to me they would be good in the parts. And also, thinking of the actors helps me write the roles. It all works together. And I think that it all has to work together.

You know, this is an old idea of mine. I'm terribly wary of plans. And I believe, I firmly believe, that the inferior side of our civilization – which, of course, has superior sides, great beauty – I believe that all its lesser sides, all that is ugly in this twentieth-century civilization, comes from plans. Plans are ugly. Blueprints. Architects' blueprints. That's why there is no architecture, because there are blueprints.

I believe that great architecture consists of constructing a building and in saying afterward: What are we going to do in here? Here, well, we could put the kitchen, this really looks like a kitchen, and then we can put the bedroom in another place... but it's all constructed already, and everything adapts. Matter adapts to the spirit; it fuses with it after the fact. In other words, long live Sartre, and long live the idea that the existence comes before the essence!...

Oh yes, I really believe that. Because all in all, everything today, absolutely everything, is planned. Imagine this: I know some people who have a house that will be built soon, whose blueprints all are finished, and who have a drawing ready in advance indicating the place where the sofa and the table and chairs will go! It's really incredible! It's just like creating a framework for oneself in life, but how can life enter this framework? It's a destructive framework. But too many things today are done this way; they start with a blueprint.

CAHIERS: Will each of your short stories work on a different principle, with a different tonality?

RENOIR: I hope the tonalities will not be so different as to give the idea that each story belongs to a different film. I hope there will be some stylistic unity. I'll work to that end, in any case, I'll try. But aside from that, the meaning of the story, the tonality – I mean the individual meaning of each story, within the general meaning – will, I hope, be different.

And the differences can be great. For example, I have a story that is quite simply the story of a man's revolt against an electric polisher.

There is a woman who likes beautiful wood floors that shine nicely and who polishes, and polishes... with a nice electric polisher. So he revolts against the electric polisher. You see, it isn't a violent story, but note that it's an extremely important one, because our minds are destroyed by household machines now, with vacuum cleaners and everything else; it gets to you, it's abominable. So here, you have a minor story about this kind of thing.

And I have another story, for example, the last one in the film,

The Little Theater of Jean Renoir: Marguerite Cassan in "The Electric Waxer" (the second sketch).

which is a revolt against war. You see people who don't want to fight any more. Who have had enough...

But I would also like this film to illustrate something that I believe to be important: It's the idea that there are no gradations in the events that affect us. Every event is important. Or no event is important. There are no different classes, no gradations, first and foremost, because we all are one.

Newspapers and advertising today give weight to events according to the number of people who are affected. They say, Such an event is important because there were six thousand victims. Fine. But if there is only one victim, and if I'm that victim, then the event, with its one victim, is as important to me as is the event with six thousand victims is to each of the six thousand victims. The quantity, in my opinion, is not very important, and I don't believe in rankings, either. Einstein's death, if you like, was no more important than the death of a Mexican worker digging holes in Los Angeles, because for the family of this Mexican worker, for everyone surrounding him, his death is just as important. And even for the world's equilibrium... how do we know, maybe he'll leave a gap as important as Einstein's. We don't know, how can we judge that?

This obsession with ranking things, with numbering things: He's number one, he's number five.... I don't think it's true. Each person is number one for certain people, in a certain place, in certain circumstances, and then he becomes number five or number one hundred thousand in other circumstances. There are no gradations.

But there are certain people who claim to pay no heed to different gradations, in order to be democratic. In my opinion, that's also false. These people say, "Oh! Excuse me! The worker is more important than Einstein!" It seems to me that there is a demagogic side to this judgment that makes it false. Because equality is absolute and the worker may suddenly be more important than Einstein in certain circumstances, but Einstein will be more important in other domains. The one thing we don't know is the importance of these domains. The worker's domain may be more important than Einstein's... and there again, I don't believe that, because in saying that it's more important, I'm still establishing gradations. Let's just say, as important... or as unimportant.

We forget one thing, which is that relativity doesn't exist only in time and in space. Everything, absolutely everything, is relative. We're surrounded by relative truths; there are only relative truths; everything depends on the circumstances, on the moment.... So, to get back to my short stories, I don't give the one about the waxer any more importance than the one about people who don't want to go to war. It's always a matter of seizing a certain aspect of life seen at two moments, probably different yet related aspects, without establishing a hierarchy within this relationship.

CAHIERS: Seizing life, for you, also means seizing the voices, the noises of the moment.

RENOIR: Yes, I don't like postsynchronizing dialogue, because I still belong to the old school that believes in life's surprises, in the documentary, which believes that it would be wrong to neglect the sigh heaved unconsciously by a young girl in a certain circumstance, and which can never be reproduced. Or if it is reproduced, it becomes what we were just talking about, a blueprint, a plan.

The Little Theater of Jean Renoir: Fernand Sardou, Françoise Arnoul, Dominique Labourier, and Jean Carmet in "The King of Yvetot" (the fourth sketch).

I think that film, and all art in fact, is made up largely of lucky accidents, and obviously there are people who are lucky and who happen to have these fortunate accidents more than others do. But if these chance occurrences are planned and determined by the director, they're not as good, in my opinion. A director is a fisherman. He doesn't make the fish, but he knows how to catch them.

Now, I think that as soon as you have to follow a precise plan... You do have to follow a precise plan for postsynching. The expressions, the voice intonation, that one tries to bring back during the postsynching, whether it comes before, during, or after a playback are planned, are part of a framework, a limited framework that cannot be changed. Note that I believe in frameworks, but only if you can forget them. For example in ancient architecture... Let's use the example of Greek temples, which are very beautiful. Greek temples were very convenient for the artists who worked on the architecture and sculptures for them. They didn't have to draw up a blueprint, because the blueprint was the same, throughout the world and throughout time. They had a blueprint that was so unchanging that they wound up forgetting it, and it was as if it no longer existed. The blueprint was changed only for practical reasons: Because of a boulder, for instance, in the middle of the plot of land, the architect was forced to add a curve in a particular wall in order to go around it, but those were real reasons, not just the genius of an architect who decided to add a curve because it would be nice. In other words, I'm enormously wary of my own ideas when I make plans, and I'm wary of other men's ideas. I feel that what we find around us – and especially what others, what the richness of other people's personalities can bring us – is more important than our personal pride as a director.

CAHIERS: The theme was there. Only the variations remained to be found.

RENOIR: Right! And it's the same thing with all music, until, say, Bach and Vivaldi, and you still have the same thing with music when it's classical, as it is still played in many countries, in India, for example. And it was the same with literature. *The Song of Roland* was probably told a million times by different troubadours. They worked within a framework, the *Song of Roland* framework, but they were absolutely free within it. And they were writers. The big mistake today is to think that being a writer means inventing a story. I don't believe that. I think that being a writer is in the way you tell a story.

We have the equivalent today: It's the conventionality of certain American genres like the western. Westerns are good because they always have the same script. This fact has helped the quality of westerns enormously. Refined people often claim the right to scorn them because they always tell the same story. In my opinion, that's a quality, an advantage, in any case, an aid.

CAHIERS: While we're on the subject, do you agree with the definition of originality that Bresson gave us the other day: Originality is trying to act like everyone else and not succeeding?

RENOIR: Absolutely! That's a very good way of putting it! You can see that simply in the way people dress. In the clothing people wear who call themselves artists, for example. And first of all, the word *artist!*... There are people who use the word *artist* and who define themselves by it, which is dangerous enough, but there also are people who dress like artists. That's even more dangerous. The artists that I knew because of my father, in my youth, all dressed like middle-class people. Or like upper-class people, in the case of Monsieur Degas who was very rich, but they didn't dress like artists.

CAHIERS: Since you just mentioned India, James Ivory, a slightly intimidated but always admiring student of yours at the University of California, spoke about you. He got interested in India because of *The River*, and he is now producing Anglo-Indian films, one of which is the very beautiful *Shakespeare Wallah*.

RENOIR: Oh, I've heard about him. Yes, yes... And he's right in not trying to do totally Indian films, because I think that there is another thing, which comes in spite of you, which is unplanned, and which is what you are, your own personality, and I think it's better to work on things that are close to you and that you can easily absorb.

But I must say that my classes were totally uninteresting.

CAHIERS: Why do you say that?

RENOIR: Because I don't believe that it's possible to have a class on film. I believe that the only possible film class would be to watch films. What else can you do? It seems to me that that's the way one learns to make films. Just as for a painter, I believe that the only good school consists of looking at paintings and saying to yourself, "Look at that!" I would love to do that, but if I were to do it, I would do it a bit differently.

CAHIERS: What did you do in your classes?

RENOIR: Well, since most of the boys who were there – or the girls – wanted to direct, I tried to make them understand my ideas about directing actors. I limited myself to that. And I tried to convince them of the merits of what we call the Italian method, which you must know, which Molière and Shakespeare practiced.... Louis Jouvet, among others, rehearsed this way. It consists of reading the text in the same way that one reads a phone book, forbidding yourself all expression. You wait for the expression to come unconsciously. It's the fight against the blueprint, once again. And once in a while, you get fantastic results. When an actor reads a text and gives meaning to it immediately, you can be sure that he's giving it the wrong meaning. It has to be wrong, it has to be a cliché, it has to be banal, because you don't find something original like that immediately. You pull out a file, take out something already used, and apply it to this line, to the words you're speaking. If you don't let yourself do that, if you reread, reread, reread a text, at some point – I don't know how it happens, I can't explain it physiologically – at a certain moment there is a kind of spark that springs from the actor, or from the actress, and sometimes it's the beginning of discovering a role.

So I made them work like that. We took a text from a book, or from just any play – very short – and obviously, we replaced the neutral knowledge of the entire role with an explanation, because we had limited class time and therefore couldn't do what one does with a caste preparing a play, who can read the text for two months until this spark that I was talking about appears or sparks or... What does a spark do? Yes, sparks, shines, flies...

CAHIERS: Have you always used this method yourself?

RENOIR: Whenever possible!

CAHIERS: Yet, with actors like Michel Simon...

RENOIR: I did it with Michel Simon first. And he agreed to it, and I'm even convinced that he believes in it.

CAHIERS: Do you think all actors can do it?

RENOIR: I think that actors, great actors, don't do it on the set (nor do the directors), that they don't do it during official rehearsals, but I'm convinced that the work a great actor does privately on a text comes down to that, comes down to absorbing the text while forbidding himself, in the beginning, from giving it meaning, and basing himself only on the sound of the words.

And it's the same with everything, isn't it? You have to wait for things to be built. Things must exist, at least a bit, before you can discover their meaning.

CAHIERS: But Ivory had the impression that through the actors, or whatever else, you were speaking of cinema as a whole. He also said that the courses were completely unplanned.

RENOIR: Well, personally, I could never give anything but unplanned courses, given what I am and what I think. It's very difficult to teach in an organized way, so I preferred using the explanation of this Italian method as a base, and from there I went on to talk about other things concerning films in general. But I might have gone too far in this direction because... because there is the famous question of technology, and I wanted to convince these young people to ignore technology, to convince them that a camera is made to serve you and that you're not there to serve the camera. You know, in many productions the camera is exactly like the god Baal. Yes, the god Baal, to whom little children are thrown. That's exactly it... but in another sense, since there is no absolute truth, if you say that, people might conclude that you don't have to know your profession, which isn't true. On the contrary, you have to know it very well, you have to know it by heart, so that you can forget it.

I even think, contrary to what I said to these students, that one can even imagine that the technology is, if you like, its existence, one can imagine that it can determine style, even the foundation, even...excuse me for repeating a comparison that I've repeated a thousand times, but it helps me understand the question – it's the story of impressionist painting. My friends and I were talking about this, and someone had an idea that I've adopted and kept, which is that impressionism is based in part on the invention of paint tubes. Before that time, before 1865, say, paint for painters was in little pots, little bowls, that were difficult to carry around. When the idea came along to put paint into lead tubes, well! – you could put these tubes in your pockets or in a box, carry them, and paint outdoors. That's not the main reason for the birth of impressionism, but it's one of the reasons that certainly helped bring it about, a purely technical, even purely material, mechanical reason.

CAHIERS: But didn't these young people have a hard time convincing themselves, when you spoke to them about how – as you just said – one must scorn technology?

RENOIR: I don't think so. In any case, at the time it seemed all right. Because there is one thing that I have been sure of for a long time, from way before I taught these classes, and that is that you never convince anyone.

People are not convinced by arguments. They're convinced by the sound of a voice. For example, I'm sure that the people who followed Hitler weren't convinced by what he told them. I'm sure that it was the little man's strange personality.

CAHIERS: The magical side?

RENOIR: The magical side! I think that convincing people is magic. People think that one convinces with arguments, with logical reasons. It's not true. Logic never convinced anyone. Absolute truth is absolutely invisible.

CAHIERS: And Socrates' dialogues?

RENOIR: Ah! I'm sure it's the same thing. There was a magical side. Because Socrates' reasons are excellent, but the truth is that if one cares to, one can respond to them, one can oppose them. But I'm sure that the element that convinces us, in what we have of Socrates' dialogues, is probably a kind of magic in the writing. It's in every writer, in fact. It's by means of the magical side that one can reach the reasonable, or the reasoning, side. Of course it's a paradox, but paradoxes are true. In any case, they have as much chance of being true as logical truths do.

This question of technology for technology's sake is a formidable question, so we don't dare talk about it. But I'm sure that we don't convince anyone – I'm back to that – our discussions are purely personal. Thus (one must always go back to the small things to understand the large ones) you can have a discussion with a friend, and you can prove to him that he would be wrong to leave his wife, because he's leaving his wife for a mistress who is the absolute picture of his wife – which always happens. Most men who leave their wives for another women wind up with another woman who is exactly the same. Exactly. Her appearance may be a little different, but the truth is it's the same woman. I even think that a man loves only one woman in his life. This woman turns up under different masks, may have ten different identities, but she's the same. So why change? So you convince a friend that he's wrong in changing when it really won't be a change, and he says, yes, you're right, it's true, it's the truth, in fact, all women are the same. He's convinced. Then the next morning, he leaves his wife. Because the next morning, he does what he wants. You never convince anyone. And art... People in America must have asked me twenty times: "Do you think that motion pictures can influence politics?" So I answered that I think that motion pictures can influence customs. But not politics. Films can determine the way people think but cannot be at the root of an action. For example, people were nice enough to think that *Grand Illusion* (*La Grande Illusion*) had a great influence and told me so. I answered, "It's not true. *Grand Illusion* had no influence, because the film is against war, and the war broke out right afterward!"

But films influence morals, yes. For example, today the world is condemned for being violent. Films cannot help but add to the violence, or they cannot help but add to the peace. Obviously, the literature from the Cathari in the Middle Ages helped give a certain gentleness to the end of the Middle Ages, which was an extremely gentle period. People weren't cruel at the end of the Middle Ages; people became cruel when they knew too much. The Renaissance was cruel. But we've strayed from your question....

CAHIERS: One last question: Have you seen any films recently that you think reflect the morals of our times?

RENOIR: English films do, in my opinion. I saw a few films in England that I think reflect the morals of today and that are extremely important. For example, the first film with the Beatles [*A Hard Day's Night*]. For me, it's an extremely important film, which even reflects the unconscious desire for change in the English nation.

CAHIERS: But can we find an accurate reflection of a time if we want to find it – too deliberately?

RENOIR: I believe, at least in this film, which is excellent, that it was entirely by accident. That's just what we were saying before: The essence was confirmed only by the existence.

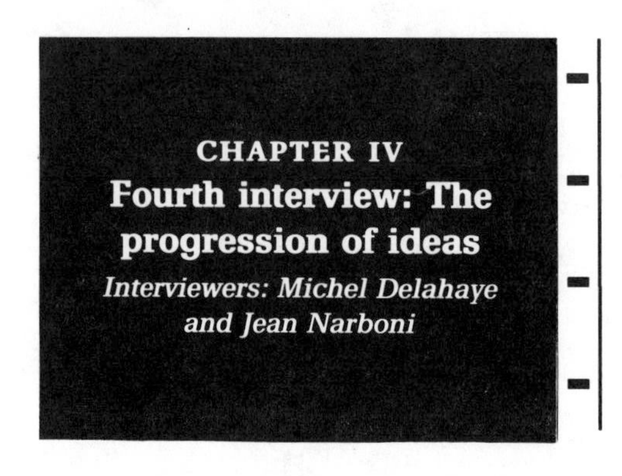

CHAPTER IV
Fourth interview: The progression of ideas
Interviewers: Michel Delahaye and Jean Narboni

CAHIERS: In your opinion, what were the reasons for the commercial failure of *La Marseillaise* before the war?

JEAN RENOIR: I don't think we ever know the real reasons for a success or a failure. I consider it to be based on coincidence: A film is successful when certain of its qualities – perhaps not its main qualities – coincide with the public's taste, with the public's demands. Many people liked it, some people were even enthusiastic about it, but the general public wasn't interested in the subject as a whole. I have the feeling that today's audiences would be much more interested in it. I'm not saying that for any logical reason. I seem to sense a certain interest in the French Revolution around me. People from before 1939 might have been more indifferent than people are now. But since then, certain events have awakened a sense of nation.

CAHIERS: There were perhaps other reasons that people may not have been conscious of, such as the extremely realistic sound track, which destroyed many conventions and clichés. You show the Marseillais speaking with their local accents, for instance, and audiences may have been a bit surprised to see something as serious as the Revolution acted out with a Marseilles accent.

RENOIR: Probably, because it seems out of place. But I wanted it to seem out of place, and I still do. I think that the accent played an important role in this story, in which the Marseillais go to Paris to impose the will of the people and correct the wrongs of the monarchy, because to do such a thing, one had to be a bit of a Don Quixote, and Don Quixote surely had an accent.

CAHIERS: Basically, you refused a certain "art," which would have made things "prettier," that is to say, easier to assimilate.

RENOIR: I don't like the word *art;* the word actually frightens me. Because the more work I do, the more I'm influenced by the literary forms and the language of the eighteenth century, and until the romantic period, art simply meant *doing,* the way in which you do something.

There was the *science* of medicine, and that meant that a man had read all the books on medicine and that he was theoretically familiar with all medical problems. And there was the *art* of medicine, which was caring for sick people, that is, the *practice* of this science. I find that this idea of practice applied to art ennobles the word. Whereas today, the word *art* is often given a rather vague meaning: something that relates to dreams, to sublime and incomplete creation, all of it tied up in a certain attitude toward life, in a certain tone that is often used in saying, "Oh, he's an artist!"

One becomes an artist only *after the fact*, and even then, sometimes one doesn't even notice, and even if one notices, nothing has to change! People may have wanted me to give more solemnity to the Revolution in *La Marseillaise*, but in making this film, I tried as hard as I could to avoid being solemn. I believe, here again, that one becomes solemn only after the fact. The awareness of a mission's importance comes only after the mission has been accomplished. I believe, in any case, that the importance – or the unimportance – of *everything* we do is noticeable only after the thing is done. I don't believe in plans, what the Americans call the *blueprint*, in films any more than I do in life, I don't believe in scripts. They must, of course, be carefully written, but there must be enough room for change so that the inspiration of the moment isn't killed, which is, in my opinion, the only inspiration that contributes anything.

So it's the same thing with these people from Marseilles. They leave with certain ideas in mind, but they haven't an inkling that they will end up bringing about the fall of the monarchy. They're even convinced that they will just relieve the king of his bad advisers, and they are therefore far from imagining that they are going to lead him to the guillotine. That's how things happen in life. I've met a few heroes in my life, heroes of a war or an ideal. I have never seen them adopt attitudes that would make them seem inflated with the importance of their mission. I have the feeling that down deep they did realize the importance of their mission, but so deep down they didn't express it.

For example, during World War I, I met Guynemer; I was in aviation myself. Now, Guynemer was obviously – to the extent that we accept fighting and killing, but there were forty million Frenchmen who accepted it at the time, and sixty million Germans – so, to the extent that we accept that, Guynemer was obviously a hero. But this hero didn't know he was a hero! He simply thought – and it was probably true – that he was a very good shot, and he was mostly concerned with the accuracy of his aim, the quality and rapidity of his shots. That is, his concerns were mainly technical. At least that's the impression I had. But I may have strayed from *La Marseillaise*. . . .

CAHIERS: Not at all, because in experiencing the war with nonheros you understood the nonheros of *La Marseillaise*.

RENOIR: It was in experiencing the war – as everyone experienced it at the time – that I wound up getting involved in film, because I wasn't involved with fighter planes but with photography. It was somewhat risky, however, because at the time we flew in... tanks, twin-engined Bréguets. The Germans were much faster. Luckily, there was someone named Pinsard who saved my life more than once with his little plane, coming to my rescue when the Germans were attacking me. The strangest thing is that one day, while I was shooting *Toni* and I was pulling my hair out because the noise from the airplanes was ruining my sound recordings, I went to see the commanding general at the base at Istres to try to make a compromise. As soon as we saw each other, we fell into each other's arms: The general was none other than Pinsard! He told me that the pilots were fascinated by all my filmmaking apparatus and that they were flying overhead to see what was going on. I told him that it was quite a nuisance. So we worked things out. After that we saw each other again. Pinsard had lived through some extraordinary adventures. In particular, he had to his credit a number of impressive escapes. He recounted them to me, and that was my point of departure for the film that turned into *Grand Illusion* (*La Grande Illusion*).

CAHIERS: There may be something else that troubled the public when *La Marseillaise* was released. First, the fact that French audiences have difficulty accepting the mixture of genres that you have always used.

RENOIR: Always!

CAHIERS: And then, the fact that it's difficult for the public to follow several narrative lines at the same time. This is the case in *La Marseillaise,* and at the time, the public wasn't ready for it.

RENOIR: Yes, but since then there have been several fragmented films that the public hasn't had any trouble swallowing. I feel that the public accepts technical experiments in film much more than it could in 1937, which gives much more freedom of expression to the directors. I know perfectly well that my method, which is to jump from one idea to another and to follow not a tangible line but a spiritual line (if I may say so), may have shocked people. I hope it will be less shocking to them now.... For example, I have always liked, and I always will, scenes that target a feeling, or even a general situation, with a particular point that is not exactly connected with the plot. As a result, I may overlook the plot, but I have neither the taste nor the talent for following a precise line in a film, starting at the beginning and finishing, without any digression or bending, with a conclusion.

There used to be an expression that was used all the time in French theater, before Copeau, in the "théâtre de boulevard." People said, "Oh! that director! He's not a poet, he's not a philosopher, he's not a thinker, what he writes is extremely ordinary, but... *but*, he's a good carpenter, he knows how to build a good structure." Well, I must admit that I'm not at all attracted to good structures.

So, in my *Marseillaise*, you obviously don't find this kind of structure. I followed an idea that grows, and grows, and grows.... I wanted to try to express not the birth – because it was latent for a long time – but one might say the coming to fruition, the development and the growth of the idea of a nation, as opposed to the idea of feudalism, that is, of personal power. One might say that it was a matter of going beyond the state of affairs in which people obeyed a lord – maybe because they liked this lord and he was very kind – but, in any case, of obeying a person who was the lord. The important thing is the *person* who embodies the lord, just as the important thing for the whole of a nation is the *person* who embodies the king. So, gradually – because this feeling took a long time to develop – we went from a personal attachment to an individual, to a personal attachment to a collection of citizens, that is, to a nation. And that's the story of *La Marseillaise*.

It was therefore a matter of developing an idea. I followed the development of a general, as opposed to a specific, idea, but I tried to do it with small strokes and with very intimate scenes.

CAHIERS: Basically, the idea of the film is of epic dimensions, but it adopts the tone of a chronicle of particular events.

RENOIR: You're right, except that your observation is based on a particular notion of the epic, because we've created a romantic idea of it. Take what are undoubtedly the greatest of the epics, *The Iliad* and *The Odyssey*. They're full of minor details, and they don't follow *one* line. They're presented with great unity in terms of the concept, which is all the more remarkable as there were more than likely many authors, but the unity is spiritual, not structural. Occasionally these works even shift abruptly to vignettes, which are sometimes quite trivial.

This isn't to say that I wanted to imitate *The Iliad* or *The Odyssey*. I had no such ambition, but I think that in trying to bring out the importance of all the minor details, even though it contradicts a certain idea we have of classicism, I didn't abandon or contradict the classical tradition.

CAHIERS: The way you show the character of Louis XVI, for example, also contradicts certain ideas, because we often think either that Louis XVI was a tyrant or else that he should have been portrayed as one. The other day at a press conference, a critic asked you, "Why did you

Nadia Sibirskaya and Alex Truchy in *La Marseillaise*.

portray Louis XVI as being nice, when everyone knows he was a tyrant?"

RENOIR: We have here film's eternal question, the fight against the cliché. In reality, the truly interesting films are those that destroy clichés. Now it happens that clichés are on the rise these days, and they're on the rise because people read more, go to the movies, listen to the radio, and so on. Propaganda has much more powerful means than it used to have in the days when it was passed on by word of mouth. I'm convinced that commonplaces are flourishing more vigorously than ever.

It happens that I'm very familiar with this idea of Louis XVI and that it was somewhat on purpose that I wanted to show him to be the opposite. First of all because it corresponded to the results of my research and then because I wanted to contradict a cliché.

I have always hated the idea that on one side there are people who are completely black and, on the other, people who are completely white. There is no white. There is no black. It's the same old story.

And I beg you to forgive me for repeating the story of how I realized this, but I find it funny, because I realized this when I entered the cavalry. The first time, in unfamiliar surroundings and in speaking of animals that I found only vaguely familiar, the first time I said the words *white horse*, I became an object of ridicule. It was then explained to me that there are no white horses, any more than there are black horses. There are dark gray horses, light gray horses, dark chestnut horses, and light bay horses; in short, there isn't a single horse that doesn't have a few hairs of another color. Clichés do not exist in nature or in life. So there shouldn't be any in my films.

What can be shown in my films, on the other hand, are people who have clear-cut opinions. But I'm not very interested in those people. And I'm not interested in them for a good reason: I can't understand such an attitude. Such an attitude makes you blind, and it also prevents you from enjoying life, because you deprive yourself of so many things. Sectarianism, like clichés, is on the rise today. Note that right now, the most serious sectarianism is condemning such and such a political idea. This kind of sectarianism remains as foreign to me as any other.

To get back to Louis XVI, I treated this character mostly according to what I knew about him or, rather, what I had learned about him, because, you see, *La Marseillaise* may be the only film in my career for which I wrote the script based on very extensive research. Normally, I write about things I know, about a place with which I'm familiar and in which I lived, and consequently, all the research is in me. But *La Marseillaise* is a historical film, and so I was forced to become familiar with the styles, manners, words, and clothing of the people of that period. So much so that I can say that I hardly wrote any dialogue for *La Marseillaise*, because almost all the dialogue is taken from existing documents. Thus, the story at the beginning, of the pigeon and of life on the mountain, was taken from the *Cahiers de revendications* of the

Etats Generaux. Farther on, the dialogue is taken from accounts of political clubs that appeared in newspapers at that time. And for the court life, I merely had to draw on the various existing chronicles.

Therefore, as a result of my research, I came to the conclusion that Louis XVI was a character who was both extremely kind and extremely distinguished. He was a distinguished man. What I mean by that is that he wasn't vulgar. That is, he didn't have the vulgarities of the aristocracy of the time, an aristocracy that had become decadent, propelled as it had been by the most absurd ideas. For example, take the idea of castes, which it had begun to cultivate. In this respect, I think that revolutions are created above all by the people whom the revolutionaries must oust: It is their errors that leave the door wide open for the others. The others must be worked up, of course, but I think that revolutions succeed only when the object to be overturned is already wobbly.

In any case, I read several documents concerning Louis XVI, and I came to the conclusion that he was an extremely nice person, and because this is what I found in my research, I wanted to show him as such.

I even think – and I think my brother Pierre did a marvelous job of expressing it – that this man knew he was a victim of destiny and knew that there was no need to fight. I wanted to give the impression of a character who *knows*. All this, even though this royal character is saddled with a wife who is sort of an aggressive chatterbox. Despite her noble birth, Marie Antoinette was an extremely vulgar woman. The idea of playing the shepherdess at the Trianon, for example, now that's vulgarity! And Marie Antoinette showed her true colors in these kinds of episodes. I didn't like anything I found out about her. She had no taste, whereas Louis XVI did have taste. He was also clear-headed. I think that Louis XVI *knew* it was the end, and he said to himself: There is nothing I can do to change destiny. I think he was a conscious victim of destiny.

CAHIERS: In creating this opposition between Louis XVI and Marie Antoinette and in making her a truly disagreeable woman, you certainly must have destroyed a few more clichés. How did you manage to push Lise Delamare in this direction?

RENOIR: There is something that surely marks the Marie Antoinette character in my film: I asked her to give a hint of an accent, which adds great frigidity to the character. I wanted to convey the feeling that Marie Antoinette was born in Austria. It's barely indicated, but once in a while there's a little something, a slight difficulty of elocution, which Lise Delamare did very well and which contributes to the character's frigidity.

That said, when I think of all the documents I read before doing *La*

Léon Larive and Pierre Renoir in *La Marseillaise*.

Marseillaise, it seems to me that Marie Antoinette was above all, and quite simply, very stupid, really an idiot. All her adventures were grotesque: her constant compromising, her preromanticism, her unbridled waste, and the story of the necklace and the Trianon and running the silk manufacturers of Lyons out of business, because she wanted her undergarments made only from fine linen and said so, proclaimed it, and waged war on silk. Not that I like silk, but many people lived off it, and needed royal publicity to sell it.

If I said before that the story of the shepherdess at the Trianon was perfectly vulgar, it's because it makes me think of the same vulgarity we find today among the people who pretend to be hippies. It's the same thing. I say that because I like hippies, true hippies, just as I've always like hoboes. God knows that true hippies, who have abandoned all comfort and who believe they have found a certain freedom in saying no, God knows they're very nice. But when the hippy goes home to his beautiful apartment at the end of the day and has his butler serve him a cocktail, in my opinion it's pointless and it's grotesque.

I would have liked to show a certain number of things concerning Marie Antoinette, but the subject was too vast. I did note another small point: At the moment when everything is falling apart, and the people are going to attack the château, she yells at her son for playing on the floor!

But all that was an attempt to address the immense events by means of digression, without forgetting the importance of the Revolution, despite my love of details.

After all, the French Revolution was the biggest event in the world since Christianity. Revolutionaries the world over refer to the French Revolution more than to any other, at least sentimentally. We owe many things to the French Revolution, if only that it gave Jewish people names, for example. That's already a contribution, because before, Jews were named, for example, Abraham, son of Jacob, but they had no family names and weren't listed with the registry office. The Revolution actually forced them to take one. The victorious revolutionary and Napoleonic armies did the same thing in the conquered countries. That's why so many Jews in Germany have the same name. They went to the town hall to get one, but they were taken by surprise. The clerk asked them, "So, what name do you want? – Well... I don't know. – OK, then, across from us is a mountain, the rose mountain. You'll be Rosenberg...." And there you have it. That gave a social existence to many people who didn't have one.

I have the impression that the Revolution continues and that this idea of a nation that I treated at the beginning of the film, this idea that we owe to the Revolution, is in the process of winning over the world at lightning speed. People who resemble one another and speak the same language get together and demand to be recognized as a group. A few years ago, I said: It's going to be very simple; the world will be divided in two. There will be the East and the West, and it will work out well because they'll fear each other, and so they'll sit one across from each other, they'll toast, and we won't have a war. That was a terrible mistake. On the contrary, we're heading toward many nations, because nationalism is gaining ground, and this current rebirth of nationalism is to a large extent due to the Revolution.

CAHIERS: Another striking aspect of your film, which is linked to the research on the Revolution you were speaking of, is its "didactic" side, the many things one learns, from the "emigration" of tomatoes to the twelve-gun charge, which contain no political didacticism.

RENOIR: My research – or what I ambitiously call my research – let's say my readings, allowed me to become very familiar with everything concerning the period and to create my dialogue, as I said, almost entirely from existing documents. Even the little things. For example, when Jouvet says to Pierre – Louis XVI – "We must leave the château," and Louis XVI hesitates and then says, "Let's march!" When I read that in the notebook of I don't remember which witness, this "let's march" struck me. I said to myself: Why doesn't he say, "Let's go" or "You're right"? No, he says, "Let's march!" There often are expressions like that with Louis XVI. In my opinion, this "let's march" has symbolic value. It almost means "Let's march to our death." I was careful to use words or expressions that were said at the time and that owe their greatness to the fact that they were said under the influence of certain emotions. There is another phrase used by Louis XVI that I quoted verbatim: When he leaves the palace and sees the dauphin playing with the leaves, the king says, "The leaves are falling quite early this year." This phrase, which I didn't invent, is rather poignant, in my opinion, and it tends to confirm this conscious-victim side, which I believe is in Louis XVI. But I believe I've strayed from your question, which was about the didactic side of the film.

I paid close attention to this documentary end. And I might not have dared make the film if I didn't have a friend who was my assistant and adviser. I had two marvelous assistants, in fact: One was Karl Koch, a German – who knew the German side of Marie Antoinette and everything concerning the German influence on the court. The other was Corteggiani. Corteggiani was crazy about historical, popular, mechanical things. For example, he knew so much about all the weapons since Azincourt that he could describe them, draw them, take them apart, and put them back together. All of them. He's also the one who helped me give the soldiers' movements the precision that you may have noticed. For example, the changing of the guard at Versailles happened exactly as it happens in the film.

Concerning this same beginning at Versailles, Koch taught me about the wake-up fanfares: the morning fanfares that accompanied the rising of his Majesty took place on both sides of the canal. There was a group of musicians on one side and another that responded from the other side.

You can't say everything in a film; it would be too long, and that's why I didn't mention this. But this explains why these fanfares in the beginning of the film answer each other: One is louder because it's closer, and the other softer. This explanation, although it isn't stated, is there just the same, and I believe that when you have reasons that aren't stated but that are correct, it helps give a certain life to the object represented. I always have been very attracted to this kind of accuracy, because it is both extremely enriching for the film and for oneself, and very amusing. And there is one marvelous film in which I find this precision and for which I have the utmost respect: It's *La Religieuse* by Jacques Rivette. Everything is right. You would think you're in that period and in a convent. It comes from this precision constructed from both details and an idea of the whole. It's a very dignified film, a very noble film.

CAHIERS: Could you tell us a few other reasons for certain episodes of *La Marseillaise*?

RENOIR: Well, here is one thing that is hard to believe – and it thrilled me when I read it – it's the aria "Oh Richard! Oh My King." When Louis XVI agrees to inspect his guardsmen, the gentlemen who are in the vestibule get down on their knees and sing "Oh Richard! Oh My King!" It looks like a nice effort by the director to give a kind of rhythm and solemnity to the king's entrance into the court. Not at all! That's exactly the way it used to happen. The song in question is taken from *Richard Coeur de Lion* which was the opera in vogue – by Grétry – and all the distinguished people knew the great aria "Oh Richard! Oh My King" by heart, and they sang it joyfully. And when Louis XVI went out, they instinctively got down on their knees to sing this aria, because they knew it and it seemed appropriate in this situation.

CAHIERS: It is sometimes said that Rouget de L'Isle was inspired to write the song "La Marseillaise" because of an opera aria.

RENOIR: It's entirely possible, but I never came across that information. It may be true because there is a great deal of information, and it sometimes is contradictory. But I am stuck with the facts that are certain, that is, that Rouget de L'Isle was at Dietrich's in Strasbourg, that a Jewish peddler who went to sell his merchandise in Montpellier made the Rhine army's chant known, and that Mirer, in Montpellier, who was commanding the city's battalion as it headed toward Paris, started singing the song because he liked it and because he had a good voice. From there, it traveled to Marseilles, and it spread.

Here again, this song, which was to become so important to French life, started with no plan, with no "blueprint." No one said: I'm going to write a song that will be the French people's anthem. It came without authors, and in fact, it had many authors. It was precisely to show that there were many authors that I had the people from Marseilles make a stop, on their march toward Paris, during which they talked about a schoolmaster who had had his students compose an additional couplet: "Nous entrerons dans la carrière..."

CAHIERS: Could you tell us a bit more about Karl Koch, who also collaborated with you on other films? Where did he come from?

RENOIR: Well...among other things, he had been a collaborator of Brecht's. And Brecht always had a very strong influence on his collaborators. He was the enemy of vague dreaming, and he gave everyone around him a great feeling for logic. That was his major influence: logic. Those who worked with him always became the enemies of useless dreams. And Koch brought this kind of rigorous logic to our discussions of scripts and scenes, a logic that for Brecht often led to conclusions that seem baroque but aren't. The problem is that the public doesn't always see the logic. The public believes that truth is not like that. We're back to the hunt for clichés.

Koch and I were good friends. He had already worked with me on *Grand Illusion*, and he worked with me again on *The Rules of the Game* (*La Règle du jeu*). His role varied according to the situation. For *La Marseillaise*, I asked him to stay with me and to help me avoid banalities, because sometimes you let yourself get drawn into things that seem easy and often you don't even realize it yourself. He was a man with a very rigorous mind, and if this were politics, we would say that in the miniature government of the film crew, he played the role of an adviser.

He helped me enormously in our cliché hunting, helped me destroy them everywhere we found them. For example, this cliché of revolutionary solemnity that we mentioned. In reading our accounts of the period, we very quickly decided that the clubs were often a mess. A lovable, charming mess, but a mess nonetheless. That's why we showed this disorder in the club in Marseilles.

So he was my adviser, but when I make films, everyone is my adviser. There is no bad advice. And that brings me back to the other collaborator in *La Marseillaise:* Corteggiani. Aside from his mechanical knowledge, his theoretical knowledge of everything concerning the armies was fantastic, unreal. One day he told me a story that I couldn't include in *La Marseillaise* because it had happened before that period, but I'll tell it to you now. A gentleman was in the Bastille, and because he wanted very much to leave, one day he had the idea of writing to Louis XVI and saying to him: If you let me out of here, I'll give you the means to have 100,000 fusiliers. The king was very interested and amused, and said: It's agreed, you shall leave the Bastille if you give me 100,000 fusiliers. And the man responded: All you have to do is give each of your policemen a gun. And it's true, at the time, the policemen carried only pikes.

CAHIERS: There is a strange connection between *Grand Illusion, La Marseillaise,* and *The Rules of the Game* that can be found in certain details: the connection between the hunters and the gamekeeper (found in *La Marseillaise* and *The Rules of the Game*) and between the two characters who are château owners, both played by Dalio in *The Rules of the Game* and in *Grand Illusion*. All that points to a single theme: class differences.

RENOIR: Oh, you know, one tells the same story throughout one's life. We have *one* story in mind, and we discover different aspects of it, little by little. That's my case, anyway. I know I always go back to the same themes. But I try to dig into them more, to discover new aspects, to express things that I haven't already said about them.

And this question of classes is definitely a question to which I have given a great deal of thought. It's fascinating, and certainly one of the questions that has always been treated, and that continues to be treated, with the greatest hypocrisy. Because people pretend that there are no more classes, that they've been abolished. In fact, we have a long way to go before abolishing them. Take a small example, very close to us: film. Film is a class! Actor's daughters marry directors' sons, or vice versa, unless they marry the son or the daughter of a producer, or a financier, or whatever. It all stays in the same small circle, and that small circle is nothing other than a class. Of course, what I am saying about film is even more applicable to other groups, but it's still the same thing: People stay together.

Classes are appearing or reappearing everywhere, even in professions. The duties change according to the profession, but each profession is like a nation that imposes its morals, reactions, likes, discipline. Take the scene in *La Marseillaise* with the man who orders the soldiers to shoot at the crowds. What I wanted to show there was the case of a man who applies the rules of his class, the military class, in a perfectly honest manner. Put a military man at a window and tell him to shoot the first person who enters. If the first person who enters is his father, he'll still shoot.

There is another aspect to this question that preoccupies me: It's the attempt to enter another class. For example, the arrival into the world of *The Rules of the Game* of a boy like Jurieu, the aviator, who is not at all a part of this world. The fact that he's honest and pure makes him even more dangerous. The truth is that by killing him, they eliminate a microbe. A very nice microbe, but a microbe that could have killed the entire organism.

CAHIERS: It's noticeable in *La Marseillaise* by the way that different groups express themselves. One often has the impression that they are not *speaking* the same language. For example, the scene between Andrex and the commander of the fort in Marseilles: They belong to two foreign worlds.

RENOIR: Absolutely. They speak words, but it's as if one is speaking Chinese and the other Assyrian. Language is the great source of misunderstanding among men: the different meanings we attribute to sounds. That's why I think that in this immense enterprise of liberation that is taking place – the destruction of the class system – of which the French Revolution was one of the principal stages, just as Christianity and the Russian Revolution were, I'm convinced that we can succeed only if we admit that certain differences still remain among individuals. But we're not there yet.

CAHIERS: In short, it's because we try to deny the differences that we wind up giving them more importance than they should have, and we allow classes to reappear. Inversely, it's by recognizing the existence of certain differences from the start that we can arrive at true equality.

RENOIR: Exactly. I don't believe in the equality that everyone today pretends exists. I don't see it anywhere. I believe, on the other hand, in differences, but I believe that they are only *material* differences. They don't have any *spiritual* importance; they don't count.

I therefore believe in differences, but not that people are of different importance. I think that the work of a head of state is no more important than that of a street sweeper, and a street sweeper, therefore, has as much importance as does a head of state. That doesn't mean they're not different. And I believe that the death of a street sweeper in the process of sweeping rue Henri-Monier can bring about catastrophes as serious as the death of a head of state. I don't believe in the difference between a man of genius – in this domain that we have agreed to call art – and a man without talent. The man without talent also has his function. What it is I don't know, but it must exist. Maybe he is necessary in order to make people understand that the other man is a genius.

CAHIERS: We're now back to your previous project, which you called *C'est la révolution!* [which eventually became *Le Petit Théâtre de Jean Renoir*]. You gave the same importance to a variety of small and large revolutions.

RENOIR: Oh, but I'm going to return to this project, because it's a very important idea for me. But I may return to it in another form. Right now I have another project.

CAHIERS: What is it?

RENOIR: I would like to do the story of a hobo, with Jeanne Moreau. I admire her very much. She's probably the actress I admire most, and I would like very much to do something unexpected with her. She has the kind of logic we were speaking of before, concerning Brecht. I've already written an outline, but I'm not satisfied with it, and so I'm going to do it over again. What I would like to show is this kind of desire for freedom through renunciation, as opposed to the belief that happiness is in production and profit. We are living in a time when we go from countries in which people are dying of hunger to countries in which there is too much of everything. But does happiness lie in having too much of everything? That is why there are people – it's the case of many hoboes, as it is of hippies – who refuse to enter this system that consists of having to work, of having to obey, of having to adopt certain forms of behavior, like, for example, having to dress suitably to go to work. Because where does all this lead you? To have certain comforts, an apartment, nice clothes, a certain ease... So, maybe by giving up everything, maybe by saying: I don't care about it, after all, I'll always be able to dig up a scrap of bread to keep me until tomorrow, maybe we wouldn't be any worse off. It's a reasonable attitude.

It's not new, in any case. They've been doing that in India for four thousand years, and I must say that it sometimes works. But I often said to myself: It works in India because the climate is warm. But it isn't true! I've never been as cold as I was in Benares. I was freezing to death, and during that time, one could see some holy men immobile on the banks of the river, with hardly any clothes on, who didn't seem to feel the cold.

CAHIERS: What was it that drew you to India?

RENOIR: Just that! I wanted to see a civilization that wasn't based on profit, a system that wasn't a matter of producing. They are the only ones like that now, because the Asians, who are so strong, intelligent, and hardworking, are going to be more productive than Westerners are.

CAHIERS: There is one perspective from which we haven't yet looked at *La Marseillaise:* the technical one. The scene with the Brunswick Manifesto, for example, is very revealing because of the extreme mobility of the sequences that were shot – like this one – with a crane.

RENOIR: Yes, we followed Louis XVI, because his reactions were very important. We therefore stayed close to him, and I moved on to a master shot only later. I didn't want to distract the audience's attention from the content of the manifesto and from the king's reaction by showing the set, the ministers, and his entourage too soon.

CAHIERS: Did you know from the start that you would use the crane, or were you prompted to use it because you felt a certain fluidity was needed or simply because of the necessities of the blocking?

RENOIR: It was the need for fluidity in the scene that prompted me to ask for the crane. I had requested that a crane remain constantly at my disposal. So when I discovered that the scene had to be fluid, as you say – which is an excellent word – I thought that the crane would be very helpful. On the other hand, I remember there being a shot of Marie Antoinette in this scene. I left that shot still.

CAHIERS: There are two other large movements noticeable in the film: the departure of the Marseillais and the crowd's storming of the Tuileries. These also are two movements that permit you do something I believe is important to you, to go from the whole to the detail.

RENOIR: Yes, of course. But it would have been difficult to do anything else, because in reality, the breaking down of this door is tied in with the feelings of all these people who are in the square. You therefore have to show both, and if you're going to show these two things, it's better to show them in the same shot. For me it's extremely important that certain shots contain both the detail that nourishes the whole and the whole that gives meaning to the detail.

CAHIERS: Did the blocking of such scenes pose many problems?

RENOIR: It demanded a certain amount of preparation, but I certainly didn't spend more than a half a day shooting each one. My cameraman had never been a cameraman before. He was an assistant. But I had a great deal of confidence in his self-confidence. He's a man who doesn't hesitate. His name was Bourguoin; I'm sure you must know him. I asked that he be named head cameraman because I knew he could do anything, and without a fuss.

CAHIERS: Can you tell us about the scene in the Tuileries that has been lost?

RENOIR: It allowed me, first of all, to show Roederer and to insist on one fact: that on that day, Roederer, who very clearly predicted that the palace was going to be overrun and who very sincerely wanted to spare the royal family from being massacred, was kept waiting all day. The scene in the beginning shows us Roederer waiting at the queen's door, which is an important detail. Then we see the queen burning letters. Roederer guesses that they are letters from her brother, the emperor of Austria, and he approves of her burning them, thinking that family matters do not concern the nation, that it is better to keep them

La Marseillaise (end): Valmy.

to oneself. It was a very good scene for Jouvet, who acted it with a kind of irony, and it was also very good for Lise Delamare, who did it with a rather nasty sort of counterirony. There was a good contrast between the ironic good-naturedness of Jouvet and the rather acerbic irony of the queen, but the scene was lost. The last time I saw it, it was in a very mutilated 16mm copy in America, a copy that lasted something like forty minutes. But the state of the copy and its subtitles made it impossible to use the scene.

CAHIERS: Were the beginning and ending sketches in the original version?

RENOIR: No, I just added them. I did them thinking that it would be good to allude to the universal side of the Revolution. The final sketch also has another purpose: explaining what the battle of Valmy meant. I was careful to give the name of the place in the film: Valmy, and to point out the mill, but I noticed that these things were rather unfamiliar to some people. Some even thought that Valmy was a battle in the 1870 war. So I figured that the line by Goethe would help by summarizing it all.

CAHIERS: It's strange to think that this film begins on July fourteenth, 1789, a day that to most people represents the moment when everything changed, whereas we know that things didn't start changing until 1792.

RENOIR: It's the fight against the cliché, once again. The main cliché, for all of life's events, is to believe that one turns a page: Before it was black, and afterward it's white. It's not true. Life is not made of sharp cuts like those in a film, but of successive dissolves. In fact, for most of the provincial nobles, and even the Parisian nobility, the taking of the Bastille did not change a thing. It's even an event that many weren't aware of.

Similarly, on February sixth, 1934, the day when there were all those struggles at the place de la Concorde, I was eating lunch in a little restaurant that might have been fifty meters away from the scene of the fighting. Many things were happening, but it was not until I returned home that a friend of mine told me what had happened during my lunch!

We always think that an event is immediately and universally noticed. We even think that it is immediately and universally understood. That's not true. The event remains underground or isolated for a long time and emerges only little by little, and only after the fact does it take on meaning.

History with a capital H is a product of historians. They are very useful, because they present a synthesis without which we wouldn't understand it. But in a film one can try to make people understand this choppy, irregular aspect that life takes on during great events.

CAHIERS: But it is precisely in historical films that one generally slaps a "sense of history" onto events. In *La Marseillaise*, on the other hand, we constantly have the feeling that history is happening in the present. Which is what prompted Truffaut to say that your film gives the impression of a collection of newsreels from the period.

RENOIR: That's what I tried to do, to allow people to remain historical figures but to find out what these men of another period had in common with us. In other words, I tried not to attribute our own current attitudes to them but to select from the attitudes of that period those that were closest to our own.

I did this kind of work especially on the speeches, because many of the speeches from that time would be almost unbearable today. In any case, they have a greatness, a beauty, an eloquence that make them great poetry.

CAHIERS: There is a scene in *La Marseillaise* that seems prophetic: that of the emigrants in Germany, which calls to mind what must have happened in 1940 with the collaborators, while others, though they were right wingers, were killed in the Resistance.

RENOIR: It's precisely an allusion to that, although it was done before all that. When I did *La Marseillaise*, I knew that a part of the French bourgeoisie would want Hitler to win. It was obvious.

There is an interesting detail in that scene: The little song they sing was really composed during the emigration – maybe not in Koblenz – by Chateaubriand, who was a young emigrant at the time.

In the same scene, I also wanted to bring in this other aspect of the situation that you were talking about, by means of the former commander of the fort in Marseilles, played by Aimé Clariond, Monsieur de Saint-Laurent. That's why I gave him an air that suggests that someday he will probably abandon the emigrants to return to the revolutionary army, which for him was above all a French army.

It also happens that deep down, he is already influenced by the idea of a nation (remember the definition of the nation that Arnaud gives), because he says to the other emigrant who is singing the praises of the king of Prussia, "Remember, we haven't always been fighting the French." It's a strange sentence, and I didn't invent it. I also found it in a report.

CAHIERS: We don't see any of the important figures of the Revolution in your film, like Robespierre, Marat, Danton . . .

RENOIR: Throughout the film, I stayed with the idea of a nation symbolized by a song. Because deep down, that's what *La Marseillaise* is, a film of ideas. Because I was following this line, if I had begun to talk about Marat, I would have gotten myself involved in doing a film about him. I had a different project. Besides, I think there are plenty of films about him. There is no lack of *Charlotte Cordays*.

CAHIERS: It's strange to see that actors like Jouvet, Clariond, and Lise Delamare all play supporting, although magnificent, roles in the film, whereas you gave a very big part to Andrex, who at that time was known as a minor actor.

RENOIR: He was known as a café-concert comic. But my decision was also made because of an almost documentary concern with physical verisimilitude. I didn't want the Marseillais to be old, and most of the well-known actors were relatively old. In addition, because I was doing a film of ideas, I couldn't do a film of stars. And as far as Andrex was concerned, I thought it was better to have this theoretician – because he is a theoretician – played by a "light" actor.

And it worked out well, because Andrex was very proud of this role. He studied it, he worked on it. The same with everyone else. It was an extremely easy film to do. I must say that I had only very good actors. There wasn't a single minor role that wasn't acted by someone very good.

CAHIERS: But if an actor is very good but he doesn't feel comfortable, what do you do?

RENOIR: In that case, if you think there is nothing to be done, that there is an irreparable divorce between the actor and his role, you

Aimé Clariond in *La Marseillaise*.

have to ask him to give up his part, but you have to do it right away, before you spend too much money. In fact, in most cases, the garment only requires a few alterations. It's a little too big, a little too tight, so you have to take it in, change the cut, fix it, and sew it back up again. You have to ask the actor to adapt some, but you also have to know how to adapt the actor's garment. Sometimes, the words aren't right for the character, and so you have to change them.

CAHIERS: Has that happened to you often?

RENOIR: Oh yes! I spend my time adapting myself to actors' possibilities. No human being is all-powerful. We all have limits. Directing means adapting one's own limits to other people's limits. When you realize that there is a total divorce between an actor and a dialogue, either you have total confidence in the dialogue, and so maybe the actor isn't right and has to be changed, or it's a matter of a few details, and so the dialogue has to be changed.

This has often happened to me. With Jules Berry, for example, in *The Crime of Monsieur Lange* (*Le Crime de Monsieur Lange*), I didn't try to impose a specific dialogue. Berry was a man who was familiar with the situation, and he was a genius as well, and he also had an astounding memory. I therefore had to try to combine all these elements so as to gain something from it. The best way was to explain the situation to him, to reach an agreement with him, to rehearse it, and then to take notes, that is, to note certain words that absolutely had to be said. It was somewhat like the pier of a bridge, but what was to be built between the piers had to be free, because Berry was so immersed in his role that I could and had to allow him the freedom to improvise a little.

What I'm saying here is really the whole question of film. In writing your script, in preparing your film, you're establishing the piers of your future bridge. If you do a good job establishing the overall picture, you know that your bridge will fit this picture, but you never know in advance what the exact result will be.

PART TWO
Television interviews

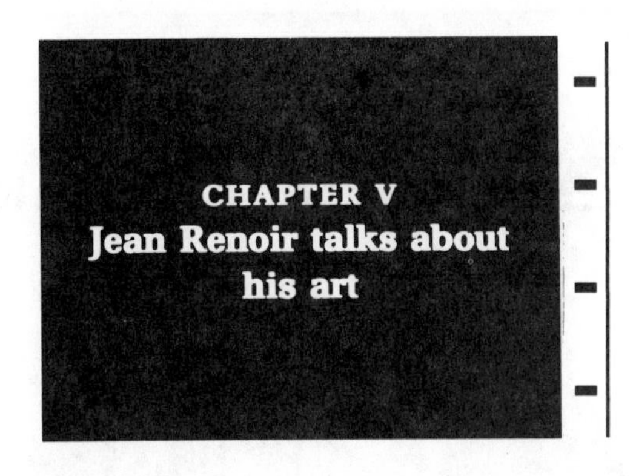

The program "Jean Renoir vous parle de son art" was produced and recorded in August 1961 by Jean-Marie Coldefy for the ORTF, the French National Broadcasting Service. Janine Bazin was the producer. The program was a long filmed interview between Jean Renoir and Jacques Rivette in a small café in the Buttes-Chaumont neighborhood.

This program preceded the airing of *The Testament of Doctor Cordelier* (*Le Testament du Docteur Cordelier*) on November 16, 1961. The interview was divided into three parts, the first ("Cinema and Speech") aired on November 11, the second ("Reflections on Technical Progress") on November 12, and the third ("The Return to a Natural Style") on November 15.

In conjunction with this interview, Renoir prepared short introductions to twenty of his films, to appear before the broadcast of each one. These introductions are presented in Chapter VII of this volume.

Cinema and speech

JACQUES RIVETTE: Monsieur Jean Renoir, you have now made close to forty films, and the only problem for the interviewer is that of choosing. Rather than beginning immediately with general questions, it might be better to begin with one or two detailed points, so-called technical details, that may perhaps lead us to other more serious, more ambitious questions. Your last two films were shot with a technique that you yourself perfected, that of shooting with multiple cameras. I believe you were quite pleased with the results of this method. Do you plan to use it for your next films or at least for your next film, *The Elusive Corporal* (*Le Caporal épinglé*)?

JEAN RENOIR: Well, I'm not sure of anything yet. I'd like to use it, but I'm not sure I'll be able to, because this technique can be used successfully, I think, with films conceived of and written in a particular way. *The Elusive Corporal* is a film that I am in the process of writing,

Sacha Briquet and Jean-Pierre Cassel in *The Elusive Corporal.*

of outlining the script, and so far, the script seems to be a regular script, so I don't know whether the multiple-camera technique will be appropriate. Nevertheless, even if it can't be used for the whole film, I'd like to use it for some scenes, just because, more and more, I believe that films are talking. I think that we have lived through the silent-film period – luckily it gave us some beautiful films – but we're leaving that stage, we've just gotten out of it. One can say that most talking films are merely silent films in which the subtitles were replaced with some sound coming from a mouth.

This is so apparent that some people even accept dubbing. Accepting dubbing means accepting that the dialogue is not a true dialogue; it means refusing to believe in the kind of mysterious connection between the trembling of a voice, the expression ... in short, it means that we have ceased to believe in the unity of the individual.

I therefore will try, even for this film, which isn't designed for it, to use several cameras for certain scenes in which I would like the actor to act out the scene from the beginning to the end.

RIVETTE: In any case, this technique is only the most recent result of the research you have been pursuing for a long time, since the beginning of the talkies, in fact, which tries to attain a maximum amount of continuity in the acting.

RENOIR: That's right. It's trying to get in the film, or at least partially in certain scenes, a continuity that comes from the development of the actor's expression, from his interior progression, in place of the continuity that is usually fabricated artificially in the editing room. In *Grand Illusion* (*La Grande Illusion*), for example, I have many scenes in which I got this result by lugging the camera around. We rehearsed a great deal, and we knew exactly where our one camera should be at any given moment, and by moving the camera we managed to follow the scene and to film it almost at a single stretch.

The other reason that I would like to use this technique from time to time in *The Elusive Corporal* is that we are going to be shooting in the winter, and the weather in the winter can be very bad and sometimes changeable. You start with a little ray of sunlight, and then a cloud comes, so that if you use a normal method, the links are difficult to make. There also is the sound, which has to be synchronized, and it's the same thing: If you shoot a scene all at one time, the links are necessarily perfect.

RIVETTE: In the end, the technique consists in taking the actors as seriously as one takes cars when filming a car accident: You always film with three cameras because you're not going to go and destroy several cars, but actors are treated with less consideration.

RENOIR: There is something rather strange in our profession, which is that the actor, who's getting paid, the actor, whose services are bought at the price of gold – the amounts paid for certain stars are incredible – in the end, despite all these expenses, he is rather scorned. We make films and forget that the person who will be seen on the screen more than the landscapes, more than the story line, more than anything, is the actor. If we manage to get a little sincerity from this actor, we're ahead of the game.

RIVETTE: That's right ... and you try to capture the actor's sincerity not just for an instant, but especially over time.... That is, there is a mo-

Marcel Dalio, Jean Dasté, Jean Gabin, Gaston Modot, [unidentified (as Maisonneuve)], and Julien Carette in *Grand Illusion*.

ment of sincerity that comes if the actor, after one minute, or maybe after five minutes . . .

RENOIR: In other words, one has to agree on the meaning of the word *sincerity*. Right now, I'm talking about the sincerity of the acting. I don't mean that the pinnacle of good acting is to have the actor express himself as he does in real life, not at all. . . . The height of sincerity in the actor's profession is that concerning his role.

We're not asking Mr. Laurence Olivier to be sincere, we're asking Hamlet; and if Hamlet isn't sincere and if suddenly Laurence Olivier appears instead of Hamlet, it's all over, it's ruined.

Now, this kind of sincerity is obtained a little bit more easily, I believe, if you've been immersed in your role for a few moments. It's rather difficult to dive into sincerity in the same way that one dives off a diving board into the Mediterranean at St. Tropez; that's not the way it's done. Sincerity fights back, you have to win it over, you have to caress it, and then, finally, you get it. I feel that if the scene is a bit longer, and especially if one can spare the actor the horrible gymnastics of having to continue where he left off... this concern with starting over does not lend itself to sincerity. You say to yourself: Oh, the last shot was a close-up, it finished with the word *hello*, said in a high-pitched voice, and so you try to regain the right voice, try to find the rhythm, and then also, perhaps, try to find the spirit, but spirit is a fleeting animal. You can't catch it as easily as that, whereas if you're in the spirit, you're there, and you stay there.

I think it's the same thing with all forms of human expression. I think, by the way, that there is an expression that says all of this in few words, whereas I'm going on and on. This expression is "get into the swing of things"... you have to be "in the swing of things" to do anything.

RIVETTE: It's like a return, in film, to the technique of certain painters like Matisse, who did perhaps thirty sketches of a painting, but then did the final painting at one stretch as well.

RENOIR: Exactly.

RIVETTE: Even if there is a shaky stroke, this shaky stroke is part of the painting.

RENOIR: We call Matisse's thirty sketches *rehearsals* in our profession. I think it's the same thing in every effort at human expression.

There is one other thing, which is that words count (I allowed myself to mention this at the beginning of our interview, we're in the age of the talkies), words are after all the means to reach truth, to reach the small discovery of the world that constitutes the goal of every work of art. Words, therefore, represent the basis for our profession, and they express something only if they've been studied. And if they've been studied, eventually you wind up forgetting them, forgetting how to pronounce them, and so only the spirit matters.

And once only the spirit matters, everything becomes extremely fragile, and an interruption can become absolutely catastrophic. The system of shooting shot by shot is full of interruptions, which is why I'm against it.

While we're on this question of the text, this is also the reason I believe one must approach the text without acting it out. One must begin simply by absorbing it, just as you absorb information, like a telephone number in the directory, for example, you don't act out the telephone number. The lines shouldn't be acted out because there is another thing that is extremely important. You see, with the system of cutting, of making a film in little pieces, you wind up acting out the moment, and I believe that good acting is not acting out the moment, it is acting out the character. Acting out the moment is always contrived. You're in a dramatic scene, and you have a man whose mistress just left him, he wants to kill himself, and so obviously, if you act out the moment, you'll have him do it with a trembling voice, which is very false, which will probably remind us of things that we've seen or heard before, which do not correspond at all to the true character. I repeat: The true character is the acted character, not the actor. We couldn't care less about the actor in real life. So I believe that the way to arrive at sincerity, to manage not to act out the moment... for example, excuse me, I'll use another example of acting out the moment. Take a very dramatic moment, the most common of all. It's possible that an actor who is really into his role, who is into his character one hundred percent, might have the idea of acting out a very sad moment by giggling, maybe he'll have a fit of laughter. Why not? People don't always cry at funerals. I've seen funerals at which everyone giggled, and it doesn't mean that they aren't crying for the deceased, that they don't miss him or her, but generally, the expression we apply to a certain moment is false, in any case, it's conventional.

That's why I believe in the method of reading the lines first, without acting them out, so that they penetrate slowly, very slowly, and finally – I don't know why – when the mysterious marriage of the personality of the actor and the personality of the author takes place, something unexpected comes out, something that even the actor doesn't expect.

If the actor knows in advance how he's going to say a word, it's bad, it's conventional. He shouldn't know. It has to come out by itself, and the only way is to ask monotony to help you, the monotony of repeating sentences and words.

So, there you have some very diverse reasons, rather off-the-cuff explanations, but maybe they can help you understand why I like this system of several cameras.

RIVETTE: Now I am deliberately going to raise an objection that isn't very subtle but that will allow me to move on. One could say that you are now abolishing the border between film and theater, that in the end what you're doing is returning talking film to the theater. What do you say to this?

RENOIR: I think it's an extremely valid objection. There is obviously a great risk there, but I believe that we crossed this border the day we accepted that films would speak. As soon as we accepted that, we were forced to accept certain rules of the theater. Silent films were grand for reasons that may be different from those of talking films, but I think that silent films were based on hypnotism. It had absolutely nothing to do with the dramatic arts, it was a matter of magic and hypnotism. Hypnotism was practiced by using close-ups. Silent films were an assemblage of close-ups. The characters who triumphed in silent films were those gifted with a hypnotic power. I think the greatest, one of the greatest, might have been Greta Garbo. You didn't go to see Greta Garbo for the story at all, the stories she acted in were perfectly idiotic. From a dramatic point of view, the acting was grotesque. When we see an old Greta Garbo film, with our contemporary frame of mind, which is that of a viewer of talking films, or a viewer of an art form that has nothing to do with silent films, we laugh, we find it grotesque. Or else if you're a film fanatic, as you and I are, you go to see it with a serious attitude, but the audiences laugh and they're completely wrong, because they forget that it's not a dramatic form of expression at all, it's hypnotism. Once you've accepted the grotesque side of this exterior, just of the exterior, deep down it wasn't any more grotesque than what we do now. You know, appearances, reality, realism, there are many things to say about all this, and maybe they'll be said one day or another, but the truth is that a close-up of Greta Garbo was something that forced itself on the public. There was the appropriate music, and the room was ecstatic. You suddenly felt as if an invisible bridge had been thrust between this enormous face on the screen and all the people who were watching it. The rather strange phenomenon that happens with very great people, and that also happens in life, took place.

I saw this phenomenon in Rome, at St. Peter's during a speech before the war, a rather dramatic speech given by the previous pope. In St. Peter's square, each spectator had the impression that the pope was talking to him, just to him and not to the others. And we had that in silent films with the big silent-film animals. I say *animals* on purpose, because the truth is it was almost an animal attraction, quite a grandiose power. For me, this isn't a criticism; on the contrary, it's a great compliment.

So now that films speak, we obviously have to deal with quality dialogue, we have to deal with rejoinders, with the wide screen. Why do we have wide screens? Some say it's to fight against television, but that's not it. Revolutions have much more profound reasons than that, reasons that those who revolt aren't even aware of, they have no idea why they're doing it. They're pushed by many invisible forces that existed, that were in the air before they were. Well, the wide screen is a type of revolution, and the real reason for it is quite simply that we wanted people to speak, and when people speak, there have to be several of them on the screen, and if we want to have several people on the screen, there has to be enough room, and enough width, or else you have to...

With a square screen, you have to move back too far, so if you want several people on the screen, they have to be full length, they have to be far away, and you are unable to see their faces, you can't see the emotion. That's why we need wide screens.

RIVETTE: The wide screen is a return to theatrical space.

RENOIR: Exactly. So whether we like it or not, we have films that speak, we have films on a wide screen, and we're getting closer to the theater. It's obvious, and why not? Aren't we in a period in which technical details are disappearing? It's unfortunate, because I think that technical preoccupations help the quality of art.

For example, I am truly convinced that this is the real reason for the quality of artistic expression in primitive periods, for example, the reason for the great quality of Greek sculpture of the Mycenaean period, compared with that of the seventh and say the fifth centuries B.C., during which they managed to copy nature perfectly, which is perfectly boring. It's not interesting. You don't even look at it, whereas we get on our knees before the poorly formed, barely squared-off figures of the Mycenaean period; they overwhelm us with emotion. Technology is against art, obviously, but it happens that we have this technology, and it happens that commercial conditions, even for noncommercial films, do not allow us to reject it. It happens that a technology, once perfected, is no longer necessary for the people who are at the root of creation. It happens that we are going to return, for example, to the Middle Ages, to the time when we were completing the technology of buildings, of performance, and of song, such as they were known. That is, the artist did everything, the artist had several professions. The troubadour was a one-man show, a troubadour arrived at a château and sang *The Song of Roland*. The important thing there was that the general theme had no importance. *The Song of Roland* was sung a thousand times, two thousand times, and each time was original, because the originality was in the form and not in the content.

I think we're wrong, these days, in giving so much importance to the story. I find that we Westerners dealt a blow, a fatal blow, to art in general, on the day we invented the idea of plagiarism. Plagiarism should be recommended, and the plagiarist should be rewarded, decorated, shouldn't he?

I know one way we can save films, and it's extremely simple. It would be to have the producers from a place like Hollywood or Paris decide that one year everyone would do one subject. Hollywood would decide, for example, that a certain western would be made, that all the directors would make the same western, and you would see the originality, the differences among the films. But instead of this, we pretend to be different by having different stories. In the end, though, we're producing exact copies. People tell a different story, but with the same faces, the same makeup, the same vocal expressions, the same emotions, but... But it's monotonous, don't you think?

RIVETTE: Yes.

RENOIR: To get back to this question for which you criticized me, very justifiably: Aren't we getting closer to a theatrical form by using this technique that makes the actor, shall we say, the master of his progression? My answer is yes, but we have no choice. We're coming to a time when, having been absolutely perfected, technology is in the process of disappearing, and its disappearance will allow the artist – and I repeat that this is not an advantage, but a fact – to practice different art forms, and the borders between the theater, film, and dance – no matter what form the performance takes – these borders will become insignificant, and more and more we'll see filmmakers and directors who will practice all the performing arts at once.

RIVETTE: Doesn't this technique of multiple cameras carry with it a danger, that the greater naturalness obtained with great actors will, on the contrary, be lost with lesser actors who are not as good, with whom one used to be able to capture flashes of truth using the old technique of filming short shots?

RENOIR: Yes, yes, yes, you're absolutely right. It's absolutely certain, obvious, that this technique requires professional actors. However, I think that we're in a period that belongs to specialists, to professionals. I think that amateurism is no longer appropriate to the spirit of our times. I see what you mean: The system basically is outwitting the subject. Say you have a child, for example. You're shooting a child, and you want this child to express the pain of having lost its mother, for example, so you merely scare him by saying "boo!" and the child opens his mouth, terrified, and underneath you add a little commentary explaining that this expresses the pain at having lost his mother. That works very well, but it's trickery, and I feel that if we want to create a new film art, we would be better off if it were completely honest.

Technical progress

RIVETTE: We were discussing the idea that speech is now an established and irrevocable part of the cinema, to which one must resign oneself as much as possible. We might add to this the progress (since that is the agreed-upon term) that film has been making for quite a few years, with color and the wide screen, progress in both the technical methods of photography and those of filmmaking. In the end, doesn't all this progress fall under the same category, which is roughly that of greater and greater realism, at least as far as the methods go?

RENOIR: Of course, but that's the story of all the arts, and we know that in the history of the arts, the arrival of absolute realism coincided with total decadence. I mentioned the example of Greek art earlier, but you can find many other examples. One comes to mind that I've mentioned many times, and I'm sorry if I'm repeating myself, but it's the example of tapestry. The first tapestry that we know of is the tapestry of Queen Mathilda. In order to kill time, the good Queen Mathilda and her ladies-in-waiting wove a tapestry, while her husband, William, was conquering England. The yarn she used was obviously very primitive, probably rather poorly scoured. Of course the colors of her yarn were very simple, they were probably vegetable dyes, perhaps a few mineral ones, but despite the tiny number of colors used, the extremely limited palette, this tapestry is probably one of the most beautiful that exists. We skip a few centuries, and we come to some tapestries that are still very primitive, the tapestries exhibited in Angers, "L'Apocalypse." We are still presented with a marvelous world, not only in the sense of dreams, but also in the sense of reality. The characters depicted are modern characters. We know them, we meet people everyday on the street who resemble these saints, these kings, these queens, all these people, the damned, the angels, and God knows the means were primitive.

Then, one day, the good King Henri IV dealt a terrible blow to the art of tapestry and killed it just like that, boom, with a big blow to the head, with Sully, which makes me wonder... I wonder if legends aren't often completely made up. This story of the stupid mistake made by Henri IV concerning tapestry makes me wonder about the truth of the legends that glorify this king so much. Here's what he did.

High-warp tapestry, a means of combining and weaving the strands in a finer way, had just been invented, replacing low-warp tapestry. At the same time the art of dyeing had made enormous progress. So the king financed and knighted people who wanted to do high-warp tapestry, thereby replacing low-warp tapestry, and so tapestry was perfected and managed to imitate nature better and better. Soon, instead of thinking up designs suitable for tapestries, simple motifs, the tapestry makers started copying paintings, paintings by Boucher, Watteau, and they almost resembled the Bouchers and the Watteaus. Today we can copy nature with tapestries, we can produce all the nuances. There are ten kinds of green, sky blue can go from cloudlike paleness to the deep blue of fine weather, with all the nuances. And the result is that tapestry is dead, the art...

Then, artificially, artists like Lurçat, for example, try to renew the art of tapestry by distancing themselves from realism. But unfortunately, there is one serious problem, which is that this attempt is artificial and just doesn't bring back the tapestry of Queen Mathilda.

So I've come to ask myself something. I've come to wonder whether people's gifts for beauty don't just happen. I wonder whether people's intelligence, this horribly destructive faculty, intelligence – we make mistakes only with intelligence – whether intelligence doesn't push us toward ugliness. I wonder whether our intelligence doesn't make us slaves, desperate admirers of all that is ugly, all that is horrible, and whether our tendency to imitate nature isn't simply our attraction to what is ugly, because the nature we imitate isn't even the beautiful part.

I wonder if the fact that in primitive times, all objects, not even art objects, were beautiful... because there is a disturbing question here. When we look at pieces of pottery, of, I don't know, Etruscan origin – old pottery – it's all beautiful. You can't tell me that all Etruscan potters were geniuses, so how is it that when the technique is primitive, everything is beautiful and that when the technique is perfected, everything is ugly, except for the things made by artists who have enough genius to master the technique?

It's quite a disturbing question.

So I wonder right now, since we're talking about the art of performance, whether our technical progress isn't simply a sign of total decadence.

First of all, technical perfection can create only boredom, because it is merely the reproduction of nature. Imagine a time when film will be able to create a perfect impression of being in a forest. We'll have trees with thick bark, even larger screens, screens surrounding the viewer. We will truly be in the middle of the forest, we will be able to touch the bark of the trees, to smell the smell of the forest; there will be automatic machines dispensing perfumes imitating the smell of the moss. You know what'll happen then? We'll get on our motorscooters and we'll go to a real forest instead of to the movies. Why bother going to a movie theater when you can have the real thing?

Imitation can only end an art.

RIVETTE: Which is to say that, finally, by pushing this way of thinking a bit too far, we'll come to regret that film has a finer and finer grain.

RENOIR: Absolutely. I'm very sorry about that. Listen, since we're both in cinema, let's note one thing, let's look at the photography of primitive films – the arrival of a train, the first American western – and let's look at the photography of Max Linder's films. In general, it's superb. There are wild contrasts, and I'm sorry... I regret the improvements in photographic film. Listen, when I was young, I fought to introduce panchromatic film for studio photography. I was even the first one to have used it. I made all my equipment myself in the attic at the Vieux-Colombier. I made a small studio to shoot *The Little Match Girl* (*La Petite Marchande d'allumettes*) on panchromatic film. Orthochromatic film was used at that time, and the lighting in studios was made for orthochromatic film; that is, there were arcs and tubes of mercury. I said to myself: Why don't we use panchromatic film, since it produces more nuances, it renders grays, it translates intermediary colors, it gives reds and avoids the contrasts that can seem ugly, the orthochromatic contrasts that make everything go right from black to white? I asked myself why we shouldn't use panchromatic film in the studios? The reason was that we didn't have the light spectrum needed, the lights we used didn't emit the ultraviolet rays required for panchromatic film. So I studied the question a bit, very generally, because I don't have a scientific mind, but in the end I found someone from Philips, the makers of lights and electrical systems, who advised me to try to boost the bulbs slightly, ordinary bulbs, which is what I did. So I made some equipment with friends, we made reflectors with zinc that we had cut, and then we made rheostats with pieces of metal that we had twisted, and we put the contacts at different points on these springs, and finally we shot *The Little Match Girl.* The photography wasn't so bad; it was very good. We developed it ourselves, in fact, in our kitchen.

We did all that. We did amateur work that was exciting, but I realize today that I was acting against my deepest convictions. I believed in progress, but now I don't believe in it any more. Currently the photography of many films is beautiful, very polished, imitates nature very well, but it is completely ordinary, perfectly boring.

We sometimes suffer from photographic boredom during screenings of perfect films. I find that the most perfect films today are also the most boring films photographically. This is very often the case. How can that be, how can we explain this, if not by this general rule that I am trying to express, which is that progress works against art, against artistic expression? Without that, without admitting this truth, how can we explain why primitive films are so exciting?

RIVETTE: And at the same time, as you were saying, we cannot attempt to produce bad photography artificially; that would be too easy.

RENOIR: I think it would be a big mistake. What we have to do is accept it... we're allowed to complain about the conditions that we work in, as I am doing right now. Note that my attitude is purely theoretical and basically conservative.

I believe in the reality of facts, and I believe one must bend before the facts. I don't believe we create our lives; rather, our lives create us. I believe that, given circumstances, given events, well... My father had a theory that I like very much and that I mentioned in a book I just wrote about him. I consider it very important. It's the theory of the cork. He used to say, "You have to be a cork, a cork in the current. You have to follow the current." Of course, the cork has to be a little intelligent, not completely stupid. It has to try to shift to the right or to the left so as to choose the moment when the current is best suited to it and to move a little in this direction, but the general direction is determined by events, by the current.

RIVETTE: That's the technique of a glider, who uses...

RENOIR: ...who uses the wind, which doesn't mean that the glider doesn't move, that he isn't intelligent. So, I'm convinced, concerning technical progress in our profession, that one has to act in this way. The problem is that if we consider the history of art, we will arrive at the conclusion that the ordinary products in times of great technical capacity were ugly; only the great artists escaped. That is, we are entering a period when you have to be either a great artist or nothing at all. I find this a serious problem, because it takes away the possibility of artistic creation from life's normal activities, from everyone's activities, a possibility that existed constantly in everything, that in nontechnical times existed even in daily activities, simply in the way one lit a fire in the morning. You'll say that we no longer have time to light a fire in the morning, that we have to run to our offices to earn a living, but that earlier there were many other inconveniences as well. Women gave birth at home, there were no hospitals, now they give birth without pain, which makes a big difference, it's great, but right now, let's not talk about the advantages or disadvantages of progress in general, I'm speaking of... of the effect of progress on art. Now, obviously, each action, during nontechnical periods, became an action of artistic creation. Lighting a fire in the morning required positioning pieces of wood in such a way that they would create a draft, and if you didn't know how to do this – using a method resembling the methods of artistic creation, they're very close – well, it was very simple, the fire didn't light. In France, there's one thing left that doesn't remain in many other countries. It sounds like a joke, it sounds trivial but I don't consider it trivial. I'm very proud that we have it: It's cooking. The French have preserved a sense for artistic cooking, for seasoning, for the amount of herbs, for the length of cooking time. They have preserved a sense of something that can't be explained, whereas technology can explain everything.

Technology brings perfect, logical solutions to everything. A true cook doesn't work technically, he works instinctively, he works with his senses. Basically, we've come to a big question, the question of intelligence and our senses.

The return to a natural style

RIVETTE: We've tried to analyze the ambiguities of the idea of progress, and you concluded that technology should not get ahead of the practical intelligence of the artisan, his sense of events and of concrete objects. Yet there may be another solution to this problem of realism, a solution that the history of the other arts suggests to us, which is to use these more and more realist means to more and more abstract ends. Can film – in your opinion – envision this solution as well?

RENOIR: As soon as we begin to have a precise theory, the facts demolish it. But I believe first that it is more difficult for film people to fight against the dangers of exterior realism by using abstraction, because film is an art based on photography, and photography photographs what we have in front of us.

The motion picture – and I'm speaking of the dramatic motion picture – is an art of expression and a photographic art. After all, the work is based on photographing actors' faces, so can we try to arrive at a certain stylization to fight against the dangers of exterior realism by means of, for example, unrealistic makeup? I don't think so.

RIVETTE: But maybe with the acting...

RENOIR: Maybe with acting, which itself would become stylized, but we must do it without its showing, because whether we like it or not, the public compares films with photography and requires them to resemble the exterior appearances of everyday photography, of pocket camera photography.

There is also another thing, which is that realism... listen, right now I'm criticizing realism, but I must say that realism was a wonderfully convenient springboard. I know that whatever I discovered in film, I discovered by using exterior reality as a base. From time to time I may have tried – I'm not saying I succeeded – to touch interior truth without respecting exterior truth, but we have to admit that exterior truth is useful, and it's still alive and kicking. The work of a great artist like, let's say, Cartier-Bresson, is based on the close observation of reality. The fact remains that there is no art in our profession if we don't base our work on the observation of human movements, on what goes on in people's minds, in their heads. It is also based on the knowledge of general ideas.

Basically, the problem is that the practice of a perfected technology sometimes distances us from general ideas.

Cartier-Bresson's greatness is that despite the realism and the detail of his photographs, they reflect a general concept. When he gives us photographs of – I don't know – of Madrid or Moscow, well, in ten photographs we have a general idea of what life is like in Madrid or in Moscow, what the people are like who live in these cities and maybe what their way of life is like. You can learn a lot.

So the big problem with our profession is that it reaches general ideas by means of details. Obviously, a perfected technology can distance us from this problem, but it can also bring us closer to it.

It can help us in this way. I think we were talking about Resnais's film earlier which is an attempt at nonrealism by means of realism. It may be an intellectual attempt, but it was a success. It's there and it's been done.

RIVETTE: It's only nonrealistic to a certain extent, since in the end he's looking for a psychological realism.

RENOIR: Obviously. That said, perfect technology is not indispensable to the practice of this kind of art, to the structure, the production, of a spectacle based on this kind of contrast.

We have an example in Shakespeare's *A Midsummer Night's Dream*, using a technology that is certainly primitive and settings that are almost imaginary. Shakespeare played with contrasts. We go from the present to an enchanted forest to a story about a duke in Athens – an Athens that doesn't exist, of course – to a detailed, realistic portrayal of the craftsmen's mentality in a small village, to a show within a show. All these different actions intertwine, contrasting with one another and creating the impression of a dream, but composed of realistic elements. They are true elements, since (though they may not be real on the exterior) on the interior they're based on an extremely thorough observation of man and his mind.

RIVETTE: This may be one explanation for the great quality of manufactured objects in primitive times. The motions that people went through to light a fire, or the actions that artisans performed in order to create an object, were actions that in the end, even though they may not have been conscious of it, were linked to some general ideas about the world. These movements were linked because they were traditional movements and were therefore linked to a civilization, a heritage.

RENOIR: Allow me to interrupt you. They were linked to something very important: to a religion, that is, to a philosophy, that is, to general ideas . . .

Jean Renoir in 1959 with the dancers of the Ludmilla Tcherina Ballet at the Sarah Bernhardt Theater on the occasion of *Le Feu aux poudres* (photo by Agence de presse Bernard). Script, ballet, and stage setting by Jean Renoir. Music by Mikis Theodorakis. This is the ballet's story as Renoir wrote it: "On the lost map of invisible countries, Strongalia and Molivia are separated by an imaginary border: the border that separates but does not protect the enemy civilizations on the other side. Strongalia is a scientific, strict, austere, virtuous, and disciplined country. Molivia is a lost corner of paradise on earth, where laziness, happiness,

RIVETTE: That's right. This is very clear in the Far East – China or Japan – where there was and still is, I think, until recently, an extraordinary way with manufactured items, and at the same time a sense for the general ideas found in the most humble objects.
RENOIR: This may be our only hope against extinction, which I believe is a real threat; I believe that we could very well see the disappearance of film. This could happen to us, and we may as well admit it. After all, television is extremely convenient, and it's an art, and what's more, it's an art that has the advantage of being at home. In the end, everything favors television. On the other hand, a new type of research, inventions, intellectual or emotional inventions, or artistic or instinctive inventions, are taking place in motion pictures. Other inventions are taking place in television, but they aren't the same, they aren't always the same. I think that if motion pictures were to disappear, they would leave a serious gap in our civilization.

What makes the struggle extremely difficult for the arts is that the public doesn't like to be surprised. I remember having a discussion about this a long time ago with Maurice Chevalier. He was explaining to me – it was in the days when he sang at the Casino de Paris; I'm talking about at least thirty years ago – he was telling me that when he sang a new program, the audience didn't like the new songs. So he wound up mixing them, always singing old songs first, songs that he had sung the year before, and even several years before, as a way of introducing the others, so that the audience wouldn't be surprised. They didn't like the brand-new songs, but they would like them the next year. That's a problem, isn't it, so what has to be done, without surprising the audience, is to try to evolve toward this kind of understanding of the object itself, of the tangible object, that is, the understanding of art and of the manufactured item that we sometimes still find in the Far East.

RIVETTE: Perhaps we can say that what created the power of these primitive civilizations, or of these Asian civilizations, was that they considered the world to be without a gap, that is, that there were no boundaries between the manufactured product and the work of art, and even their concept of the universe was part of the same system, based on their idea of the world.

RENOIR: The world is one for Hindus. Yes, of course, but I think that this concept was also helped along by the fact that the exterior differences were very clearly marked. I may be wrong, but I feel that because the world is made of contrasts, if we accept very distinct exterior differences, the interior differences will stand a chance of being less distinct. These exterior differences, for example, what we called nobility in Europe, were the castes in India. Castes are obviously very convenient. A Brahman knows very well that he need have absolutely nothing to do with, nothing to say to, even no... almost no contact with a Kshatriya or a Sudra. He knows this, it's accepted, so once the differences are marked, once man's thirst for vanity has been satisfied, he can forget it, and he can allow himself to have a greater intellectual relationship.

But this kind of intellectual unity, I believe, was also facilitated by a unity of belief.

For example, since we're talking about India, we can say that India is not so much a geographic entity, India is Hinduism. All the people who adored God by means of the same forms and the same rites, the people we call Hindus, were quickly united, first by a common language, a language that was to the Hindus what Latin was to Europeans, and that language was Sanskrit. So this obviously allowed an extreme simplification of intellectual concepts.

This doesn't mean it's good or bad. It's just the way it is.

RIVETTE: Did opposing castes have the same view of the world?

RENOIR: They definitely had the same view, and they still do, and it was the same for everyone. It was what created the unity of what we call Christianity. After that, we divided up Christianity with the idea of the nation. The idea of the nation is an arbitrary one, and it doesn't hold, it's in the process of disintegrating right now. In all honesty, one has to admit that the world is divided into ideologies, and not, in the least, into nations.

One thing obviously disturbs this unification, right now, and that's the difference in languages, but the difference in languages is being replaced by an extremely strong religious unity that is in the process of conquering the world, and this is the religion of science.

To get back to our problem, the problem of the motion picture, I believe we must proceed as the Ancients did. We were talking about, we spoke several times about, innovations, about a possible rescue, even about revolution, and I believe the most valuable revolutions were those that were based on material facts. We have just done a good job of criticizing technology, but we must admit that technology often brought about great changes in art.

For example, if the impressionists painted differently from their predecessors, it was simply because they recognized the existence of an extremely important technical invention: the invention of photography. Also, at that time, painting materials started being packaged in a more transportable form. One could go far away on foot into the fields carrying a box of paints, and this was more convenient than when paints were ground in pots and stored in heavy jars.

Similarly, I think that if, under Julius II, Michelangelo and Raphaël began to paint on large surfaces, it was probably because the manner of producing paints, the use of certain oils, of turpentine, permitted them to do that.

So you have to work with the facts. We were saying that something had to be changed in film, that film was falling asleep, and I believe that here, in France, there are some extremely interesting experiments, more interesting than in any other country, experiments that try to do something new. But perhaps these experiments are not based enough on facts, are not based enough, let's say, on the nature of the audiences of tomorrow.

Will the audience of tomorrow be an audience that will pay a lot, that won't pay a lot, that will come from far away? Do – and this is something I don't know and that we must find out – do changes, artistic revolutions, depend solely on artists, or do they also depend on audiences? We change the food in a country if the consumers want to eat differently. It doesn't depend solely on the shopkeeper selling the food.

RIVETTE: And in which direction do you see film shifting?

RENOIR: What I think right now, I think because I'm in the process of writing the script for *The Elusive Corporal* and because this script must respect exterior realities. I don't believe we have yet exhausted this exterior reality. Despite my lack of admiration for this cult, I think we have to continue in this direction.

I think that the exterior reality that we seem to have respected, we have respected only very superficially. I think we thought we were being true to life by disguising an actor who plays, let's say, a miner in a mine, with fake charcoal, with a little more black on his face. But this is still makeup, I think, and now I believe that we should also use this exterior reality to arrive at a poetic reality. But what is poetic reality? It may be the summary of emotions capable of animating a human being, it may be an attempt to say in three words what is normally said in two hundred.

Poetic reality may be a summary, may be a pleasant way of directly communicating with the spectator. I believe that in the end, that's what we have to do, just that, we must communicate with the spectator.

I believe that our role is to open windows, isn't it obvious? Listen, our profession is to look, not because we are better than others at looking, but simply because that's all we do, and since that's all we do, we have learned to see, whereas other people have to go to work in banks, in other professions, and don't have the time to learn to see. But that's all we do, which is why artists must have time. Besides, if you allow me to go a bit farther, I would like to say one thing, which is that my father hated the word *artist*, and I don't like it very much, but I don't see any other word to use. It's a distortion of the language. Until the seventeenth century, art was a way of doing something, the technique and the science were knowledge, only that and nothing else. It meant that one had read or written some beautiful cookbooks, but that one might not know how to make a soft-boiled egg. The person who did know how to make a soft-boiled egg knew the art of cooking. But in any case, to get back to our general question, I believe that in this opening of windows, which is our job, we have to choose the landscapes we will show, and if we show landscapes too different from those outside the windows already opened, the public will get angry. We must proceed rather cautiously. It's annoying, because it's no fun to be cautious. It would be marvelous to be able to open windows onto absolutely unexpected, unknown, unrealistic landscapes, but it's very difficult. Man is a creature of habit, and we are creatures, after all, so I understand why my dog likes to sleep in the same corner, in the same part of the house, every night. It's nice to return to the same spot on the floor. We also like to go home to our corners, to our nooks. So we have to open windows, and these windows are going to reveal some things. They will make people say: Look, it's true, I had never thought of it that way. Cézanne opened a window onto cardplayers, and the people around these cardplayers, in the city of Aix-en-Provence, took fifty years to see them. But after fifty years, they said: Hey, it's true, that's what these cardplayers are like. I had never noticed that their skin had reflections of this color. This revelation sweeps them off their feet. This revelation kills our enemy, the enemy of our time, which is boredom, and suddenly we're swept away.

The other day, I participated in a program on modern French painting that will be shown in America, and because the lighting took a long time to set up, I waited in a corner of the Jeu de Paume museum. I waited on the spot where the cameraman had asked me to stay, because he needed me to stay there to work on his lighting. I stayed there, and I was a foot away from a corner of the painting of a woman, a servant, by Cézanne, which is in the Jeu de Paume, and I was in front of the corner with the browns and dark greens, and a dark blue, and suddenly I was with Cézanne. By means of these few brush strokes, I had a conversation with him, he seemed to be talking to me. And I think that's it, that what we mean when we talk about art: It means opening a window onto something that the public hasn't noticed, and when you open this window, it means having a little chat. This is why I don't believe that works have different degrees of importance.

In my opinion, either an artist is interesting or he isn't. Excuse me, I'm expressing myself poorly. I should say, either I like him or I don't like him, or else he is either my friend or he isn't. If he is my friend, if

I love him, he can say anything. Anything coming from a man one loves, from a friend, is much more interesting than profound truths coming from a person to whom one is indifferent. I believe this is extremely important in art. You have to love the artist. I have a little memory concerning my father. I remember I played the piano when I was young, and I played very poorly, and one day I was playing, poorly, but I was putting real emotion into it, as all bad pianists do, and my father interrupted me and said, "What's that you're playing?" "It's Mozart...," I answered. "Oh, that's good," he said, "I was really scared!" "You were scared of what?" And he said, "Well, I liked it, and I was afraid it might be Beethoven..." whom he hated.

I think that this question of friendly contact is the essence of art. Film producers may have even made a mistake: They looked for perfection instead of looking for personality, but no one is interested in perfection, who cares about perfection. It's as if someone were to claim that a woman is loved because she is beautiful. I've known some very beautiful women who were not loved, and men weren't interested in them, and I've known some very ugly women who were adored, who were chased by all the men. Beauty doesn't mean a thing, perfection doesn't count, it's personality. So film producers are wrong when they look for perfection, when they use a dozen script writers and a director, thinking that the result will be better. Yes, it's true, the result is better, but it isn't interesting. Sometimes one corrects the other, and so on, and so on – there are constant improvements at each stage – and finally you have a very beautiful finished product, a manufactured product that no one is interested in. I believe that's another thing that works against us in film, perfection.

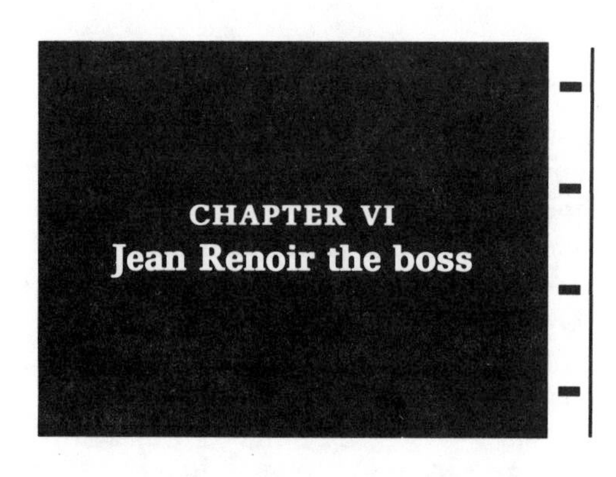

Three television programs were grouped under the title "Jean Renoir le patron" (the boss). The programs were produced in May and June of 1966 by Jacques Rivette for Janine Bazin's and André S. Labarthe's series "Cinéastes de notre temps." Of these three programs, only two were aired, the first ["La Recherche du relatif" ("The Search for Relativity")] on 13 January 1967, and the third ["Le Règle et l'exception" ("The Rule and Its Exception")] on 8 February of the same year. Although the second, entitled "La Direction d'acteurs" ("Directing Actors") and consisting of a long mealtime conversation between Jean Renoir and Michel Simon, was scheduled, it never aired.

We have published "The Search for Relativity" and "The Rule and Its Exception." "Directing Actors," a remarkable visual and aural document, is interesting more because of tone, accents, attitudes, and emotions than because of what was said, and would have lost a great deal in being transcribed.

In the following pages, we try to give a kind of shooting script of the programs, by indicating, as precisely as possible, the place, the date of the shooting, the names of the participants, and, in parentheses, the titles of the films from which excerpts were shown. In addition, "The Rule and Its Exception" had thirteen subtitles indicating the themes discussed. We've shown them in bold type wherever they appeared during the program.

The photos accompanying these texts do not necessarily correspond to the clips shown during the program.

"Jean Renoir le patron." *Photography:* Pierre Mareschal. *Composition:* André Neau. *Script:* Marinette Pasquet. *Sound:* Guy Solignac. *Editing:* Jean Eustache.

THE SEARCH FOR RELATIVITY

[Begins with an excerpt from *Toni*]

27 May 1966. Restaurant du Lac, in the park at the Buttes-Chaumont. Jean Renoir is with Pierre Braunberger. It is the end of their meal.

JEAN RENOIR: This is a film that should seem like a documentary and yet not be a documentary. It should seem as if it were filmed carelessly, without paying attention, by putting the camera just anywhere, very freely. But in fact the film had to be extremely well prepared, extremely well composed.

[Excerpt from *Nana*]

JACQUES RIVETTE: What was your perspective on the character of Nana in relation to the American films that you admired?

RENOIR: Nana seemed like a character who was sufficiently haphazard, sufficiently rough around the edges, sufficiently – I don't want to say primitive – to allow us to approach our ideal, which at that time was, we must admit, American film. I think that Pierre and I got into film because we admired – of course we also admired Swedish and German films – but most of all we admired American films. Isn't that right?

PIERRE BRAUNBERGER: That's right. Moreover, we met because I had just returned from America, I had just worked, in a small capacity, on the film by Valentino called *Monsieur Beaucaire*.

RENOIR: But I think our admiration for – I'll name them – the Chaplins, the Griffiths, the Stroheims, the Fred Niblos, the Clarence Browns, to name a few . . . in short, the directors of the period, I think our admiration went beyond reason. Our admiration was a kind of cult that was probably not always justified. And as a result, my God, we had very little desire to see French films. French films at the time, which were called artistic films, bored us. They seemed sort of monotonous, slightly gray, slightly slow. The truth is that our dream, which was very ambitious, was to contribute to French film, which we loved, and to France, in which we were thoroughly immersed, to contribute the possibility of more active, livelier filmmaking, and our model was the American motion picture. Isn't that true?

BRAUNBERGER: Basically, I consider *Nana* to be one of the first modern French films. It's a very important film. There was a great reaction against it, but I think one could argue that it served as an inspiration to a good part of modern film today.

RENOIR: I think I remember one reaction to it. There was a preview of *Nana* at the Moulin Rouge, with the Moulin Rouge orchestra accompanying the film with some airs by Offenbach, if you remember. The audience seemed to follow the story very well, but the people who were in the business were not at all pleased. And one very important person in the motion picture business . . .

BRAUNBERGER: Madame Perret.

RENOIR: . . . at the end of the screening, got up and said, "This is a Kraut film." I had just returned from the war, and I was really hurt. After all, I was anything but a Kraut, and that made me laugh. But it's always like that. The truth is that we wanted to contribute something to French film, and we thought that, as in all arts, to contribute something you had to search elsewhere, you had to search abroad. After all, think of the Renaissance. The French Renaissance came from the desire to imitate the Italian Renaissance, but that didn't prevent the French Renaissance from being purely French. Nothing is more French than Ronsard, than Rabelais, than Montaigne. Obviously, though, in their minds, they accepted the idea of seeking inspiration abroad, even in different centuries, in antiquity.

BRAUNBERGER: The Italian Renaissance is Greek and Latin antiquity.

RENOIR: That's right. Of course, we discovered the French genius little by little. In any case, as far as I'm concerned, I discovered that we could feed off ourselves in France. But at the same time, I believe this period of wild admiration for foreign films was useful. It helped sweep away certain routines, certain superstitions, that were then a part of French cinema. That said, there were French films that I really admired. You can never form an absolute judgment about anything, they just don't exist.

BRAUNBERGER: Just the same, the great French productions were mediocre, there's nothing left of them today.

RENOIR: The great French productions were above all very boring, extremely "artistic." The word *artistic* was our enemy, we hated it. Just the mention of the word *art* gave us goose bumps. We didn't want to produce art, we wanted to produce films with a fresh spirit that would attract the public's attention.

[Excerpt from *Nana*]

ANDRÉ S. LABARTHE: There was much talk of an American influence concerning *Nana*, especially Stroheim's.

RENOIR: It's obvious. Stroheim influenced me in the beginning and [turning to Pierre Braunberger] he influenced you. It's obvious that he was our teacher.

LABARTHE: Which may explain *Nana*'s reception, the people who called you a Kraut.

RENOIR: Maybe. That's possible. I believe mainly that there is a kind of fear in people who can be labeled *reactionary*, a fear of what they're not used to seeing every day. Coffee comes with one lump of sugar, give them a coffee without sugar, or with two lumps, and they're outraged: It's Kraut coffee.

[Excerpt from *Nana*]

BRAUNBERGER: I don't think that the audiences were against it, it was the producers, those who believed they had an interest in this profession or who actually did have an interest in it.

RENOIR: That's possible, but I think that it went even beyond people's personal interests; it was a kind of religion. It's the same thing when we explain to believers today that mass can be said facing the congregation, instead of turned away from the congregation. Many believers don't accept this and consider it a dangerous revolution in the Church. I think that man is a creature of habit, that's his role, and that's why, from time to time, God creates artists, and my God, it's a difficult role because you have to bear the wrath of all the people who don't like to change, that is, the majority.

BRAUNBERGER: Who can't change...

RENOIR: Or who can't change. But Pierre, you shouldn't be sorry about it; that's the way it is. It does us a lot of good. I think that having opposition gave us strength, and the only danger is if we now consider our contribution to be the rule. The greatest danger for all innovators is that their innovations seem like gospel to them. Personally, I know I have one fear, and that's of becoming rigid.

BRAUNBERGER: Cocteau used to say that the problem with youth was not a problem of age, but of always being ahead of others.

[Excerpt from *Nana*]

RENOIR: In any case, one thing is for sure: You carry on your profession, you continue, you try to make films. The important thing is never to do anything concerning the details that is against your true beliefs. I'm starting to think now that the main theme of a film isn't terribly important. I believe more and more in the inspiration of the art of the Middle Ages, or of traditional Indian art, for example, in which the frame is somewhat fixed; it doesn't change much. Within this structure, you're free, and within this structure you must be innovative. We can tell the same stories as do other directors, whom we didn't like in the beginning. We thought these stories were pitiful, but we were wrong. It wasn't the stories that were pitiful, but the way they were told.

[Excerpt from the prologue of *La Chienne*]

RENOIR: I had just worked with Michel Simon in my earlier films, in *Tire au flanc* and *On purge bébé*, and I was very enthusiastic. I found him to be an exciting actor, and it seemed to me that the male role in *La Chienne* would allow Simon to do some new things. At that time, the American influence was wearing off, but the Americans still contin-

Michel Simon and Nicole Fernandez in *On purge bébé* (photo by "Avant-scène).

ued to amaze me, and I thought that Michel Simon would surpass the Americans in this movie. And in fact he did surpass them – not all of them – but many.

9 June 1966. A screening room at ORTF, located on the rue Cognacq-Jay.

RENOIR: Details, details, that's what counts the most. I heard his voice, you see, I heard Michel Simon interpret this character with a slightly monotonous voice, with the voice we hear in the film now, a voice that avoids outbursts, highs, and lows. That's why I was very happy to run across . . . I didn't choose Madame Berubet for the wife, Michel Simon brought her to me. He said to me, "I see what you want, you want me to have a slightly somber, slightly dull voice, and opposite me you want a wife with a loud voice. In that case, I'm going to bring you Berubet," and he brought Berubet, who is, in any case, an admirable actress. But this question of Michel Simon's voice was one of the driving forces in the film.

LABARTHE: The beginning is synchronized? The meal . . .

RENOIR: Everything is synchronized. There was no postrecording.

LABARTHE: There was no sound mixing either.

RENOIR: No. There was no mixing at the time. You had to splice the tracks together end to end without combining them. Of course you could overlap the sound when you spliced it, and I did that several times to try to mask the passage from one shot to the next, but it doesn't fool anyone.

[Excerpt from *La Chienne*]

RENOIR: Michel Simon had just played Clo-Clo, for which he used a booming voice, and it seemed to me that this man could give the dramatic intensity of the greatest actor in the world, simply by using these seemingly drab methods – the contrast between the exterior means and the effect, the dramatic effect. Now, as far as the other characters went, I think that little by little, not in the beginning, but as we shot, I realized that I needed other characters with loud voices. And I also thought it was good to bathe this so-called realistic story – that's a ridiculous word – what does realistic mean? It means nothing – this story, such as it appears – what people call true to life – it seemed necessary to bathe it in a kind of slightly hazy poetry. I counted a great deal on the actors' diction to help me get this effect, and I think they helped me a great deal and the effect was achieved. This question of voices obsesses me terribly in film. I may be wrong, but I took great care with this question of voices, and I still do. It made me notice that accents, bad accents, the bad ways of expressing oneself on the screen or on the stage, are the same in America, where I worked sometimes, and in France. It's the same, especially with girls. The girls who come from acting school or from a conservatory all have the same obsession: They finish their sentences on an upswing, the ends of sentences are always interrogative. They don't say "It's nice out" affirmatively, they say "It's nice *out*?" as if they were asking if it were nice out. I think it's a kind of coquetry, a way of offering oneself. They say "Isn't the sun shining *today*?" as if they were saying "take me"... I like people to say "Isn't the sun shining today," and for the end of the sentence to drop, and that's my great struggle with beginning actors, and especially with beginning actresses.

RENOIR: Excuse me for jumping to another topic and for going back to *La Chienne*. I just saw something that I found delightful. I have an obsession, when I shoot films, which is that I try to make the viewers think that the main characters shown on the screen are not alone in life, that there are other people who live as well, who love, who suffer, who drink, and who have joys and pains. I hate the idea of isolating the main characters, and when I did the meeting between Michel Simon and Warrant Officer Godard, I didn't know... I couldn't add anything since it was in front of a boutique, and I couldn't have it in front of anything but a limited setting because it had to be raining, and my means for making rain were limited. I had only two or three waterhose nozzles, and that was all. Consequently, I had to keep a rather limited field, a wall and no depth. So I had an idea, that I'm so pleased with because when I see the film, no one sees it but me: It's the curtain going up. I said to myself: Keep that move, that will give me a backdrop, people may imagine that there's a shopowner on the other side, who's living, who has his own problems too.

RIVETTE: And at the same time, a curtain being lowered is still a curtain. You like curtains. There's a hint of the theater that suddenly hits you when the curtain goes down.

LABARTHE: But why did you have to have rain, since it wasn't raining?

RENOIR: Oh! there's no reason for it. It seemed to me that a meeting like that could happen only in the rain.

Restaurant du Lac.

RIVETTE: There is one thing that stands out in *La Chienne*, which is its relationship to other films, not only silent films, but other films of the period. It's a film that was shot with many long takes, with shots that follow the actors for a long time.

RENOIR: There are two reasons for that. One is that I already believed in the necessity of not cutting the actor's inspiration by making him work with short takes. I still believe that. I believe that once an actor gets started, you have to let him finish his race. The technique of shooting this race bit by bit is therefore dangerous, in my opinion, because you also risk cutting the actor's inspiration. There is also the fact that I was still influenced by the techniques from the beginning of the talkies, in which, because there was no mixing, you tried to work with several cameras and only one sound track. In fact, you tried to avoid sound editing. So the idea of not doing sound editing meant not doing too much picture editing, either. It wasn't just a question of style, of a sought-after style; it was also a question of habits I had acquired while shooting *On purge bébé*, which was still when one had to be careful to not cut up scenes too much.

RIVETTE: But if I remember correctly, *On purge bébé* is a film that was shot with several cameras.

RENOIR: *La Chienne* was, too. I often used three cameras in *La Chienne*, and I like working this way now once again. I've always come back to this technique for the same reason: so as not to cut the actor's inspiration. In *La Chienne*, when two people had a conversation, for example, the conversation between Michel Simon and the warrant officer in the bistro, I had one camera for the master shot, one camera on Michel Simon, and one camera on Michel Gaillard, who played the officer. And after that, you work things out by means of sound editing, because the sound is the same.

RIVETTE: But you also had scenes that were shot with only one camera, or else if you had several cameras, you kept the shots from only one of them.

RENOIR: That happens, too, and I also had many scenes in which I moved the camera, not to create a stylistic effect – I never believed in that. I'm the slave of the acting, and I don't ask the actors to work for the camera. I ask the camera to work for the actors, and you can see that I already had many shots in *La Chienne* in which I moved the camera so as to follow the actors, just so I wouldn't cut off the acting. I used this technique later, and to a much greater extent, in *Grand Illusion*, for which an acrobat like my nephew Claude, the cameraman, was required in order to film certain shots like that of the "Marseillaise." Seeing him shoot that scene, you really would have thought he was a pretzel, or an ivy vine curled around the foot of the camera. I started to work this way in *La Chienne*. But nonetheless, if we're talking about my concerns in *La Chienne*, my main concern was above all with the actors, even more than in *On purge bébé*. It was mainly a matter of expressing a certain character, of bringing him to life, of making him digestible for the audiences. I'll go a step further, it was a matter of making the audience love this character, who is basically a man who cheats on his wife, who behaves in a dishonorable fashion, and who winds up being a murderer. So it was a matter of making him likable, and in order to make him likable I had to follow the slightest detour of his thoughts. I also had to show the people around him, to show that if this man became a murderer, it was because those around him were insufferable and that when you have people around like that, you become a murderer, like it or not.

[Excerpt from *La Chienne*]

LABARTHE: We were talking about the character of Michel Simon who, despite what he is, makes himself likable to the viewers.

RENOIR: He builds a bridge. All great actors are bridge builders. They build a small bridge between themselves and the audience. In my opinion, Michel Simon is one of the greatest bridge builders. The bridge he builds is a boulevard.

LABARTHE: It also has to do with your technique. The fact that we follow him continuously means that we're always close to him.

RENOIR: But you can't follow all actors. With many actors, if you follow them all the time, you wind up getting very annoyed because they're empty, their heads are like little bells with nothing inside, whereas Michel Simon is so stuffed with thoughts, with doubts, even with unpleasant thoughts, often with a lack of confidence . . . is so stuffed with questions, with introspection, that following him is exciting.

LABARTHE: So the character that Michel Simon brings to life, or even that your other characters bring to life, are never condemned in advance. They're nasty characters, but one realizes that they're not as nasty as all that or that they have other sides.

RENOIR: Of course. When I joined the cavalry, I learned something essential to film, to literature, and to art in general. I learned that there are no black horses and no white horses. Only civilians or infantrymen say "a white horse" or "a black horse." A true cavalryman says "a chestnut bay horse" or "a light gray horse," because there are always a few black hairs in the white and always a few red hairs in the black, for example. That's my answer. Nothing is absolute, there are no absolutely mean people, and there are no absolutely good people. Good people are often very mean, and mean people very good. I think that Gorki says something like that. I vaguely remember a sentence in my film *The Lower Depths* (*Les Bas-Fonds*). It's that murderers are not murderers every day, that there are times when they are not murderers.

[Excerpt from *Toni*]

8 June 1966. At Robinson, an estate belonging to Pierre Gaut, the production director for Toni. *A picnic. Jean Renoir is surrounded by Pierre Gaut, Sylvia Bataille, Charles Blavette, and Blavette's wife.*

LABARTHE: When you shot *Toni,* you had already worked with Pagnol?

CHARLES BLAVETTE: Yes, I had shot a film called *Jofroi* and another called *Angèle*. And this is exactly how it happened: I turned up in the courtyard of the studio in Marseilles, at the Peupliers, and someone named Bourelly said to me, "The boss wants to see you." The boss was Pagnol. I went up to see Pagnol, and he said, "Look, Jean Renoir

Michel Simon and Jean Renoir during the filming of "Jean Renoir le patron" (25 May 1966, The Pomme d'Api restaurant in Joinville).

is working on a film, *Toni*. He's looking for a lead, and I told him you had the part." At that point I was stunned, and I said, "It can't be. What?" and the light in the room began to dim. It was simply Jean Renoir who had entered the room and who was standing in front of the window.

Charles Blavette in *Toni*.

[Excerpt from *Toni*]

BLAVETTE: It's you. *Toni* isn't Blavette, it's Jean Renoir.

RENOIR: You're joking!

BLAVETTE: Yes it is, it's your method, Jean!

RENOIR: It's a marriage.

BLAVETTE: You take an actor, whether he's an actor or not. He acts like this and you make him into that, and when he's finished, he doesn't even realize it.

RENOIR: I don't either. Because I ask the actor to teach me my profession, as you say that you learned yours from me, but the actor gives me as much as I give him, probably more. When I start, I don't know a thing, my friend. There are some guys who are really lucky. They come to direct, and they know exactly what they're going to do, they know everything. They say, "Here's the script, I'm going to follow it, I'll do this, close-up, that, like this . . . and the feelings are this, that." As for me, I admit, I don't know a thing, not a thing.

BLAVETTE: And you know everything.

RENOIR: You're joking, I don't know anything. I know nothing, so I start with the actors. We talk, I explain the idea, and then suddenly the actor has a kind of flash, a kind of inspiration. He says to himself, "That's it, here it is, I've found it, we'll start there." And once you've found the point of departure, you're set, but you never find the point of departure on your own.

[Excerpt from *Toni*]

RENOIR: The truth is that what happens with me is that I'm not always able to understand the meaning of a scene before I've actually seen it. I find the true meaning of the acting, a scene, even a word, only after the words have materialized, once they exist. As Sartre would say, I believe that the essence comes after the existence. Let's exist first, and then we'll see. I have to see something that exists in front of me, and then I begin vaguely to understand the meaning, but deep down I'm really an exploiter. I ask the others to give me all the elements; I try not to bring anything to it myself; I want everything to come to me from without.

PIERRE GAUT: Yes, but you manage just the same, and I find that extraordinary, because I see progress from the third rehearsal to the fourth. But I would be truly incapable of transforming that third one into the fourth and of making improvements in it.

RENOIR: Yes, but there is also another thing I believe in, which is that the benefits of rehearsals are superficial and mean nothing. It's the famous Italian method that is often talked about, which is reading lines but not letting yourself give them any expression. You read it as if you were reading the telephone directory, and then, little by little, a spark flies from a word, and from this spark a good scene may follow.

GAUT: That's also called hypnotic suggestion.

RENOIR: It's also called suggestion, yes. But the important thing is not to start off believing that you know the meaning of the scene. You have to start off knowing that you know nothing and want to discover everything. Each scene has to be an exploration.

GAUT: It's like Picasso always says, "When I paint, I start and I don't even know what I'm going to do."

RENOIR: That's very important. And I think that's the number one rule in art, whatever art it may be. You must allow the elements of the act to conquer you. Afterward you may manage to conquer it, but first it has to conquer you. You have to be passive before you can be active.

[Excerpts from *Toni* and from *The Crime of Monsieur Lange (Le Crime de Monsieur Lange)*]

Restaurant du Lac.

RENOIR: At that time, and even now, I was absolutely convinced that technology was at the root of intellectual changes in a profession, of stylistic changes. I often tell the story of the impressionists and paint tubes. I claim – and I talked about this with Reichenbach who thinks the same – I claim that one of the reasons for the impressionist revolution in painting is the invention of tubes of paint. Before they were invented, paint was sold in little pots, and when you put them in your pocket, they turned over, they weren't very practical. You couldn't go outside. But with tubes, you could put them in your pocket, you could put them in a little box and carry a palette, the tubes, a little bottle of oil, and a little bottle of turpentine, and you could go outdoors and paint there. This purely technical invention probably determined all the nontechnical stylistic discoveries of impressionism.

[Excerpt from *A Day in the Country (Une Partie de campagne)*]

1 June 1966. The banks of the Ource, near Essoyes, where the Renoir family house is located. As a child, Jean Renoir used to play there with Paul Cézanne.

RENOIR: I think there is a relationship among all the arts. After all, it's a question of expressing oneself. The big difference between film and an art like painting is that many people express themselves in film. The actor has to express himself, the director has to express himself, the technician has to express himself. There is also another big difference, which is that the means given to film directors are complex, whereas the means given to painters are extremely simple. The truth is you can paint with a piece of charcoal on a white wall, or at least draw, whereas to make a film you need a camera, film, sound, so many things. This is not to film's advantage, because I think that technical resources are against what we generally call art. The more tech-

Jean Renoir, Marinette Pasquet, and Janine Bazin.

nical resources you have, the more difficult it is to express yourself. You wind up drowning in wealth. I believe it is a great advantage for a painter to be able to paint anywhere; he doesn't need much equipment. Second, when one's technical concerns are limited to the essentials, these essentials become much more profound and become more special as well. I believe that a good painter is harder to find than a good filmmaker, because a good painter, since he doesn't have very advanced technology, since he is limited in his means, has to be more clever. You know the expression "Don't spread yourself too thin." I think that this is extremely important in art. The painter has the advantage of digging into the same little hole, and he can go very, very, very, very deep. He can even go so far as to find the relationship between eternity and the instant, between the world and the spirit, between the body and the mind. Painting can go very far. I believe that right now, painters are the great philosophers of our time.

[Shot of Auguste Renoir in *Ceux de chez nous* by Sacha Guitry]

RENOIR: There are a few filmmakers who have at times come close to something like that, but in film, let's be frank, we're limited by the immensity, by the magnificence of our means. I hope, I believe, I have tried in all my work – ever since I started to make films – I have always tried to make films because it was fun. My main goal was my own joy, a joy that exists during the fabrication. The truth is that the result doesn't really interest me. I have several films that were successful, I have some that were notoriously unsuccessful . . . but it's all the same to me, the important thing is to create. I think it's the same in all aspects of life. I think that all people who are hooked on results and who pursue goals, I'm convinced that they are extremely unhappy and that when they arrive at their goal, they realize that the goal wasn't worth all the effort they made. Whereas the joy of working, the joy of creating an object – once the object is created, you put it aside – the joy that the sculptor has in pushing the clay with his thumb or in chiseling the stone with his hammer, or the joy the painter has in guessing the relationship between a blue and a red and in expressing a little piece of eternity with this relationship. . . . It's *while* you're doing it that it counts. After that people say, "It's good," "It's not good": So what, that's their problem.

[Excerpt from *A Day in the Country*]

Hôtel de Brinon.

LABARTHE: What strikes me when I look at your films is their experimental side. You experimented with photography, with the choice of lenses, with the choice of actors.

RENOIR: Yes, of course. Often it backfired. It's not always a good thing. I really believe that to succeed in anything in life, you have to persist, you have to dig in the same hole, and I personally spent my time digging in twenty different holes, and I wonder whether I wasn't wrong in doing that.

LABARTHE: But don't you think that this experimentation . . . You have to go very far with it?

RENOIR: Of course, you have to go all the way. It's because I'm extremely wary of the abstract. I'm terribly wary of my own reactions. I don't believe that the world I may create will be as good as the world as it exists now. I believe in surroundings, and believing in surroundings, I obviously believe in technology – not just because it's technology, but to the extent that it's a hurdle, maybe. It's a good hurdle, one that you have to get over, and in getting over it you acquire spiritual wealth that has nothing more to do with technology. Because in the end, when the film is finished, the photography may be good or bad, it's not all that important. Some very great films have bad photography

The filming of "Jean Renoir le patron": Jean Renoir and Jacques Rivette.

or bad sound. Certain films with magnificent photography and magnificent sound are nothing at all. But I repeat that this technology is necessary. Because if you're not careful, if you don't try to arrive at a kind of perfection in the form, I think you lose it.

[Excerpt from *A Day in the Country*]

The banks of the Ource.

RENOIR: The motion picture is way behind painting. What's done in painting is done in the motion picture fifty years later. Fifty years later. Obviously, some of my fellow directors and I are preoccupied with considering the world to be as one, if you like, that things are not separate, that there aren't people, and then animals, and then trees, and then ponds. No, we think there is a whole world and that this world, each element in this world, governs the conditions of other elements and that we can't think of a fly without thinking of the bird that will eat the fly.

RIVETTE: So that in the end, the setting is essentially pantheistic in your eyes.

RENOIR: I think so. Of course it's a question of temperament. It's extremely difficult for me not to see divinities all around me and not to imagine that nature is alive and that the trees are speaking to me. That's a bit pretentious, because the trees are much more clever than I am, much wiser, but I do try to listen to them and learn their lessons.

[Excerpt from *Picnic on the Grass* *(Déjeuner sur l'herbe)*]

27 May 1966, in Catherine Rouvel's apartment, rue Caulaincourt in Paris.

RENOIR: Catherine, do you remember when we met for the first time?

CATHERINE ROUVEL: It's something I'll remember all my life!

RENOIR: Where?

ROUVEL: It was at the Cinémathèque, on the rue d'Ulm. You were presenting Flaherty's *Louisiana Story* and there was a little cocktail party, and I saw you there. I was so shy; I had just arrived from Marseilles and still had an accent. I was a redhead, and I had a big hat on my head.

RENOIR: A fur hat...

ROUVEL: Incredible! That's right, a white fur hat. I came up to you. A friend introduced us, and you said, "I'd like some pictures of this little lady."

RENOIR: The first thing that surprised me was that this southerner, who was such a typical southerner, was wearing a Russian fur cap. I said to myself, "That's really strange, something's out of place." So I looked again and I found – and by the way, the impression I had could perhaps be helpful to you in certain roles – I found that you had a 1900s look to you. You made me think of a character, one who was magnificently acted by Simone Simon, in fact, in one of my films, the character of Séverine in *The Human Beast* (*La Bête humaine*). You made me think of Séverine. I said to myself, "Well, here's a Séverine." And I like Séverine very much, and I liked you in turn.

ROUVEL: That's fantastic! I didn't know all that was going to happen to me. I simply know that I turned red and – I was shy – I hid in a corner, I backed up as much as I could, and I didn't see *Louisiana Story*!

RENOIR: That was just the beginning. After that we worked together.

ROUVEL: Yes. You wanted to do a test for *Cordelier*.

RENOIR: A little test that I didn't keep. I didn't leave it in the film, it wasn't very good, but it did allow me to get to know you. And after that we rehearsed *Picnic on the Grass* together using a method that I'm entirely against now. You remember my method at the time... describe it.

Catherine Rouvel on *Picnic on the Grass.*

ROUVEL: It amazed me. I wasn't at all familiar with television, as I had never done any. We rehearsed with markers, you had drawn some things on the ground.

RENOIR: That is, I had drawn with a piece of chalk the outline of the exterior set in which we were going to shoot, so that the actors could get used to the distances. That's something I'd no longer do. We're young at any age. I was a baby then, now I'm young.

ROUVEL: Yes, but it allowed me to get used to television methods, and afterward, thanks to you, I was no longer surprised. When I worked on the "Colettes," I knew where I was.

RENOIR: That's it, that's exactly why I don't like this method. I don't like it. It's practical, it allows you to shoot with a certain security, it permits you to avoid spending too much money, to avoid going over schedule, to shoot the number of shots planned for the day, but in my opinion, it kills one extremely important thing, which is the actor's surprise when faced with the set, and in my opinion this surprise is very interesting. I think that the actor must assimilate the set himself, and not through a director who draws some chalk lines on the ground. If I were a dictator – let's pray that I never will be, because I wouldn't like it! – but if I were a dictator, I would start by forbidding all pieces of chalk on stages and on sets – because theater directors work only with chalk now, they mark the spots where the actors' feet should go. I hate that, I think that actors must have freedom of movement. What's really important is to bring to life a certain character – it's the marriage of Nénette and Catherine – and the rest is a joke, it's not important.

ROUVEL: But it allows you to work more quickly.

RENOIR: It allows you to work more quickly, but I'm no longer a partisan of working quickly. Not really. I've learned a great deal since, while I wasn't shooting. I've filmed very little since, and I've learned a great deal. I've learned, for example, that the hurdles of the film are useful. Say you have a shot that's difficult to light: It takes a long time and the actress's mind goes blank because the lights are so hard to take, but during this seemingly wasted time she plunges into a world that allows her to become more familiar with her character. I think that inconveniences wind up being advantages, I'm convinced of that.

ROUVEL: I think that most of all you get into a climate, you swim in this climate because anything outside it is a matter of indifference.

RENOIR: It disappears. You're surrounded by lights, by familiar faces. That's why it's very important that no visitors be on the set, not even friends, if they're not part of the film. The face of an electrician you know is the face of a friend, it's part of the world to which you temporarily belong, whereas even the face of your mother who has come to visit is extremely dangerous. So next time, no visitors.

ROUVEL: We'll get rid of them all.

[Excerpt from *Picnic on the Grass*]

Hôtel de Brinon.

RIVETTE: Shouldn't the viewer be added to the list of people who are active in the birth of a film?

RENOIR: Obviously. It's impossible to have a work of art without the spectator's participation, without his collaboration. A film must be completed by the audience. That's why absolute precision is dangerous. On the other hand, however, intentional imprecision is dangerous as well. I think that one of the ingredients for success is to have a lot to say, to have too much to say, so that you do say it, but you don't say it all. There are certain parts that you cannot manage to formulate,

Fernand Sardou, Jean-Pierre Granval, Jacqueline Morane, Jean Renoir, and Catherine Rouvel filming *Picnic on the Grass*.

that you forget, or for which you simply can't find the words, the terms, the camera movements, the lighting, or the right expressions for the actor to express it. The audience compensates for it. What's interesting is that each person in the audience, each viewer, compensates in his own manner. The truth is that a film is as many films as it has viewers. If there are a thousand viewers, you have a thousand films, if it's a good film. If it isn't a good film, it's precise, and it's the same film for each viewer.

[Excerpt from *Picnic on the Grass*]

RIVETTE: We could therefore define the success of a work by the many interpretations it allows for?

RENOIR: I think so.... You see, the big mistake in commercial filmmaking right now is the search for perfection. Often people say to me, "Oh! producers are disgraceful people, disgusting people, they think only of money, they think only of how much they'll make, they think only of what's financially successful." It isn't true! I claim that producers are the most disinterested people in the world, they are people who really love film. My only criticism of them is that they want to make good films, which in my opinion, is completely ridiculous. It's not a matter of making good films, it's a matter of bringing in a little piece of humanity. It's a matter of opening a little door onto what we think we have discovered about the human mind or about a situation, a situation that leads us to characters. It's a matter of getting to know people, and that's all. When producers seek technical perfection, as they often do, with the earnest desire of producing a work of art, I think they are making a huge mistake. What happens is that these absolutely perfect products, these products to which nothing can be added, wind up being boring, and audiences wind up getting tired of films because they've been shown too much perfection.

[Excerpt from *The Lower Depths*]

RENOIR: The audience's collaboration is even a necessity now, because there are many people whose lives are not much fun. These are people who live in big cement apartment houses, and every morning they go to an office or to a factory and they do the same thing, make the same motions. They drive their cars on highways where they stop and start – they stop for the red light and they start at the green. It's rather disappointing, isn't it? Other periods had their disadvantages as well. I'm talking about the disadvantages of our times without suggesting that they are better or worse. But our period has its disadvantages. One of the disadvantages is solitude. Everything leads to solitude, and in addition, people want solitude, they think solitude is good. Someone who tells you they bought a house in the country says, "I have a marvelous house. Just imagine, there isn't a soul around me, not even a mouse, only fields, nothing." They don't realize that human beings are the interesting part of life. What's interesting is meeting people, not meeting trees. Trees are magnificent if they exist in relation to a human being, but I couldn't care less about trees by themselves. In any case, they don't interest me. They excite me as soon as they bring me closer to the people who planted them, to the people who created the civilization around them, or when they bring me closer to the people in my area, to emotions I've felt, when they bring memories to mind, but trees by themselves don't interest me. So one of the ways of fighting against modern boredom is art. Art is a little bridge that you erect. The director of a film, if he has a little talent, sometimes succeeds in creating a little bridge between the screen and the audience, and then we're all together, and we create together, we build the film together. The audience makes this contribution, and this contribution is very important.

[Excerpt from *The Human Beast*]

LABARTHE: You said in *Cahiers du cinéma* that films are not eternal, that reels of film deteriorate, so where does the importance of this art lie, since one hundred years from now there may be no more films?

RENOIR: Of course. But would you ask me where Homer's importance lies, because between you and me, no one has read Homer. Suppose there were six thousand of us here, and we asked the question, "Has anyone here read Homer?" If the people are truthful, they'll say no. Homer is very important, nonetheless. Something strange happens with a work of art: It outlives its existence. I don't know why, but it's a fact, there's an indirect influence. Think about it, let's be honest, take any great work of art, take the best painting in the Louvre. How many French people have seen it? A tiny proportion, maybe one in a thousand, I don't know, yet its influence is obvious, the influence of French works of art on French civilization. Take, for example, something we have all around us: good architecture. After all, we do still have a few prodigious houses in Paris, we have a few old houses in the Marais, we can see doors with sculptures, columns on each side, and it makes us feel happy, ecstatic. But not many of us are walking around ecstatic. I believe, in the end, that a work of art works mysteriously. I believe a great deal in radar in life, in human radar. There is a kind of radar that causes the work of art to influence people, but not directly. I think that going to the Louvre and saying, "Ah! I'm going to look at the *Mona Lisa*!" "Ah!, I'm looking at the *Mona Lisa*, how beautiful!" I don't think that does much for you. But if you feel the presence of the *Mona Lisa*, and if you know... You have to hang paintings on your walls at home, not so much to look at them, but so that they can influence you.

[Excerpt from *The Human Beast*]

RIVETTE: It's like throwing a stone...

RENOIR: In the river, into calm water, and the circles, even the farthest away, reach you.

LABARTHE: In the end, a work of art is not made to be looked at, it's made to permeate living people, people in the street.

RENOIR: *Permeate*, you've found an excellent word.

LABARTHE: So that goes against all current practice, which is to create a monument, a sound-and-light spectacle, or whatever.

RENOIR: Oh, let's not talk about all that! I'm completely against these things. First of all, to begin with, I find the lighting of monuments to be very ugly, it flattens them, and you can't see the difference between a picture postcard and a monument, when it's lit in this way. Everything is flattened; you can't see the difference between a good sculpture and a bad sculpture when they're harshly lit. Of course I'm against spectacular art, except if it's the art of the spectacle, which by definition has to be presented as a spectacle but which also acts not so much as a spectacle but as an influence. It's like the paintings that are lugged all around. They lug paintings all over the world at the risk of damaging them, of seeing them slashed, stolen, only to show them to people who say, "My God, it really is beautiful," "Oh yes, the hand is very well drawn, and there's a faint expression in the eye." They don't get anything out of it; they would get a lot more out of a painting painted by their neighbor or their child. You can get very good paintings just from children. Until the age of six, children generally are good at painting, so all you need is a drawing on the wall done by a child, and you'll get a lot more out of it than from a three-minute stint in front of the *Mona Lisa*.

[Excerpt from *The Human Beast*]

THE RULE AND ITS EXCEPTION

2 June 1966, on the steps of the Château de La Ferté-Saint-Aubin, in Sologne.

JEAN RENOIR: Here we are at the Château de La Colinière. In real life it's the Château de La Ferté-Saint-Aubin, and in my film *The Rules of the Game* (*La Règle du jeu*) it's the Château de La Colinière. What may be interesting about this film is the time that I filmed it. I shot it between Munich and the war, and I shot it at a time when I was very affected, very upset by the state of mind of a part of French society, of a part of English society, of a part of world society. And it seemed to me that one way to present the world's state of mind would be precisely not to talk about the situation, to tell a light story, and I sought my inspiration in Beaumarchais, in Marivaux, in classical authors, in comedy.

[Excerpt from *The Rules of the Game*]

Screening room at ORTF.

RENOIR: What happened with *The Rules of the Game* is what happened with all my films, with everything I've written, with all I've tried to do. Generally, and throughout my life, I've been obsessed by a certain general idea. It's very strong, but in the beginning I can never find the right way to present it. I don't know how to express this idea, it's just there. It's very strong, it obsesses me, but I have no idea how to express it, how to give it a form, and then, very often, when I'm lucky, I find a little idea, an idea that relates solely to the plot, a purely vaudevillesque idea. For example, here, I had the idea of trying to imitate one of Musset's comedies. That's the exterior. Sometimes this secondary idea can be used as a vehicle for my general idea, and then I'm happy, and it works out well. That's what happened with *The Rules of the Game*.

[Excerpt from *The Rules of the Game*]

1. The shooting script

LABARTHE: I'd like to ask you a question about the shooting script, because I suppose you didn't have one written down?

RENOIR: I had a shooting script written down, but naturally, as usual, I wasn't able to follow it because I made many discoveries through the characters. The characters came alive and confirmed their need to move and to speak in a way that I hadn't foreseen. And because the links from shot to shot are difficult – since there are many characters – fewer shots are shown, but still a certain number. Therefore what I did was I had a little outline on a little piece of paper, on a note pad, so I'd know where to position the characters in the next shot. But I hardly ever looked at the outline. You don't need it. You remember.

LABARTHE: Your initial shooting script didn't change as much?

RENOIR: It was more complicated. I hadn't yet adopted the method that I adopted much later, which is having many off-camera voices and an enormous number of observations made by people, observations by people who are rather far away, if necessary, that sometimes reach us – not always, sometimes you don't hear them, but it doesn't matter. In other words, during the shooting I was more concerned with creating a certain ambience than with precise dialogues and characters. I was very careful to keep the principal characters out of this kind of disorder and to have them stand out. But when I wrote my first shooting script, all this was done with too many separate, overly precise shots. Notice that I don't have many long shots, but I do have many people whom I show in the background, and what they're doing in the background also counts. The audience therefore catches what it can, but I think the film does a good job of giving the impression of a crowd, of people getting together, coming and going with no specific position with regard to the camera. That was a great concern in the scene we just saw: unity. I wanted the audience to have the impression they were seeing a single shot following the people and that there had not been any cutting.

RIVETTE: Yes, it's a 360° panorama.

2. The depth of field

RENOIR: It's the depth of field. For that, Bachelet and I ordered some special lenses, very fast lenses, but ones that still gave us considerable depth, so that we could keep our backgrounds in focus almost all the time. And, as far as the background went, allow me a small digression: I just saw the shot in *The Rules of the Game* in which the lady of the house talks about her adventure with the aviator, in which she explains her role in the exploit, and in the background I put Marcel Dalio and myself. Nora Grégor explains her relationship with Toutain, and in the background I said to Dalio, "We're going to have some fun, we're going to counterbalance this scene." And the two of us look like two ham actors in the background, indulging in a series of absolutely unspeakable grimaces, but I found it very funny.

RIVETTE: It was to balance out the scene with Nora Grégor, which is a little too serious?

RENOIR: We had a great time! We let ourselves go, and I couldn't restrain myself, because I wasn't on the other side of the camera to see my acting. I think if I had directed this scene, I wouldn't have allowed myself to do that.

LABARTHE: And the fact that you acted in the film didn't pose a problem when it came to blocking the shot?

RENOIR: I arranged the blocking, and then I went over to the other side. Note that since all the characters carry themselves very stiffly in this film, when I directed the others, I directed myself. I became a kind of complement to the others. This character, my character, is in fact a complement to the other characters. He's a kind of cork that can be fit into the necks of different bottles, a kind of wedge used to steady the furniture. I arranged the furniture first, and when a leg was wobbly, I put the wedge in, that is to say, myself.

Marcel Dalio and Jean Renoir in *The Rules of the Game.*

3. The characters: Octave

[Excerpt from *The Rules of the Game*]

RIVETTE: One of the questions one asks oneself after seeing *The Rules of the Game*, and it may be one of the things that disturbed viewers in the beginning, is Who is the main character? Is it Dalio, is it Nora Grégor, is it Roland Toutain? Octave? I don't think there is one, but...

4. The main character

RENOIR: I agree with you, there is none. And while I was shooting, from time to time I said to myself, "It's this character" or "It's that character." The truth is I didn't know. And it's one of the rare cases in these stories of making films that the concept I had in the beginning – it's a detail, in any case, but my ideas relating to this detail were confirmed – that is, that it was going to be a film about a group, a film representing a society, a group of people, and not a personal case, it's one of the rare cases that this concept was still present in the end. I may have forgotten it sometimes during the shooting, but it was the same at the beginning and in the end, when I found myself with all the footage for the editing. In the end, I was united with my original concept. I wanted to show a society, a group of people; I was even rather ambitious, I almost wanted to show an entire class.

RIVETTE: And you didn't look for a center, for security's sake?

RENOIR: Well, I may have looked for it, and I didn't find it. I think I did look for it and didn't find it. Such as it stands now, the film seems to be rather well balanced, but I think I was constantly plagued with doubts. I wondered, "Maybe I should put more emphasis on this character, and that will give me a kind of mast to cling to, a security blanket." And then, I came to think that with this subject, it wasn't possible. The subject overwhelmed me. But you know, when you're faced with a good subject, and *The Rules of the Game* is a good subject, it devours you. You can't do what you want, you're drawn in, you shoot many things you hadn't foreseen, in spite of yourself, because that's the way it is, because they belong to the subject. I like to let myself be absorbed, but in this case, in *The Rules of the Game,* I allowed myself to be completely absorbed by the subject, and also, of course, by everything that reinforced the subject, like the actors, who were extraordinary and who were completely immersed in the inn where we went together. We lived there, we were far from Paris – it's very important to be far from Paris for a story like that – you forget all the fuss. Other little problems came up with the cast and crew, but it was very nice, it was wonderful. We were really cut off from the world, and this whole ambience – the actors and the landscape and also the subject, as I said – wound up devouring me and made me do lots of things that I hadn't planned on doing.

[Excerpt from *The Rules of the Game*]

LABARTHE: And one has the same impression with the scenes. I don't think you can say, "This is the key scene." Rather, there is a center somewhere, but one can't say, "This is *the* scene."

5. Seeking the center

RENOIR: If there is one, I don't know which one it is. I don't know, and seeing that I made the film, I don't think that those who didn't make the film know, either. No, I don't think there is a center. Note that in *La Chienne,* for example, I was working constantly, constantly, for the moment when Michel Simon kills Janie Marèze. That's really the center of the film. One could say that I conceived of the film in two parts: what comes before the murder and what comes after the murder. The scenes we just saw [from *The Rules of the Game*] symbolize the entire film because we flit around. We follow one character, we follow the other, we get an impression of the whole, we have characters who pass by, who come and say silly things. Talazac says, "Are we going to finish our bridge game?" Someone else says, "I hate bridge," someone else says "I love sea salt" or "I don't like sea salt," they say anything. They say anything, but I had hoped that this anything would wind up creating a whole, and I think that, in part, my wish came true.

LABARTHE: Yes, if we suddenly pay attention to a seemingly insignificant line, it takes on importance.

RENOIR: One thing is for sure: The reason I pulled it off is because of the actors. Each actor was immersed in his character, and the truth is that when I asked them to come to the set to shoot the scene that followed the preceding one, they were in the swing of things, they knew what was going on, and they were immersed in their roles completely. Sometimes I felt that I had no directions to give, that they were so involved that all I had to do was to sit back and watch people work.

[Excerpt from *The Rules of the Game*]

Château de La Ferté-Saint-Aubin. Marcel Dalio arrives, climbing the lawn steps. He and Renoir embrace and then sit on the steps.

MARCEL DALIO: Ha, ha, ha, ha, ha, ha, Octave! How nice, how nice of you to come back and see me after so long! You see...

RENOIR: Not too tired? Everything OK?

DALIO: After twenty-five years... no, see, I bought myself some black glasses.

RENOIR: Remember the cars, right here? Your Delahaye? And the rain...

DALIO: I didn't provide the rain.

RENOIR: No, I did.

DALIO: You know, there's one thing that impresses me here. I suddenly realize that I'm very familiar with the terrace – of course, I live here! What surprises me is seeing these two wings in the front; I realize that you economized. You didn't use certain places, certain parts of the château. You have to explain that to me, because all of a sudden I realize, "How pretty! Why didn't we use these two beautiful wings?"

6. The characters: La Chesnaye

RENOIR: For one very simple reason: We weren't doing a documentary on this building, we were doing a documentary on the marquis de La Chesnaye played by Dalio.

Jean Renoir and Marcel Dalio in "Jean Renoir le patron."

DALIO: And these wings certainly couldn't have given me my cue!

RENOIR: And then also, I'm convinced that landscapes serve no purpose on the screen, landscapes don't count. What counts is that they help the actors and the director to immerse themselves in a certain atmosphere.

DALIO: Yes. What you say is quite true because I know I got into theater not because of real châteaus, I got into it because of the backdrops, the painted châteaus, and I was really moved to see these painted châteaus on the stage in the old melodramas of my childhood.

RENOIR: We should add that a painted château can be much more real than a nonpainted château!

DALIO: What can we talk about, my dear Jean?

RENOIR: Well, we could talk about the luck we had in finding a fluid character in your character, a character who isn't quite sure of what he wants. A character who doesn't know what's important in life, whether it's his toys, his little animated dolls, or the mechanical organ, or if it's his wife, his friends, or Octave. So the audience also wonders, it bothers them, you see, they collaborate, they become authors, they complete the character.

DALIO: They give you your cue, which they should always do, in any case.

RENOIR: Always. And that helps us avoid presenting the kinds of characters who are carved in stone and all polished, who know what they want, who have a definite diction, who have a goal in life. You had no goal in life, and I think that helped us tremendously. In any case, the way you did it, it was fantastic.

DALIO: You're too kind, but while we're on the subject, I have always been asked why you chose me. I had been more of a burlesque character, a traitor, or even a Rosenthal, and that always surprised people, as if a marquis or a count had to have a certain face. Maybe they have one in magazines. Why don't I look like a marquis? Tell me: my frizzy hair? My eastern look?

RENOIR: There are some marquises who look eastern. First, I chose you because I think it's always very helpful, in film, in whatever you're writing, to go against conventions. You were the opposite of the convention, and then, I'll tell you something, I always work by memory. And I used to know some aristocratic guys who looked like you.

DALIO: That's very nice for me, I'm thrilled!

RENOIR: I know your character very well, and you also knew him through and through. You were drawn into him.

DALIO: I got to know him little by little, I may as well admit it. I was born here, and in six weeks I became the marquis de La Chesnaye we now know.

RENOIR: That's right, but we discovered him as we went along. What thrills me in this instance, and what still thrills me in my memories, is that we created both your character and the film's entire story – since it's built around your character – we created it as we went along, we didn't follow the plan. You see, I think that plans are fatal these days, you know, blue with white lines, the architect's blueprint.

DALIO: They resemble the buildings we see on our roads these days, unlivable buildings!

RENOIR: Exactly, unlivable!

DALIO: Yet they're well made, they're made by qualified, prize-winning engineers.

RENOIR: Well, the marquis de La Chesnaye was not made by engineers, he was made with memories, and I've known several marquises de La Chesnaye.

[Excerpt from *The Rules of the Game*]

RENOIR: Say, do you remember the shot in front of the mechanical organ?

Jean Renoir and Marcel Dalio during the shooting of *The Rules of the Game.*

DALIO: Yes, I have to admit to having had a lot of trouble there, I was rather ashamed of having to redo the scene, and I said to myself, "But it's simple, I'm going to go in front of the mechanical organ, and I'm going to look joyous," but...

RENOIR: But what a shot! I think that it's the best shot I've ever done in my life. Oh! It's fantastic. The mixture of humility and pride, of success and doubt. Nothing definite. It borders on many things.

DALIO: You're right, because we, as actors, often need words, you understand, to give us a little balance. It's because we're lazy, we lack courage. Words are like crutches, you know what to do with your hands, your legs, your eyes. But there, all of a sudden, to be surprised, you have to have a certain naiveté, or genius... and since I don't have genius...

RENOIR: You do have genius, and the proof is that you did it. It took time but you did it. I realize that at the beginning I was wrong, I thought it could be an improvised shot. It couldn't be an improvised

Marcel Dalio in *The Rules of the Game* (the mechanical organ scene).

shot, it had to be worked on. We worked on it by shooting it and re-shooting it.

DALIO: It was the culmination of an entire life, of his life in any case. La Chesnaye's life. He was an amateur, an amateur of everything.

RENOIR: An inspired amateur.

[Excerpt from *The Rules of the Game*]

7. The characters: Christine

Screening room at ORTF.

RIVETTE: I find that one character is particularly mysterious in the film, it struck me when I saw it again two days ago – Octave, or even Dalio who is a complex character, are clear characters – but the character who is really rather opaque is Christine. Throughout the film, it's impossible to know who she is, what she thinks, what she wants.

RENOIR: She probably doesn't know herself.

RIVETTE: She's the character one wonders about the most.

RENOIR: Of course, because her logic is so clear. What she says is so simple, so direct, so clear and transparent, it winds up seeming mysterious. But I think that all absolutely simple and direct beings are like that, they seem mysterious. You say to yourself, "My God, he said, 'It's raining.' That must mean something!" Not at all, it means that it's raining.

[Excerpt from *The Rules of the Game*]

RENOIR: The truth is she never says it, it isn't shown, I have no shot explaining this feeling, but I think that this woman is in the process of suddenly being confronted with some of life's realities, realities that she doesn't find very pretty. Although she isn't very young, she's a woman who was probably rather innocent, and that's why I wanted to have a Viennese woman play this rather romantic part. Suddenly the romanticism, the pure love, the eternal love, the moonlit walks hand in hand are all replaced by a much more brutal reality: by the purely physical need to be thrown on a couch and to make love – or rather by the need to throw her on the couch and to make love to her that she sees in this man, in the others, in the people chasing after her. It probably wasn't that way with Dalio, it probably wasn't that way with Toutain, but this evening, that's the way it is. This celebration – which I tried to make slightly unreal – this celebration is an opening onto reality for Christine, and it immediately causes a turnabout in her behavior. Since that's the way life is, let's go, I want to make love to the first person I see, I don't love him but I'll do it. If those are the rules, well, I'm going to play by them, even more than the others do.

RIVETTE: There is, however, a moment in the film when Christine has a revelation and realizes that these are the rules, which is why there is a center after all: It's the scene with the field glasses.

RENOIR: Oh! Of course! Nevertheless, I believe that Christine's character is the character of a woman who is innocently romantic, an old-fashioned romantic. She represents a character clouded by an old-fashioned romanticism in a society of modern people – or at least they were modern when I shot the film. She doesn't belong to their times, and she is also a foreigner. So suddenly this foreigner discovers a reality that she probably finds very ugly. And I tried to express this in several shots. I didn't have her say it, but I hope it can be guessed, that it can be seen.

8. The search for the center (2)

LABARTHE: Yes, to get back to the shot with the field glasses. This shot is just about in the middle of the film, and it's only after it that the action begins. Starting then, things happen. Before it was a kind of gigantic exposition, the relationships among characters . . .

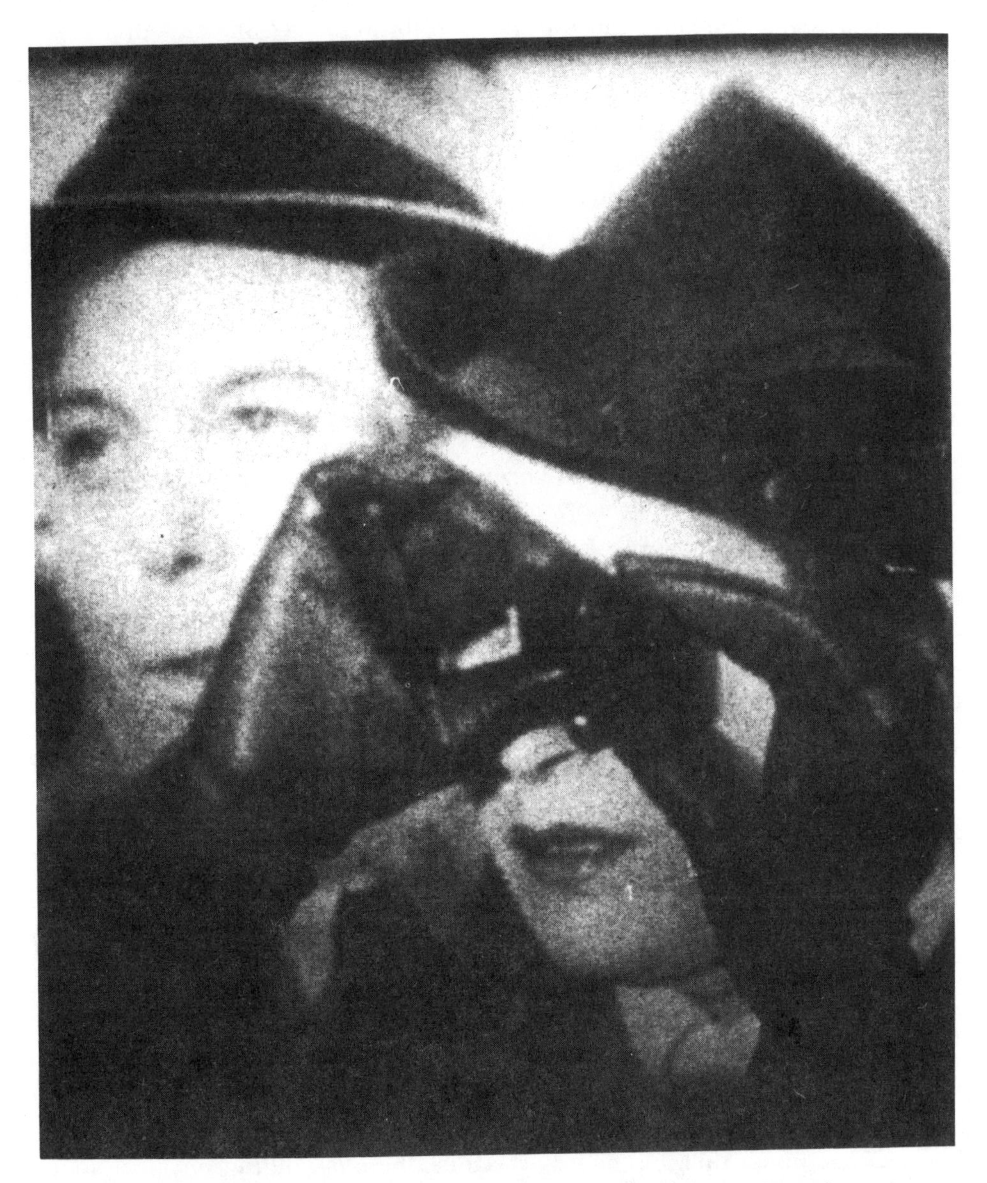

Jean Renoir and Nora Grégor in *The Rules of the Game* (the field glasses).

RENOIR: The action was only in the progression of already-existing conditions, whereas starting then, the situations change, evolve.

RIVETTE: As a result of Christine's using the glasses: If she hadn't used them, there would be no reason it still couldn't be going on.

LABARTHE: So she changes in relation to this shot? She saw this scene in the field glasses.

RENOIR: Absolutely. But all this corresponds to my great belief in the importance of one's surroundings. I think that people turn, change, evolve as the things around them evolve, and I think that here, if we follow Christine's character in the middle of all these characters whom I tried to show, if we cling to Christine especially, I think we see a character who is very clearly influenced by the people around her, by what's happening around her.

[Excerpt from *The Rules of the Game*]

9. Improvisation

LABARTHE: Yesterday we talked briefly about those field glasses, and you told us that the scene was almost improvised.

RENOIR: It was completely improvised, but improvisations correspond to things you have in mind. The truth is that in a film like this one, 50 percent of the film is improvised, but it's an improvisation that corresponds to what was deep inside me. In other words, the general feeling isn't improvised, but the ways of expressing it often are.

LABARTHE: That is, if the field glasses hadn't been there...

RENOIR: Something else would have been. I don't know what, but the binoculars were wonderful.

LABARTHE: The kissing scene still would have been included?

RENOIR: Perhaps somewhere else, perhaps differently. But there certainly would have been the revelation for Christine that her husband and Parely were having an affair and that the world wasn't what she thought it was, that the world isn't beautiful. Notice that even she probably let herself get very close to Jurieu, to Toutain, but given that she was a romantic and that romantics are blind and don't see things, she probably forgot that. But the fact that her husband is having an affair, which probably shocks her... She immediately guesses that the relationship between her husband and Parely is purely physical. She's wrong about this, by the way, because there is nothing physical about Dalio, he's also sentimental. All these people are sentimental, as are all these types of societies, as are all the people who give in to their instincts and close their eyes to the world. They're sentimental.

LABARTHE: But did this slightly ambiguous, slightly mysterious aspect of the characters come to you from the start, or, rather, did you have very standard characters in the beginning, for example, whom you later reworked?

Jean Renoir and Nora Grégor in *The Rules of the Game.*

RENOIR: There were some very standard characters whom I changed. Note that in the beginning, Christine wasn't like that. There is one thing that helped me, influenced me tremendously – yet it was the reason that made me ask her to play this role – it's her accent. I felt that this accent was the little barrier, the little curtain that separated her from her purely French circle.

LABARTHE: In other words, were there specific adjectives in your project: Christine is like this, Christine is like that?

RENOIR: No. I had these adjectives in mind, but I never wrote them down, I never them put them on paper. The truth is that the subject was so deep inside me that just about all I had to write down was the plot, the movements, so as to not make any mistakes. But the meaning of the characters and the meaning of the action, and especially the symbolic side of the film, were things I had been carrying inside me for a very long time. I had wanted to do something like this for a very long time, to bring a rich, complex society to the screen. You know what the expression is, it's a historical expression that may have led me to do this film, a historical expression that, I believe, originated during the reign of Charles X. I forget who said it, whether it was a general, a lawyer, or a poet. It is: "We're dancing on a volcano." My goal in undertaking this film was to illustrate "We're dancing on a volcano."

[Excerpt from *The Rules of the Game*]

LABARTHE: Were the metaphors in the film, or the symbolic side – say, the death of the rabbit – the parallel between the rabbit's death and Jurieu's death, were they very clear?

10. The sacrifice

RENOIR: It's too clear not to have been intentional. It's obvious. I had the idea of Jurieu's death such as it is – Jurieu was condemned before the film began – but the idea of having him die in this way came to me from the rabbit's death, which I filmed first. My idea was that the hunting prepared Jurieu's death in a primitive way. Jurieu was the innocent one, and innocence couldn't live in this world. It was a romantic, decaying world. It happens that we are dealing with two extremely innocent characters, Christine and Jurieu. A sacrifice was needed. If things were to continue, one of them had to be killed. The world lives solely off sacrifices; some people must be killed to appease the gods. The society will continue a few more months, until the war and even after, and this society will continue because Jurieu was killed, Jurieu is the creature sacrificed on the gods' altar in order to continue this kind of life.

LABARTHE: Right, just as it's the rabbit's death that permits the hunting to continue.

RENOIR: Yes. We spend our lives living off sacrifices. The ancient world, and the modern world even more, kill, kill, kill, kill many, in the hope that these killings will allow us to continue.

[Excerpt from *The Rules of the Game*]

RIVETTE: And the death of Louis XVI, was it necessary?

RENOIR: Louis XVI's death was probably necessary, it was needed for the Revolution to begin. The first symbol, or the first important story, not the first, but an extremely important story in which sacrifice changes the world and allows certain ideas to develop, is, of course, the story of Christianity. Without sacrifice, there would be no Christianity; it's obvious, and this necessity appears constantly, and even now we live only with the help of constant minor sacrifices. Louis XVI's sacrifice probably allowed the theoreticians of the Revolution to express ideas that are now in the process of overturning the world, because the effects of the French Revolution are being felt only now. The ideas behind the French Revolution were very quickly seized upon by the bourgeois classes, who, by the way, with total honesty and great innocence, tried to make them adaptable, digestible, but I have the feeling that the results of Louis XVI's death are only being seen now.

[Excerpt from *La Marseillaise*]

RENOIR: I think there's also something else that I didn't show in *La Marseillaise*, and I regret it, because it's an extremely important event. It's the fact that the king, maybe not primarily the king but, rather, the queen, and the king because of the queen's influence, had forgotten that the monarchy had survived for centuries and centuries only by being the natural ally of the people against the aristocracy and the middle classes. I think that Louis XVI and Marie Antoinette allowed themselves to be immersed in the aristocracy, allowed themselves to be taken in. They lost their role as the decapitators of the aristocracy.

RIVETTE: Which in the end was the role that the Capet played at the beginning.

RENOIR: Not only in the beginning but also later in the game. The kings spent their time beheading the noblemen who had become too important.

RIVETTE: Yes. About Nora Grégor's character in *La Marseillaise*, we could make a perhaps rather arbitrary comparison between her and aristocratic characters in general, and between her and Louis XVI and Marie Antoinette in particular. They all are characters who, from their own point of view, are right but who find themselves suddenly displaced.

11. Synchronism

RENOIR: And who are obsolete. *Displaced* is the right word. I think that in most dramas, not only historical, but also in the dramas of daily life, there is almost always a question of displacement. One of the actors in the drama lives in one period, and the other actor lives in another period, and they're not synchronous. I believe that synchronism is the secret to life. The problem with Agnès and Captain George in my novel [*Le Capitaine Georges*] is that they are not completely synchronous. That is, they are except for Agnès's beliefs, they are synchronous on all but one point, and this point destroys everything.

[Excerpt from *The Rules of the Game*]

RENOIR: There's also another thing. There is a force that I give in to in my films and that I believe in a great deal, and that's fate. I really believe that you can't go against the current, that we're caught in a kind of river that pushes us, carries us, and that men are not mean or good or traitors or not traitors. They are simply the playthings of destiny, and in this film I tried to show that, too.

RIVETTE: It's the theory of the cork . . .

LABARTHE: Yes, but at the same time, an entire segment of your career was politically committed.

12. Political commitment

RENOIR: Of course, but I was involved without wanting to be. I was involved because the events that revealed themselves to me required that I become involved. I didn't go looking for the events. I didn't go looking for things. I was voluntarily or involuntarily a witness to certain things and it's the outside world that acted on me and led to my convictions.

LABARTHE: Because for certain events, witnesses don't exist. You can't just watch an event. Either you're on the outside or you're on the inside.

RENOIR: Right. You can't be a mere witness to events. You have to get involved, and the only way for me to get involved in a useful fashion, I'm afraid, was by means of the characters in my films. For example, in my book *Le Capitaine Georges*, I tried to show a man who doesn't want to get involved but who in fact must get involved, because the events are much stronger than both his selfishness and his will not to be involved.

LABARTHE: And at the same time, the characters you depict, when you depict them, are always – maybe not right – but at least they have their reasons for being as they are, and you always understand these reasons.

RENOIR: I try.

[Excerpt from *La Marseillaise*]

RENOIR: You know, there are some lucky directors who can plan, who can put their ideas in order and follow plans, and who know exactly what they want, who can direct their thoughts and even their destinies. As for me, I admit to being the victim of my surroundings. A happy victim, in any case, since I'm quite content, but what I see around me limits my reactions. I belong, I belong . . .

RIVETTE: Yes, but just the same, in seeing your films, one doesn't have the feeling that they are lessons in giving in to fate. There is a certain surrender, but it's always a positive one.

RENOIR: OK, but I don't think that my characters or I give in to fate, not at all. I think that we belong in a context, that we are integrated, and given that, we wind up accepting this integration. And so whatever we do, we accept the idea of doing it within the framework of this integration, not all alone.

[Excerpt from *La Marseillaise*, followed by a shot of an article from *Le Figaro* of 4 May 1966 (on *C'est la révolution!*)]

Restaurant du Lac.

JEAN RENOIR s'intéresse aux "petites révolutions" quotidiennes

JEAN RENOIR est revenu à Paris. Mais pas pour des vacances. Quand les autres en prendront, tout de suite après le 14 juillet, il tournera *C'est la Révolution*.

— Il s'agit, nous dit le célèbre cinéaste, d'un sujet que je viens d'écrire et qui est composé de plusieurs épisodes — de quatre à six. Chacun relate une de ces petites révolutions de la vie courante où les gens s'insurgent contre les préjugés, les habitudes ou même le progrès. Par exemple, on verra

électrique, prototype des instruments ménagers qui font aujourd'hui une usine d'un simple logement. Cependant, il y aura aussi quelque révolution plus sérieuse. Ainsi l'épisode dont l'héroïne est une dame d'un certain âge qui fait du strip-tease dans une boîte de nuit, ce qui lui vaut de recevoir force tomates. Mais un jour, dans le port où elle gagne, de la sorte péniblement sa vie, les marins se rebellent et la vieille dame assiste joyeusement au massacre de ses persécuteurs.

A clipping from the 4 May 1966 issue of *Le Figaro*. ["Jean Renoir turns his attention to the 'little revolutions' of daily life"].

RIVETTE: What is the guiding idea of the whole, since I imagine they are sketches that . . .

RENOIR: Yes, they are linked solely by a general idea, and not at all by exterior means. There is no plot, there is no story about a character who goes from one sketch to the next. It's just a general idea, and the general idea is explained in the title, I think, *C'est la révolution!* [later *Le Petit Théâtre de Jean Renoir*]. It's about revolutions, about certain revolutions. For example, the revolution that is expressed in war is an antiwar revolution. This doesn't mean that armed people destroy all the military sites. No, it simply means that some people decided that they had had enough. In the sketch that I just spoke to you about, "La Crème de beauté" (Beauty Cream), the lover has had enough of his mistress's coquetry and gives in to the absolute simplicity of the servant. It's a revolution. In "La Duchesse," it's a revolution against the shameful way the duchess is made to work in a nightclub. That one takes a bad turn, because at the same time, there is a real revolution, and people come in with machine guns and fire into the crowd. You can imagine. I have one revolution against an electric waxer. There's a husband who is sick of hearing his wife, who is always going "bz-bz-bz," constantly polishing the floor. In that case, I use two husbands, because the first one slips on the floor, falls, and dies. So the second husband avenges the first.

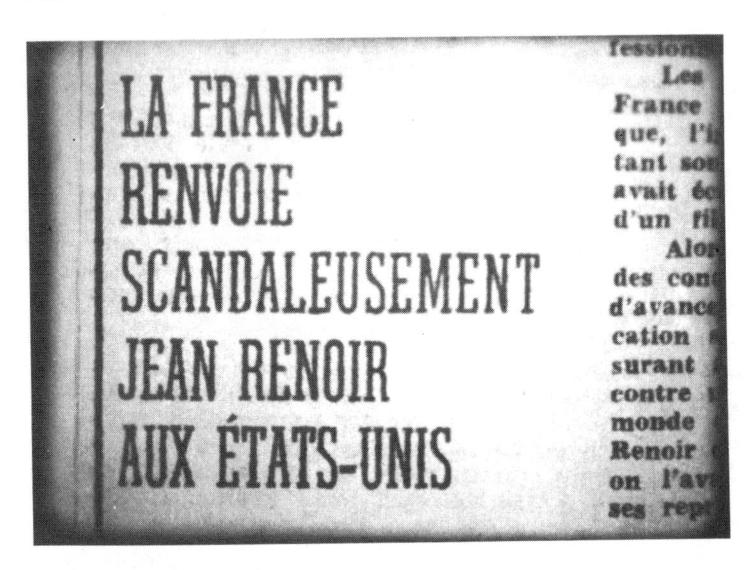

LA FRANCE
RENVOIE
SCANDALEUSEMENT
JEAN RENOIR
AUX ÉTATS-UNIS

A clipping from the 1 August 1966 issue of *Combat* ["France scandalously sends Jean Renoir back to the United States"].

RIVETTE: And you think that whether small or large, revolutions are always positive or good? You're for revolutions?

13. Revolution

RENOIR: I'm for constant revolution, though I recognize that they often fail. I don't claim that a revolution is the best way to resolve something, I simply show them as they are in life, as they exist, whether they concern very important things or nonsense. I think that our lives are made not of revolutions but of the desire for constant revolution. We feel like revolting all the time. Constantly. Generally we don't do it, but from time to time we do. So, what I show in this film are the rare cases in which we take a deep breath and go for it, we revolt. What I like about revolutions is also the idea of violence. I think that from time to time, violence is necessary in our lives. From time to time, you have to be like Samson, you have to shake the columns of the temple. Now that's a revolution. Samson's story is a good revolution. We're not going to show it. Next time.

[Clipping appears from *Le Figaro*, 4 May 1966. Two other newspaper clippings then appear: One, from *Combat*

JEAN RENOIR est revenu à Paris. Mais pas pour des vacances. Quand les autres en prendront, tout de suite après le 14 juillet, il tournera *C'est la Révolution.*

— Il s'agit, nous dit le célèbre cinéaste, d'un sujet que je viens d'écrire et qui est composé de plusieurs épisodes — de quatre à six. Chacun relate

Le Figaro, 4 May 1966.

(7 August 1966), "The Renoir Affair: A Scandal or Sinister Plot?" The other, also from *Combat* (9 August), "The Renoir Affair from Day to Day."]

LABARTHE: About revolution – how can traditions that are perpetuated, for example, French traditions, how can we reconcile the idea of even small revolutions with the idea of the permanence of French traditions?

RENOIR: I think they reconcile very well. In any case, it happens that revolutions have often preserved traditions more than nonrevolutions have. It seems like a paradox, but politically, for example, we can see that revolutionary governments are generally closely attached to what we call folklore, and so they try – often very sincerely – to gather together all that corresponds to the glorification of the past grandeur of a country where a revolution has taken place. Whereas the evolutionists... Take painting, for example. One can say that from the Renaissance to Bouguereau there was an evolution ending with Bouguereau, an evolution that, without any revolutions, by descending through people who never revolted, through a particular evolution, came to be opposite of those who were at the beginning of the process, who were at the beginning of the story. What could be further from Raphaël than Bouguereau? Whereas people like the impressionists – who did create a revolution – are really closest to the national tradition. So there is no contradiction, and I believe, in any case, that the answer to your question, "Are revolutions against the maintenance of traditions?" is, frankly and definitively, "no" and, often, "on the contrary."

[Excerpt from *La Marseillaise*]

PART THREE
Remarks

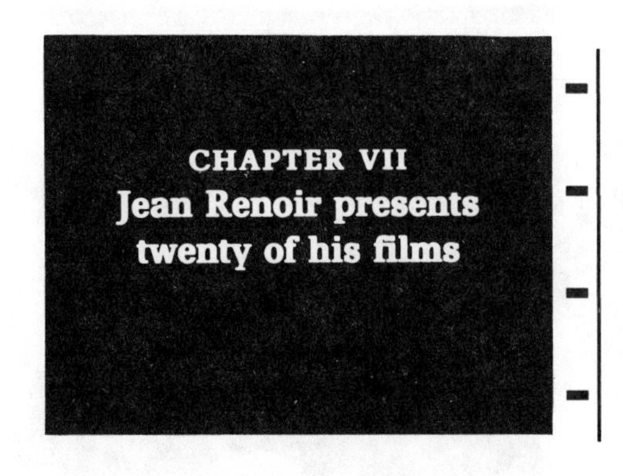

These "Propos" ("Remarks") by Jean Renoir were recorded and filmed in August 1961, in conjunction with the program "Jean Renoir vous parle de son art" [see Chapter V].

Each of these presentations was meant to introduce one of the twenty corresponding films, all of which were to be shown during a retrospective of Jean Renoir's works. We found no trace of this anticipated homage in the television guides of the following months.

The Testament of Doctor Cordelier (*Le Testament du Docteur Cordelier*)

I wanted to tell a story about rich people. Obviously, if instead of dwelling on Cordelier's story, that of a multimillionaire doctor, I had told the story of a coolie working in a Pakistani or Indian rice field, or the story of a French country doctor with many children and many debts who can never manage to make ends meet, the spiritual problems would have taken a back seat, and the problem of finding bread for his family would have been on our little doctor's mind more than it is on Cordelier's mind. True, Cordelier is a rich man, but this rich man is still a man; that is, he is subjected to the common law of men. The common law of men, as we know, is that of original sin. We cannot forget that at the beginning of the world, the Lord kicked us out of the garden of Eden and told us, "In the sweat of thy brow shalt thou eat bread." So, when we try not to earn our bread by the sweat of our brows, we wind up paying for it. We pay for it with a horrible illness: boredom. People like Cordelier are bored, and I believe the only way to cure oneself of this illness is to address spiritual questions.

La Chienne

La Chienne takes me back thirty years. Maybe even a bit more. It certainly dates me. *La Chienne* was not easy to shoot. It happens that be-

Teddy Billis and Jean-Louis Barrault in *The Testament of Doctor Cordelier.*

fore *La Chienne,* I had made, I had directed, silent films with lots of extras, even with an army, with horses, with lances, with lots of things. These films were very expensive, and people were convinced that if they added microphones and sound, the result would be disastrous. So they didn't want to give me a talking film.

To prove that I could shoot a talking film without bankrupting the producers, I made a little film called *On purge bébé,* taken from Feydeau. It was a tremendous financial success. I wrote it in six days, with one of my assistants, of course. You never do anything all alone in this business, you know. So I wrote it in six days, shot it in six days, and edited it in six days. Six days later it was showing at the Gaumont Palace, and six days after that it was making a profit. After that I was a great man, and they gave me, they allowed me to do, *La Chienne*. I had many reasons for wanting to do *La Chienne.* One of the most important is that I adore, I love, I'm quite excited – platonically – by the women one meets on the streets of Paris. I think there is nothing more charming than a young working-class girl taking a walk or rushing to catch a train at Saint-Lazare or at the Gare du Nord. It's one of the world's unique and beautiful wonders. So I wanted to tell a story with a girl like that at the center. It happens that in La Fouchardière's novel, the girl is a prostitute. After all, it's a profession like any other, you can't throw stones at everyone, she's a very nice, very seductive girl, and I was happy to tell her story. I also had another reason, a very strong reason, for wanting to tell this story, which was my admiration for Michel Simon. We all agree that Michel Simon is a great actor, and I thought *La Chienne* would be a good vehicle for him, that it would allow him to reach certain heights. He reached them. He didn't need me for that. In any case, I brought him the framework, and he worked within it, and it was a great success. I also remember Flamant. I remember my associates. In short, I can't mention everyone, it would take too long and would be meaningless.

Toni

Toni is a film that corresponds to one of my realism crises, one of those times when you tell yourself that the only way to make a film is by recording with photographic precision everything you see, including the skin texture of the people you put before the camera. To satisfy this desire for realism, I chose a true story, a news item. A very good friend of mine was a police commissioner in Martigues, and he told me Toni's story. It's an extremely sad, extremely gripping, extremely true story, and a story that, in addition, took place in the foreign workers' section of Martigues, which itself is very interesting. And the portrayal of this section allowed me to dwell on a theory that has always been dear to me, which is that the people of this earth are not divided into nations but are perhaps divided into work categories. What we do is our true nation. My friend and I went to visit all the places where Toni had lived, where he had loved. He reenacted his investigation for me, and little by little the story built itself in my mind. He established a short summary of the facts for me. With this summary as a base, I wrote *Toni*.

I had another preoccupation at the time of *Toni:* camera angles. I've changed a great deal since, but at the time it seemed to me that such a story would require certain angles that interested me.

Toni is therefore a story that, to a certain extent, represents what we now call neorealism. I left for Martigues, I lived with the people of Martigues, and I brought a camera. I entrusted my nephew Claude with this camera, by the way. It was one of his first major films. And that's it. We shot it like that, with local people, while breathing the local air, while eating the local food, and while living the life of these workers.

Grand Illusion (La Grande Illusion)

I've written and repeated several times my reasons for filming *Grand Illusion.* I don't want to repeat myself again. There were, of course, many reasons. There is one that I may not have mentioned. I wanted to show French officers as I had known them when I was in the army before and during 1914. Military style has changed much more than we think. The way a soldier or an officer presents himself today is completely different from the way this same soldier or this same officer would have presented himself thirty years ago. And the change has not occurred in the direction people think. People think that behavior was much more rigorous, much stiffer before, but it was the complete opposite. There was a kind of ease that seems to have disappeared. The expression or phrase in the military code on which military instructors put the most emphasis was the expression "without affectation or stiffness." Now it seems to me that today, military men carry themselves with a bit of affectation and a great deal of stiffness. You can see it, for example, in the way arms are presented. What does "Present arms!" mean? It means that you show your gun or your rifle to an officer or a superior so that he can see if there's powder in it. And if there is powder in it, he throws you into prison for eight days. That's exactly what "Present arms!" means. It has become a kind of fixed symbol, and in my opinion it makes no sense. It probably relates to some very profound ideas, but in my opinion these very deep ideas are not consistent with the French spirit. The French spirit is an easygoing spirit, a relaxed spirit. It's an aristocratic spirit, whereas this new stiff manner of holding oneself is, in my opinion, more plebeian than aristocratic.

La Marseillaise

In *La Marseillaise,* I tried to recount one of the greatest moments in French history in the same way I would have described an adventure that took place next door. I wanted to treat this great moment from an intimate perspective. I tried to imagine that I was witnessing true events, current events, and that my camera was hidden in a corner and

Filming *Grand Illusion:* Jean Gabin, Eric von Stroheim, Pierre Fresnay, and Jean Renoir.

was revealing the trivial side of these great events. I also tried to evoke the greater side, of course, but I stayed mostly on the other side. I don't think I would have used different technical methods if I had been telling a love story that took place at Les Halles.

The characters in *La Marseillaise* are important. The revolutionaries are great men; the king was a great man. And my brother, who played the part, and I, did everything possible to maintain the nobility of Louis XVI, a nobility that we were persuaded this king possessed.

La Marseillaise also corresponds to something extremely important; it corresponds to the time we shot it. It was a time of enthusiasm, it was at the time of the Popular Front, a kind of boom before the bust. During this time, we even believed that the disputes in France were finished, that we were coming to a kind of union. A union of all Frenchmen, a union of the French belonging to the most varied classes, to the most varied professions. People with the most varied concerns. We even believed we were coming to the end of this kind of perpetual dispute that has divided the French for so long, that of the religious wars.

The Diary of a Chambermaid

The Diary of a Chambermaid was taken from a novel by Octave Mirbeau. The novel was written before 1900, and it has stuck in my mind since my earliest childhood. As soon as I began to work in the cinema, I tried to make *The Diary of a Chambermaid* into a film. I often tried but it never worked out. In France, the producers were somewhat horrified by the subject. In America, I tried once again to shoot *The Diary of a Chambermaid* and I succeeded, thanks to the help of Paulette Goddard and Burgess Meredith. We formed a little group, and this little group was able to find the means to shoot *The Diary of a Chambermaid*. Now why shoot *The Diary of a Chambermaid*, which is such a French subject, in America? Why in English? Well, this is why: *The Diary of a Chambermaid* represents one of my antirealist crises. I told you during an earlier interview that I had had some crises of heightened realism. I also had some crises, and I still do, of heightened antirealism. There are times when I wonder whether the only truth isn't interior truth, and whether the accuracy of makeup, of costumes, of appearances, of furniture, the exterior truth, if all that shouldn't be neglected so that we can plunge a little deeper into this interior truth. *The Diary of a Chambermaid* represents this concern. That is, I was, of course, thinking of the commedia dell'arte while shooting it. I was thinking – this sounds pretentious – of classical tragedy. Classical tragedy takes place with the same costumes, and commedia dell'arte takes place with the same costumes, which didn't prevent either of these two genres from treating extremely important, extremely profound subjects, whether comedy or drama. Are human beings helped or hindered by appearances? That is the question. So I shot this film in English and in Hollywood, and I situated it at the time of Mirbeau, not so much to be faithful to Mirbeau, but because I believe that if one day we arrive at a kind of commedia dell'arte style in cinema, the period to choose, the only period, the period that would allow us to abandon our concern with exterior truth, the right period to choose just might be this 1900 period. I can see all films taking place in 1900, very simply, just like that. There would be no more research, there would be no more concern with exterior accuracy. We'd be set, we'd have to worry only about what happens within the characters shown on the screen. I shot *The Diary of a Chambermaid* right after a film that was exactly the opposite: *The Southerner*. *The Southerner* took place in the cotton fields. I chose the main character, Zachary Scott, because he was the son of a farmer who grows cotton, the son of some big Texas ranchers, and the truth is that I shot *The Southerner* in much the same way, although way before, I shot *Toni,* the film I made in Martigues and in which I used local people, in which I used a true story... in short, total realism.

The Diary of a Chambermaid is a film that surprised people in America and that, oddly enough, was successful only long afterward. It's successful now. I see it constantly on television. One of the minor consolations of our profession is that if we miss our chance commercially, we sometimes have a chance to catch up.

French Cancan

French Cancan is above all the story of Nini. Nini is a little laundress who walks around with a basket under her arm. Nothing is more seductive than a laundress walking in the street with a basket under her arm. There are no more of them today, of course, but when I was little, there were many of them, and I used to watch them.

It's also the story, of course, of the brilliant individual who invented what we now call the music hall. This guy is responsible for shows, for nightclubs, for everything that now exists to distract people who are bored. But Nini is very important to this film. Nini is Lulu's sister. Lulu is the little woman in *La Chienne*, who is Célestine's sister. Célestine is the chambermaid in *The Diary of a Chambermaid*. She may even be more closely related to Magnani – Camilla in *The Golden Coach* (*Le Carrosse d'or*). In any case, Nini is walking in the street with a basket when the great impresario stops her: He'll teach more than just a better way to earn money, a way to shine, he'll teach her

French Cancan.

the beauty of a trade. This is extremely important. I believe in professionalism. It seems to me that we should base our lives on it. I believe that *French Cancan* may be above all a homage to trades, and what a trade this one is, since I chose dance! In any case, even if I had tried not to believe in professionalism while shooting *French Cancan,* I would soon have been forced to return to my original conviction by the girls who worked with me. It was absolutely fantastic! We lived in an unbelievable atmosphere! The courage, the good faith, the sweetness of these dancers, who went to such lengths and who really hurt themselves at times – it's often very painful to do a split, it's no fun at all.

So I present *French Cancan* to you by way of asking all of you to think of your trade and to love it. Because there is always a way to love one's trade. First, because there are no distinctions, no rankings in trades. We can say that everyone is an artist in life: The baker who manages to bake the best loaf of bread is just as important as Picasso. What you have to do is be the best baker, make the best loaf of bread, and if you're a painter, you have to be the best painter, and paint the best, with genius. In the end, that's how we express ourselves, because that's essentially the big question. The problem is that if we want to explain ourselves too much – perhaps as I am doing right now – it's a mistake. But I apologize. If we try to explain ourselves too much, we end up explaining nothing at all. If we try to explain ourselves simply, by perfecting an object, if we express ourselves through something we want to do or tell, then we have a small chance, while remaining hidden, of modestly expressing ourselves.

Nana

Nana is both a marvelous and a much less beautiful memory. It's a marvelous memory because it's a film that I did under exceptional conditions, in an atmosphere of warmth and friendship. I did this film with all my friends. There was Pierre Champagne – a few years later, the two of us had an automobile accident together, and unfortunately he died. There was Pierre Lestringuez, who also died, and there was Werner Krauss, the German actor; Jean Angelo; and, of course, Catherine Hessling. You see, I shot *Nana* because I admired Stroheim, and I wanted to do something that would not be an imitation of Stroheim's art but that would be an homage to him. I did it with my own money, and I lost this money. That's why it's a bad memory. Note that I'm not sorry about it. I don't regret it, since because I didn't have any money, I was forced to work for others, and while working for others, I learned filming discipline. That wasn't a bad thing. It's very good not to do what you want. So after *Nana* I worked on other films. I don't know what's become of them, but thanks to *Nana* I entered the business as a full professional.

Winna Winfried, Georges Koudria, and Pierre Renoir in *La Nuit du carrefour*.

Le Nuit du carrefour

I did *La Nuit du carrefour* (*Night at the Crossroads*) because of my admiration for Simenon. I admired him then as I admire him now. I was therefore just a step away from trying to bring to the screen what he is so able to accomplish in his books. That step was the filming of *La Nuit du carrefour*.

I asked my brother Pierre to play the role of the commissioner Maigret and found a strange creature, a kind of bizarre seventeen-year-old girl, with a very pale face, whose name was Winna Winfried. I don't believe in the term *photogenic*, but it happens that this girl justifies its use. Just put her in front of a camera, and everything works. Her voice also works. She delighted the sound engineer, and she also delighted me.

A passerby and Michel Simon in *Boudu Saved from Drowning.*

In *La Nuit du carrefour* I tried to recreate Simenon. I don't know whether I succeeded, but in any case, let's just say that it was an absolutely wonderful communion with him. I tried to give the impression that the mud sticks when you walk in the mud and that the fog blocks your view when you walk in the fog. I tried to do what Simenon does in his books: He surrounds the spectator with a particular atmosphere. To arrive at this goal, I may have exaggerated the obscurity. I put darkness everywhere, not only in the scenes, but also in the story, in my script, in my shooting script, in the dialogue. I wrote the shooting script and the dialogue in collaboration with Simenon, by the way. We tried to keep the mystery. I don't know whether we were successful. I haven't seen the film in quite a while, but in any case it is an important memory for me; it's once again the memory of a friendly enterprise, Simenon, my brother, and myself, my brother, the first Maigret. You'll see.

***Boudu Saved from Drowning* (*Boudu sauvé des eaux*)**

Boudu is Michel Simon. That is, he is one of the greatest living actors and one of the greatest actors in the history of the theater and film. *Boudu* is an homage to Michel Simon. It's Michel Simon, by the way, who suggested that I do *Boudu*. When we had finished *La Chienne*, we tried to find another subject to work on together. We had many ideas but couldn't really come up with anything. Then one day he said to me, "We should do *Boudu*." At first I didn't understand. I read the play, which I admired a great deal, it's a beautiful play. But I couldn't see how we could make it into a film. One day it came to me, it hit me. I saw Michel Simon dressed as a hobo. I had already shot a hobo with Michel Simon, in fact. It was at the end of *La Chienne*. So when I went to see the end of *La Chienne*, *Boudu* hit me. I said to myself, "That's it, we have to shoot *Boudu*. We've already shot it." So I shot *Boudu* using various means. Excuse me for talking about the technical end, but I wanted to take advantage of the fact that Michel Simon was so real, that he was a hobo among hoboes, he was all the hoboes in the world, and it was interesting to see whether all the hoboes in the world could be absorbed by the Parisian crowd. For this kind of shot, I obtained a very long lens, the kind of lens that is used in Africa to film lions from afar. But instead of filming a lion, I filmed Michel Simon. I stationed my camera in a second-floor window, so that I would be above the roofs of the cars going by, and my Michel Simon walked on the piers, through the streets of Paris, among people who didn't notice him. And I shot many scenes like that. Excuse me for talking about the technique, but some of you may find it interesting.

Boudu is a film that I see quite often, not because I take pleasure in contemplating my former work, but simply because of Michel Simon. When I see *Boudu*, I forget that I made the film, I forget what happened, I only see one thing: a great actor on the screen.

Madame Bovary

Madame Bovary was a strange undertaking. It's a project in which I tried to combine a real background with the most stylized acting possible. I tried to give the actors an extremely formal text. By the way, I'm not really to be credited for this text, I took it almost entirely from Flaubert, but in any case, it's a text that is not made up of everyday conversation. It's a text with a beginning, an end, a progression. It has a kind of rhythm. It's a text that is not what we call *natural*, an odious term in films today. I hate the word *natural*. The text of *Madame Bovary* is not natural, it's good. It's good because I didn't write it, I repeat, Flaubert did. So these words had to be spoken, and spoken in front of real farms with real straw roofs, and around these real farms were real cows, real geese, real chickens, and the people who were seated in the dining rooms or kitchens of these real farms were drinking real cider. When someone opened a door, he opened a real door, a heavy door. The accessories were real accessories. I was very careful about all that. I insisted on the absolute realism of the location, of the background action, and I insisted, on the contrary, on the absolutely

Charles Granval in *Boudu Saved from Drowning.*

composed character of the foreground. I insisted that my actors act as if they were in the theater, in good theater, of course.

This wasn't very difficult to do, since I had Valentine Tessier. She's an absolutely extraordinary, staggering, touching Madame Bovary. I saw clips from the film not too long ago, and I forgot that I had made it, and I hardly saw Valentine Tessier. Rather, Madame Bovary was there before my eyes. My brother, who was so at ease and moving in his part, and also the unforgettable Max Dearly, an absolutely fascinating actor. His training as an actor had been quite strange. He started in Marseilles, where he played in fairy plays in the little thea-

André Fouché and Valentine Tessier in *Madame Bovary*.

ter behind the Canebière, and generally he played the wicked fairy. He played it on his knees, with a very large robe, and with large pointed shoes attached to his knees that stuck out from underneath the robe, and the train of the robe hid his feet. He walked on his knees and looked like a midget fairy. A man who played midget fairies is a man who can play the pharmacist Homais, and he did a very good job.

I had one of the greatest rewards in my life concerning *Madame Bovary*. You know, you make successful films, you make unsuccessful films, it's very important, but not as important as one thinks. What's important is the opinion of people you admire. And there was a man whom I admire a great deal who saw my film. He saw the uncut version – because I must tell you that the film was drastically recut. It's a film that lasts at least three hours, but the public saw it in a version that lasted no longer than an hour and a half. In particular, the scene was cut in which Max Dearly discovers matches, which at that time was the latest in progress. You took a little piece of wood, dipped it in a sulphur compound, then you opened a bottle of phosphorus, and dipped it in, and a flame appeared. It was beautiful, I was very proud to have reconstructed that. The man who liked my film was Brecht. And since I admire Brecht a great deal, Brecht's opinion was the greatest reward for this film.

The Crime of Monsieur Lange (*Le Crime de Monsieur Lange*)

The Crime of Monsieur Lange is above all a wonderful collaboration with Jacques Prévert. We didn't start together on this film. I started with a friend named Castanier, and we wrote a story that wasn't bad, I think, and that a producer decided to film. But all in all, we weren't very sure of ourselves, and I had the idea of asking a friend to take a look at our work. The friend was Jacques Prévert. And Jacques Prévert worked on the film with me, and something quite different came out of it. This doesn't mean that the film was written in advance – it isn't often in the history of my films that I've had a script that was followed exactly. I don't even think it has ever happened, and this was no exception. What happened with *The Crime of Monsieur Lange* is what often happens with me. That is, I have a well-written script. We know it's well written, and we say to ourselves, "OK, we can shoot it." Then we arrive at the set. We rehearse the actors, and we realize that it doesn't work, or we notice that there are ways of being that are more in keeping with the actors, maybe more in keeping with the extras, the set, with whatever is going on all around. Whatever it is, *The Crime of Monsieur Lange* was no exception, and I asked Prévert to remain with me on the set every day. Prévert was very kind, and he accepted. He doesn't like to get up early, but nevertheless he came and helped me with all the phases of the shooting. And much of the film's dialogue, some of which is quite brilliant, was found, thanks to this collaboration and thanks to this improvisation.

There is one example that we were just talking about with Rivette. It's when Jules Berry, who is dressed as a priest, returns to the business that he founded and finds Lefèvre in his place, and Lefèvre says, "If I were to kill you, who would miss you?" and the priest, Jules Berry as the priest, responds, "Why, women, my dear man!" I say it very poorly, so it's not very funny, but when Jules Berry says it, I think it's rather remarkable. Now that's improvisation. It was while Prévert and I were talking that he suddenly had this idea in a flash, and that was it. The film was shot in this atmosphere of amusing, bantering collabora-

tion. We were a group of buddies; if ever there was a film of buddies, this is it.

But the film represents other things for me as well. Technically, it's an attempt at linking the background and the foreground in the same shot. It's an attempt at camera movements uniting both what's happening in life, in the background action, and what's happening in the minds of the actors in the foreground. Of course this also corresponds to the idea that I spend my time trying to perfect, of not cutting the scenes and allowing the actors to follow their sequence. In this case I tried it with the help of some incredibly complicated camera movements. Believe me, Bachelet and the cameramen had a hard time. They were like snakes wrapped around the camera dolly, and this camera moved in all directions, sought out the actors, followed them, ascended, descended, and this was made all the more difficult because the set was extremely small. The sets were of normal dimensions constructed around a courtyard. The fact that we shot in this courtyard also explains the poor quality of the sound. The sound isn't good in this film, I must admit. But I prefer bad sound to postsynchronizing, and so we decided to keep the sound with all the tramway noises in the background, which from time to time prevent us from hearing the words. I prefer that, I prefer to have naturally, normally spoken words, which truly come from the bodies and minds of the actors. I prefer that to the best-done and the most artificially boring postsynchronizing.

The Lower Depths (*Les Bas-Fonds*)

The Lower Depths was Gabin, Jouvet, Le Vigan, and Sokoloff. Obviously a magnificent team. It was also an attempt to maintain the spirit of Gorki, and to transpose this spirit to the banks of the Marne. At the same time, we wanted to keep the Marne's value as a French river and the value of its banks, with their little, skinny bushes so typical of the Parisian suburbs. When I had finished the script for *The Lower Depths* – which I naturally ended up changing during the shooting, as always, but it is one of the scripts that I changed the least, I almost followed it – it seemed to me both decent and prudent to send it to Gorki. Gorki read it, and to my great surprise, despite the enormous differences between my script and the work that inspired it, he approved of it wholeheartedly. He even wrote a few lines to announce publicly his approval of it and to say that it seemed to him as though it wouldn't be a bad film, that it would be good. Spaak also helped me with the script, by the way, and there may have also been a

(*facing*) Marcel Levesque in *The Crime of Monsieur Lange.*

Robert Le Vigan, Louis Jouvet, and Suzy Prim in *The Lower Depths*.

Paul Temps and Robert Le Vigan in *The Lower Depths*.

good deal of the producer's, Kamenka's, influence, which was particularly helpful. Let's get back to Gabin. You can imagine how excited I was at the idea of shooting with this actor, and I don't have to tell you that I wasn't disappointed. We immediately got along like two peas in a pod, and shooting with him, as in all the films I've shot with him, was a kind of, not exactly research, but a kind of rambling conversation from which scenes sprang forth, as if on their own. It was truly easy, enjoyable work.

There was Jouvet, who played the role of the baron. I was able to give Jouvet lines that pretty much matched his personality. But the most stylized character of the whole group was obviously Le Vigan. I've spoken about this several times in our informal talks – I like to introduce an extremely stylized character in my films, a character to whom I try to give a very lyrical language, a language that is a step away from being false. One false step, and you would cross a dangerous boundary. I was able to do something rather funny with Le Vigan in this direction. I searched for something for him to say right at the moment when he is going to kill himself, to commit suicide by hanging himself. And I thought it would be nice for him to recite some verses. Le Vigan and I found these verses in Shakespeare. That's right, it's the lines about the cherubim and the stars that begin with "Jessica, Jessica." It's in *The Merchant of Venice*.

I said that I improvised very little in this film. There is, however, a scene that I didn't improvise – it's in Gorki's work – but that I added in a last-minute rewrite. It's a scene in which Jouvet and Gabin are sitting on the grass on the banks of the Marne, and Jouvet, the baron, speaks of the successive changes in his life, changes that he symbolizes by his clothing. "There is a kind of fog floating in my head," and it seems to him that his life was just a succession of different outfits; he went from rich man's clothing to poor man's clothing. It's a scene in which Jouvet gave me great pleasure. Yes. Basically, the main problem for me was to avoid trying to seem Russian, because I knew that if we tried to seem Russian, it would seem false. You can't seem Russian on the banks of the Marne! If you want to seem Russian, you have to shoot in Russian, in the Russian language, and in Moscow or in Russia. My problem was in keeping Gorki's spirit pure, keeping it almost uncompromisingly pure, and at the same time transposing it and keeping as they were the exterior setting, the clothing, and the French people who were to bring this spirit to life. And the actors I had, who were nice enough to act in the film, helped me tremendously.

A Day in the Country (*Partie de campagne*)

For a long time I had wanted to do a short film that would be as carefully done as a feature-length film was. Normally, shorts are done in a few days, are botched up, and are sometimes shot with actors who aren't very good and with inferior technical means. It seemed to me that if we filmed a short carefully, it could be part of a film composed of several shorts. My idea was to make a film lasting about forty minutes, and with three forty-minute films, you would have a film as long as a feature-length film and that might be more varied. In any case, it might have attracted certain viewers. Some people like that sort of thing. Some people do like that, because today (at that time it wasn't done, but it has become popular since) there are many films with vignettes. So it was basically a matter of a first step in the direction of a film of vignettes.

I decided on Maupassant for one very simple reason: I love him, and it seems to me that there's a little of everything in a little story like *A Day in the Country*. It has many problems, and it sums up a part of the world. Of course, there are few love stories as touching as *A Day in the Country*. This is common for Maupassant; it's common for many great authors.

Another thing was that this extremely short story didn't limit me. It's not like a play that forces you to use certain dialogues. *A Day in the Country* didn't force anything on me. It only offered me an ideal framework in which to embroider. I truly believe in this idea of a framework within which one embroiders. It's a question of plagiarism.

I must admit something: I'm absolutely in favor of plagiarism. I believe that if we want to bring about a great period, a new renaissance of arts and letters, the government should encourage plagiarism. When someone is convicted of being a true plagiarist, we should give him the Legion of Honor right away. I'm not kidding, because the great authors did nothing but plagiarize, and it served them well. Shakespeare spent his time writing stories that had already been written by little-known Italian authors and by others. Corneille took *Le Cid* from Guillén de Castro [*Las Mocedades del cid*] and made a French *Le Cid*, and Molière ransacked the Greeks and the Latins, and they both did a good thing. The habit of using a story already invented by someone else frees you from the unimportant aspect. What's important is the way you tell the story. If the story has already been invented by someone else, you're free to give all your attention to what is truly important, that is, the details, the development of the characters and the situations. I'm sorry for this digression, which has nothing to do with *A Day in the Country*, but too bad. We're here to talk, to tell stories, and I'm telling you some.

A Day in the Country takes place on the banks of the Seine. I couldn't shoot on the banks of the Seine, because the Seine in 1935 – the year I shot *A Day in the Country* – was no longer the Seine of eighty years earlier, it was no longer the boating Seine my father knew. The Seine in 1935 was a Seine with factories, steamboats, and lots of noise. So I shot on the banks of the Loing. I was lucky enough to have a friend, Anne-Marie Verrier, whose husband, Monsieur Verrier, was the ranger in the forest of Fountainebleau, and he was living in this little, absolutely marvelous, absolutely delicious house in the forest, right on the banks of the Loing, near a bridge. So we wrote *Auberge* [inn] on the front of this house in the forest. We were a bunch of friends, and we moved into Anne-Marie Verrier's. We shot *A Day in the Country* at her house.

The most important incident concerning *A Day in the Country* is that I had written the script for the sun. I had written a script in which we would be sitting in the dust, all sweaty. But it didn't stop raining. I was able to sneak in a little sunshine between showers, but because it kept raining, I decided to change the script and write it for the rain. So the long rainy scenes that you see are simply an adjustment to the circumstances.

In *A Day in the Country* there is one thing that you might find interesting. I had some assistants who since have won a great deal of acclaim. I had Visconti, who was a great help, Jacques Becker, of course, Cartier-Bresson. We were a bunch of friends, and it all seemed like a kind of happy vacation on the banks of a very pretty river.

The Human Beast (La Bête humaine)

Shortly before the war in 1939, Monsieur Hakim, a producer, had the idea of shooting *The Human Beast*. He had a feeling that Gabin would play the lead role. I don't know whether Hakim and Gabin came to me themselves, but in any case, Gabin asked to have me direct the film. Gabin came to see me, and Hakim came to see me. I thought about it a little, I said, "I'd like to know what it's all about, after all." I have to admit that I hadn't read the novel. I skimmed over it quickly, it seemed fascinating, and I said, "OK, let's do it." We had to start right away. I'm very proud of the following athletic feat: I wrote the script in twelve days, which isn't bad! I brought it with me, but we didn't follow it, I'll tell you that right away. But we had it, it's always good to have a script when you begin a film, and we started the production. To prepare for it, Gabin and I wanted to learn a bit about railroads, about locomotives, because the locomotive is one of the most important characters in the film. It's basically a kind of triad of two women and Gabin. One of these two women is Simone Simon and the other woman is the locomotive. So Gabin, and Carette as well, rode on locomotives, learned to drive them. Gabin drove the train several times from Le Havre to Paris with some good chaps who didn't know they were being driven by a great actor. They may not have felt very comfortable with the idea, in any case, so it was better not to tell them. Finally, we began to shoot *The Human Beast*.

One cause for discussion – not merely discussion, let's call it controversial conversation – with the producers – who understood immediately what I wanted to do, by the way – was the selection of the female role. They wanted a woman who was clearly a vamp, you know, one of these dark women who you know right away is going to be dangerous, is going to spell catastrophe. I claimed, and I still claim, that vamps have to be played by women with innocent faces. Women with innocent faces are the most dangerous ones! Also, you don't expect it, so there is an element of surprise! I insisted that we use Simone Simon, which we did, and I don't think we were sorry.

The Human Beast was a rather difficult film to shoot, since much of it takes place on locomotives. You can't shoot on a locomotive the way you can in a studio. There was so much to install. I must say that the state railway system was marvelous, they helped us, gave us some extraordinary assistants who took part in the film, who advised us, who prevented us from making mistakes. Because here again I insisted on exterior reality, I wanted very much for it to be respected. Believe me, there isn't a detail in this film that isn't exact. They gave us a track

(*facing*) Simone Simon and Jean Gabin [– from] a poster for *The Human Beast*.

that wasn't being used during the time we were shooting the film. On this track we put a train, composed of a locomotive, our locomotive, our character, the Lison, the one we photographed. Behind it, we had a flatcar on which we had two generators to provide the electricity. We lit the locomotive exactly as if it were a character in a studio: instruments, lights, backlighting, everything you need. And of course all that was connected with wires, with straps, all that. It was all very complicated, because we were moving at sixty miles an hour! To reach sixty miles an hour in a hurry, we had another train push us from behind, so that we picked up speed quickly. We did it with two locomotives. We also had a few normal cars in which the actors could wash up, relax when they weren't shooting, reapply their makeup, have something to eat, and so on. It all was very organized. I must say that the photography was exciting and rather dangerous at times. My nephew, the cameraman, Claude Renoir, was almost knocked off once. He was in charge of a camera that was against the side of the locomotive. We had measured everything. The camera was fixed against the locomotive, but we had miscalculated, and the camera stuck out maybe one centimeter, and when we entered a tunnel – we were filming in a tunnel – the camera was knocked off and smashed. Luckily Claude saw what was coming just before it happened, he guessed it, and he flattened himself against the train and wasn't knocked off too. Luckily he's still alive.

The film was also shot at Le Havre, where we lived in some of the railway's buildings, in the freight depot. I have to tell you that Gabin and I had a great time with this film. It's wonderful to drive locomotives, it's an absolutely marvelous thing, and I don't think he's forgotten it. I haven't forgotten it, anyway. The other day, in fact, while looking through an old wallet, I found the card that allows me – I hope it's still valid, I plan on using it from time to time when the trains are full – to ask the engine crew for a place to sit.

The Rules of the Game (*La Règle du jeu*)

I love talking about *The Rules of the Game* because of all the films I've done, it is, of course, the one that was the biggest failure. When it came out, *The Rules of the Game* was a perfect flop! I've had quite a few flops in my life, but I don't think I've ever had one like this! It was a complete and total flop. One day, not too long ago, I was presenting *The Rules of the Game* to an audience of young people at a school in America, in New York. Some of the young people had heard about the reception *The Rules of the Game* got in Paris, and one of them asked me, in French, "Tell me, Monsieur Renoir, what makes *The Rules of the Game* a controversial film?" One uses the word *controversial* when translating from English to French poorly. So I answered, "Well, young man, this film can be considered *controversial* for the following reason: On the first night, at the Colisée, I saw a man in the audience very solemnly unfold his newspaper, take out a box of matches, light one, and set the newspaper on fire, with the obvious intention of setting the room on fire. I think that a film that provokes reactions of this sort is a *controversial* film." So there you have it: I made this *controversial* film in 1938–39. I had no intention of making a *controversial* film, believe me. I had no intention of startling conventional people, I simply wanted to make a film, I even wanted to make a good film, but one that, at the same time, would criticize a society that I considered to be rotten and that I continue to consider to be absolutely rotten, because this society is still the same. It's still rotten, it hasn't finished drawing us into some very pretty little catastrophes. All right. That said, in making *The Rules of the Game*, I wanted to make a likable film, so I used as my source a writer who is a lovable creature, someone whom you can't help loving. I used Musset. *Les Caprices de Marianne* was my source, but a very distant source indeed! The resemblance is very slight, but there is something in my plot that reminds us of *Les Caprices de Marianne*. And then, you know, you always need a point of departure, so let's just say that *Les Caprices de Marianne* was my point of departure.

The Rules of the Game also represented my desire to return to the classical spirit, my desire to escape from *The Human Beast*, from naturalism, even to escape from Flaubert. It represented my desire to get back to Marivaux, Beaumarchais, and Molière. This is quite an ambition, but allow me to point out to you, dear friends, that if you're going to have mentors, the bigger they are, the better. It doesn't mean you compare yourself with them, it simply means that you try to use them as your models.

So, this was an attempt at a classical work. I accompanied it with classical music, and I had it acted in somewhat of a commedia dell'arte fashion, a bit of a pantomime style. I used extremely simple characters, but ones who, simply stated, took their ideas to the limit, developed their thoughts to the limit. They are candid characters. I hope that the portrayal of this society leads us to love it, delinquent though it may be, because this society has at least one advantage: It wears no masks.

When *The Rules of the Game* was shown in July 1939 at the Colisée – I told you the story about the man with his newspaper – many people wanted to destroy the seats. I went to these screenings, and I can tell you that it breaks your heart. It's all very well to say you don't care, but it isn't true, you do care. It's very upsetting to hear people whistle at you and insult you. I received plenty of insults because of *The Rules of the Game*.

All that's over. I have, in any case, recently been compensated, but

Marcel Dalio and Mila Parely in *The Rules of the Game*.

haven't forgotten it yet. What I wanted to tell you is that because of the whistling that broke my heart, I decided to cut it, and that is why the full and complete version of *The Rules of the Game* no longer exists. There is one, and I hope it's the one you are going to see. There is one that is almost complete, which was reconstructed by some film laboratory technicians, who were able to find the negatives, develop them, and remake a complete copy. In short, they were able to reconstruct the film. There is only one scene missing in this reconstruction, a scene that isn't very important. It's a scene with me and Roland Toutain that deals with the maids' sexual interest. You see, it isn't very important!

I said that I was later compensated. Three years ago, in fact, I was in Venice, and the people from the Venice Film Festival very kindly had the idea of showing this full version, which had just been completed, one afternoon in their large auditorium. I went, and I had the pleasure of seeing a truly packed theater. There were many people standing, sitting on the steps, and the people applauded a great deal. They were very kind. I had the feeling I was getting revenge for the insults of 1939.

The Southerner (*L'Homme du sud*)

The subject of *The Southerner*, like that of *The Human Beast*, was brought to me by my friend Hakim. He brought me a script and said, "You should shoot this." I read it, but I didn't like it very much. "I see this is taken from a book," I said to him. "Why don't you bring me the book?" He brought the book, and I read it and liked it very much. I told him, "I'm going to write the script myself, and I think I can shoot it." The book is a very strange, extremely interesting book; it's almost a documentary work.

Oddly enough, the adventure of *The Southerner* reminds me a little of the adventure I just went through with *The Elusive Corporal*. *Le Caporal épinglé* is a great novel, a great book, it's almost a journal, almost a documentary. The book from which *The Southerner* is taken is the same kind of work. In English it's called *Hold Autumn in Your Hand* [by George Sessions Perry]. It means that you must preserve and store the vegetables and fruits that grow in autumn. The truth is it's a book intended mostly to convince American farmers not to eat only canned food in the winter, I mean, canned meat, salted food, but to try to eat green beans, and vegetables and fruits, in order to fight against an illness known as pellegra that was – it no longer is – at that time rather widespread in certain southern states. Children suffer from it and they get large pimples, even scabs, on their skin, and it's due to a lack of vitamins in their diet. I wrote the screenplay alone. It's one of the rare ones that I wrote alone. It may also have been my first English project. The script was presented to a big star, who was supposed to guarantee that the film would be a success. This great star read it and declared that it was very bad. This didn't bother me, I didn't care. It happened that my producer was David Loew, who is a marvelous man and a marvelous friend. He said to me, "Well, it's very simple, since this star thinks your script is bad, he won't act in it, that's all, and you can choose your own actor." And I was able to request that Zachary Scott, who was under contract at Warner at the time, be lent to us to play the starring role. I was very pleased with this arrangement, and I'll tell you why. Zachary Scott is himself a southerner, the son of a farmer in one of the southern states. He knows their language, he knows their habits, and he contributed a kind of exterior accuracy to the film that I found to be extremely valuable, because this is also one of the films that I tried to shoot while maintaining exterior accuracy. Betty Field, his wife, wasn't a southerner, she's from New England, but she adapted herself completely, she changed her accent a little. She's a marvelous actress who knew how to adapt herself. Many of the other actors were from the South. It's truly a southern story, a story of the southern United States.

I worked a great deal with rather small lenses, which gave great depth, so as to never lose sight of the fields behind my characters. The fact is that this land that my hero wanted so much to cultivate and that he counts on to become independent, this land, these fields, play a role. The land is a character in the film, so you have to see it. That's why I used these lenses, which gave me depth and allowed me to stay in touch with the background, even while our interest is focused, I hope, on what the character in the foreground is saying. Naturally, this also led me to shoot outdoors quite often. When I shot my first film in the United States, which was *Swamp Water,* the production department didn't understand why I wanted to go to Georgia, where the story takes place. They said to me, "Why do you want to go to Georgia?" I told them, "Well, because the story takes place in Georgia. It seems only natural to me to go shoot in Georgia." It seemed strange to them. But they did send me to Georgia, because I insisted.

I had none of these problems with *The Southerner*, because David Loew, the producer, understood right away. He actually had a village constructed on the banks of the river where the story takes place, in the middle of the cotton fields, and we lived in a tent for several weeks. We just stepped outside to be on location, to begin working with the cameras. The actors were there, on location. It was absolutely marvelous. We forgot the studio, Hollywood, the swimming pools, and all the rest. We were truly in the cotton fields, and we could consider ourselves to be true cotton farmers.

The film was quite successful, and from time to time it is still shown, with some success, on American television.

The River

I read this book [*The River*] and was immediately convinced that it would be a marvelous starting point for a film. Very proud of my discovery, I wrote up a short summary and went to see various producers, different studios. They all said to me, "You're fit to be tied, my friend, this subject is completely uninteresting. A film in India must have certain, indispensable elements. You have to have tigers, Bengalese lancers, and elephants. There are no elephants, Bengalese lancers, or tigers in *The River*, and so it isn't an Indian film and we're not interested." It happened that at the time, a very intelligent man, a florist, a Mr. McEldowney, wanted to make a film. He wanted to make a film for the following reason: He had been in the air force in India during the war, had become acquainted with the country, liked it, and had met some financiers who told him, "If one day you want to produce a film, we'll back you." It happened that he didn't have a subject, he didn't know what to shoot, and one day he was seated next to a lady in a plane and he found out that she was Nehru's sister. He spoke to this woman and told her, "I would like to do a film about India." She said to him, "My young friend, that's very easy to say but not so easy to do, because Indian subjects are so difficult for Europeans to understand that you risk doing something false that not Indians, or Americans, or Europeans would like. There is, however, a writer who has seen India through the eyes of an Englishwoman but who has seen it very clearly, because she was practically born in India, she lived her whole life there and speaks several Indian languages. She's an English author named Rumer Godden. Mrs. Rumer Godden lives in London now. Why don't you write to her and ask her for the rights to one of her novels? I recommend especially *The River*, which is a marvelous story." This Mr. McEldowney was so excited by this conversation with Nehru's sister that he tried to buy the rights to this novel and he found me, because I had already acquired an option on it. That's how *The River* came about. So he asked me, "Do you want to do *The River*?" I said, "Obviously. Otherwise I wouldn't have bought the option." And I told him, "I'll collaborate with you on one condition, that you pay for me to go on a trip to India so that I can see whether we can really shoot there, because if we can't shoot in India, if *The River* has to be shot in a Hollywood studio with reconstructed sets, I'd rather forget it." He agreed, I went to India and I was convinced. The word *convinced* is weak. I was overwhelmed. It's an extraordinary country, with extraordinary people, and I'll tell you right away that it's the least mysterious country in the world. For a Frenchman, India is very easy to understand. The people have just about the same reactions as people do in France. In any case, I met some friends right away who helped me understand, who opened doors for me. I'll simply mention one small incident.

The director of photography for the film was my nephew Claude, and it was his first color film. Naturally we took a course in Technicolor, and so forth; we didn't jump into color just like that, we didn't just dive in. But I needed a camera operator. While I was doing tests on some young Indian women in a studio in Calcutta, I noticed a fairly old man who handled the clapper boards at the start of each take. He had a rather exceptional way about him, and so I asked questions and found out that he was a well-known Indian cameraman who was simply curious and wanted to see how I worked. So I asked him if he wanted to be the cameraman for my film. He said yes, and he then went to London to study Technicolor. He's the one who's responsible for the film's photography.

India brought me many things by way of *The River.* India brought me a certain understanding of life. This doesn't mean I understand everything, it doesn't mean I know all the answers, it simply means that I rid myself of quite of few prejudices. India may have taught me that everyone has his reasons. India is a great country, an extraordinary country, and I believe it's a country whose moral influence on the world will continue to grow.

My introduction to India happened through several people, of course. One person who helped me a great deal was the director of the French Institute in Calcutta, who lived there almost like an Indian. She had close friends on all levels of society, and she introduced me to many people. It was through her that I met Radha the dancer, for example. Radha the dancer, of course, took me even farther, because she initiated me – yet another ambitious word, don't think I know so much – but in any case, through her, I had the idea that one extremely effective way of approaching Indian civilization would be through dance. Dance remains an absolutely essential Indian form of expression, and I think that if you understand Indian dances, you not only understand India, but as a consequence you understand what art in Europe was like, especially the performing arts, before the Renaissance.

But I think I've said enough about *The River*. I could go on and on, believe me. One year spent in India cannot help but leave its mark, and when I start talking about it, I can go on endlessly, there's so much to say. It's better for me to stop talking and let you watch the film.

The Golden Coach (*Le Carosse d'or*)

The River, which was shot in color, received some praise; some people thought the color was good. And that inspired me to push this experiment with color even further, along with my nephew Claude. At that time, just by chance, some Italian producers asked me whether I'd like to shoot an English-language film, a film aimed at the Anglo-American market, with Anna Magnani, who at the time, by the way, didn't speak English. The idea was to take the film from Mérimée's *Carrosse du Saint-Sacrement*. I immediately warned these producers, who were extremely understanding, extremely intelligent, and extremely pleasant to work with, I warned them right away that I would probably not follow Merimée's story, Merimée's play, because I thought it would be more interesting to go back to the subject's sources, to seek a slightly more cinematic story from among the stories that had inspired Merimée. Merimée's play has a wonderful dialogue, but you can't go beyond it, you have to make it into a kind of tennis match in which the balls are replaced by words. That's not quite suitable for a film, in my opinion. So I told them that I would accept, under the condition that they allow me to turn the subject around, and they very kindly agreed. So I went to Italy, I met – and I am very happy to have met – Anna Magnani, who is an extraordinary character, not only a great screen actress, but also a great woman in real life. To begin with, we agreed that I would try to deviate from the naturalist style, the so-called realist style, which had been the style of most of Magnani's films until that point.

I suggested using the commedia dell'arte as a foundation and making Magnani into a commedia dell'arte character. She agreed. I then began to study the commedia dell'arte and to look for music – it's very helpful to have music, even when writing a screenplay; it puts you in a certain frame of mind – and at that moment a name sprang up, forced itself on me, and I immediately asked this illustrious character to be my associate in composing the film. His name was Vivaldi. It's wonderful to have someone who has been dead for several hundred years as your associate, because he never objects, he always agrees with you. Vivaldi was very kind. So, with Vivaldi's melodies as my foundation, I tried to write the script, which I wrote in conjunction with several friends. I had more help on this film than on any other film I've shot in my life. It was a difficult film. It was a film in which I tried to enclose one performance inside another. I tried, if you like, to erase the borders between the representation of reality and the reality itself. I tried to establish a kind of confusion between acting on a theatrical stage and acting in life. I don't know whether I really achieved my goal, but in any case it was truly interesting to try it.

Magnani's work was particularly delightful, especially when she was tired. When she was tired, she came to me in the morning in a horrifying state. She had probably spent the night in bars, and naturally she arrived looking beat. She looked at herself in a mirror, then she called Claude and said, "Listen Claude, do you think I can be filmed like this, look at this face, my eyes are down to my mouth, it's impossible, you can't photograph me like this!" And so I said, "Listen Anna, we may not photograph you, but we can still rehearse." And we began to rehearse. We began to rehearse with the other actors, and the first rehearsal was rather pitiful. At the second rehearsal, things started getting better, and at the third rehearsal, the words started

The filming of *The Golden Coach:* Anna Magnani and Jean Renoir.

coming out of her mouth, taking on a resonance, and she began to absorb them, to make them her own, and her face began to change. At the fourth and fifth rehearsals, Anna looked exactly like a young girl. I like to tell this story, because that's what characterizes a *great* actor or a *great* actress. The art is stronger than the physical self, the power of the spirit overcomes the body.

I must say, by the way, that Anna deserves a great deal of credit, because she didn't speak English, as I said. She learned it for this film, and the result, in the English version... I don't think that you are going to hear the English version, and I regret that, because in the

English version her speech is absolutely delicious, her Italian accent is very pronounced, very strong, and it gives the English words an absolutely unexpected resonance. I think that's one of the reasons the English version is good. It's the contrast between the Italian accent and the English language.

The Golden Coach is a film that I was able to take to the limit with great meticulousness, thanks to the producers' patience and kindness. It's a film in which Claude and I were able to study color contrasts with a great deal of care. Sometimes, for example, we didn't shoot because the costumes didn't work with the set background. Sometimes we had the sets entirely repainted, had the wigs changed, had the makeup changed. I think that from the point of view of the color, some of you may find the results interesting.

Paris Does Strange Things (*Eléna et les hommes*)

Eléna et les hommes is Ingrid Bergman, who takes on a rather unusual form, I think. What inspired me to do this film was above all the idea of filming Ingrid Bergman. Deutschmeister suggested this project, and naturally I accepted it happily because Ingrid is a marvelous woman whom I love both in life and on the screen. So my idea was to have her act in something comical. I had the feeling that she needed it, that comical situations would fit right in with the development of her career. I must say that I wasn't thinking very much about the film's success and that I might have been wrong; rather, I was mostly thinking of her.

After that, other things came and grabbed me, pulled at me, and excited me. I was very happy to work with Jean Marais. Jean Marais added an inimitable kind of grace and elegance to the film. The film also gave me the opportunity to meet Juliet Gréco, to admire her, and to appreciate her.

But let's get back to Ingrid, since she was the cause of the film. I had suggested several subjects that didn't work, when an idea struck me. My idea was to do a film on General Boulanger. So I suggested we do a film on General Boulanger, and everyone agreed. Everyone said, "Ah! What a splendid idea, that could be very funny." Of course, the ending is rather sad, but he's a character who can be portrayed with a certain sense of humor these days, perhaps a bit more lightly than he really was in history. So I wrote a script for General Boulanger. I must tell you that I also had some other reasons, very minor reasons – minor reasons are influential – for thinking of General Boulanger. I had an old friend, who is dead now, and during a military revue this friend was able to hold the reins of General Boulanger's horse, and he never forgot it. This friend remained a partisan of Boulanger even fifty years

Paris Does Strange Things: Ingrid Bergman.

after Boulanger's death, because he was able to hold the reins of his horse.

There was another thing that struck me and that I wanted to show in the film, but I couldn't – I wasn't able to, simply because I didn't have the material means to do it; we shot the film in winter, and it would have to have been summer – and it's the story of a revue, General Boulanger's last revue, the revue that prompted his flight into Belgium. You know that General Boulanger prepared a coup d'état, but he thought that it would fail, and so he fled to Belgium where he committed suicide on his mistress's tomb. Well during his last revue in Paris, a strange incident occurred. Many of the regiments were very faithful to Boulanger and to show their loyalty these soldiers had grown a little pointed goatee, just like the general's. Then on the day of the revue, these faithful soldiers appeared before the general with clean-shaven chins. The republican triumph expressing itself in the form of a shaved chin seemed appropriately cinematic to me, and I was very sorry not to be able to show it in the film.

To get back to working with Ingrid. I wanted to try these comic scenes with her. Unfortunately, at the last moment, Deutschmeister and I realized that Boulanger had relatives, heirs, who were extremely nice people and that evoking the memory of their ancestor might bother them, annoy them, disturb them, hurt them. So we decided to forget General Boulanger and to shoot another film, to shoot a film with the same subject – it's still about a general, a plot, a coup d'état – but this change of direction at the last moment, I must say, did not help me make a very good film. I did what I could, considering it was almost completely improvised. From time to time, I was still able to dig up some situations in which Ingrid was marvelous and to dig up some situations in which the other actors were marvelous. For example, I was able to give a big part to an actor I like very much, Jouanneau. He was absolutely marvelous. Pierre Bertin was also rather extraordinary.

All in all, I was able to try some things I like, to take a crack at a kind of burlesque pushed a bit too far, which is something I like tremendously. In short, the fact that we changed the story at the last minute may have harmed the commercial side of the film, but it did allow me to try some experiments that delighted me no end. Maybe the most interesting experiment was our attempt to find the most superficial aspect of the burlesque genre and to combine it with a plot played by normal, serious actors.

CHAPTER VIII
Hollywood conversations

These "Hollywood Conversations" are excerpted from a conversation that took place in Hollywood between Jean Renoir and Jean-Louis Noames, during the summer of 1963. They were published under the title "Propos rompus" in *Cahiers du cinéma*, no. 155, in May 1964.

David and Lisa

I was very impressed by *David and Lisa*.* I feel that this film represents a turning point in the history of film, not only in the history of the American film, but also in the history of film as a whole. I believe that there is a way of writing dialogues, and of having them spoken by the actors, that allows us to know better what is going on inside these actors. After all, our profession in motion pictures, as in all the arts, is to try to lift this kind of "veil," this curtain between the viewer and the subject, the human being presented on the screen, which in the end is the director himself. I think that in *David and Lisa* – by means of very high caliber, extremely moving actors – we achieve a certain contact with the director, which is, all things considered, the essence of art.

Night of the Crossroads (*La Nuit du carrefour*)

This film is quite different from many other films, first, because there was very little money to make it and circumstances forced me to work under unusual conditions. Jacques Becker was my assistant at the time, and we had many friends, very close friends who helped me, by the way, on many other films. So we all went to live in a kind of a barn at these crossroads. The crossroads were forty kilometers from Paris; barely thirty or thirty-five taking the northern highway. There was a kind of inn that wasn't occupied, and so we went to live in it.

*A 1962 American film by Frank Perry, with Keir Dullea and Janet Margolin.

We had someone do a little cooking, make a little hot coffee, and we slept on straw. From time to time when we weren't too tired, we woke up and shot a few scenes, we didn't have to worry about union rules, of course; we could work when we wanted. When the crew wasn't too tired, we went outside. We worked in the fog, in the rain, and of course, whatever happened in front of the camera depended as much on the actors' improvisation as on my own wishes, but we all were immersed in the subject. The result was obviously a rather incoherent film. We couldn't finish it because we ran out of money, but in the end, this incoherence for which it has been so criticized comes, I think, mostly from the method used to shoot it, that is, this kind of commedia dell'arte.

Subject matter

I'm very influenced by and become very engrossed in actors, and so I try to have a subject firmly in mind before I start, because once I start, I forget it. I think of only one thing: how to express the personality of the actor within the framework of a defined role. But often the actor and I break away from this framework . . . too often. It's the commedia dell'arte once again, but with one great difference: The commedia dell'arte was geared to an audience that was completely different from the film audience, the twentieth-century audience. Another thing: The troupes changed cities; they didn't stay long in any one; and there weren't millions of viewers seeing the same play, or at least they were spread out over different locations. Whatever the case, it was possible to reuse the same material; and it's a good thing because in my opinion, if you can free yourself from the subject matter, you stand a chance of doing better work. I think subject matter is necessary, I believe in great subjects, but I also think it's a terrible weight to have to drag around; I believe that the director's first task is to rid himself of the subject. In the commedia dell'arte, they had an enormous advantage, which is that they had already worked on their subjects five hundred times, they knew them by heart. The subject matter no longer counted, and the character's appearance no longer counted either, since the harlequin's costume, movements, and appearance were always the harlequin's costume, movements, and appearance. Once the appearance and the subject were out of the way, they could concentrate on the essentials, that is, on the character, the situations, and the way to deal with them. This is exactly what all the great classics did, it's what Shakespeare did. Shakespeare very rarely invented his subjects; even *The Tempest* is said to have been taken from Montaigne.

A Day in the Country (*Une Partie de campagne*)

This film grew out of my desire to do something with Sylvia Bataille. It seemed to me that a film with costumes would be right for her. I was already beginning to share René Clair's opinion (he's the first one to have stated this idea) that there should be a "cinematic period," just as there was a commedia dell'arte period, and that this period should be the second half of the nineteenth century. This is an idea that I approve of one hundred percent: Get rid of realism entirely, and do all our films with costumes from a period that would be the film period. It's the opposite of cinéma vérité. To get back to Sylvia, I had the idea of working with this Maupassant short story because I saw things in it to say that would work well with her voice. It was totally improvised. I often improvise my films, I always write an absolutely rigorous screenplay at the beginning. I don't follow it, but I write it, and I often write it several times. For example, for *The River,* which is also extremely improvised, Rumer Godden and I wrote three complete, very detailed scripts before leaving. Then during the shooting, well, we shot something else. For example, the passage like the little Indian story we tell about Radha came to me while walking along the banks of the Ganges during the shooting. It wasn't in the script. To get back to *A Day in the Country,* if certain landscapes, certain costumes, bring to mind my father's paintings, it's for two reasons: first, because it takes place during the period and in a place where my father worked a great deal in his youth. Second, it's because I'm my father's son, and one is inevitably influenced by one's parents. If I were the son of a nursery gardener, I would probably know a great deal about trees, and I would have an extraordinary taste for gardens. But I'm the son of a painter, so I'm more or less influenced by the painters who surrounded me, who surrounded the little person I was when I was young.

Whether *Grand Illusion* (*La Grande Illusion*) is the best Renoir film

I don't have such definite opinions about my films. I don't think that any film deserves to be called the greatest, or the worst. On the other hand, I feel that sometimes voluntarily, often involuntarily, I've been following the same line ever since I began making films. I've basically shot one film, I've continued to shoot one film, ever since I began, and it's always the same film. I add things, I see things that I haven't said before and that I have to say, but the truth is it's the same conversation that I began with an audience, a rather limited audience, by the way – the audience interested in this kind of cinematic art is extremely limited – it's a conversation that I continue with this public and that I shall continue. I don't know whether it gets better or not, but I know it continues.

You see, all that comes from the unfortunate idea – which is shared by many people, by the majority of people, whether it's the public, critics, film people, producers, or directors – that the important thing in art is perfection. For example, when starting a film, most people, most producers, say very honestly, "We're going to try to make a good film." In my opinion, this is a stupid proposition; making a good film is uninteresting. The only important thing is to make a film, a book, a dish, in which the personality of the cook, the author, appears. What counts, as I was saying, is the conversation. There are weak points and strong points in these conversations, but what counts is the contact, the establishment of a bridge. Perfection is an insane joke. I can cite proof of this right away: Chaplin's films were considered by all the technical specialists as having been shot with poor technique, poorly lit, poorly photographed, with poorly conceived scripts, and so forth. In my opinion, his films are still masterpieces. I believe that none of us is ready to come close to Chaplin, and yet all the lovers of perfection criticized him. I would give you any... Listen, take art, for example, great works of art are not perfect. The academic works are perfect. The paintings of Luxembourg, of battlefields with swordsmen flourishing sabers are perfect works. They're perfect, all the shadows, the mustaches, everything, everything is there, they're perfect. They're perfect, and they're unbearable. I can give you an even better proof: that of life. The most important thing in life, after all, is love, and I don't think that one is attracted to a woman because she's pretty; I don't believe that. I have here a little book with pictures of women who had the most successful love affairs of the past century. That's right, these are the women on whom millions were spent, people committed suicide for them, they were Nanas, but they were not at all beautiful, and I'm sure that their chambermaids, who were very beautiful, wouldn't have gotten five cents out of a man. No, what matters is human contact. And that's what's interesting in cinéma vérité: It aims to establish this contact. The attempt to establish a human contact by... whether by means of cinéma vérité or abstract painting, is an attempt at something that in my opinion is extremely noble. It's an extremely difficult task, it's a task that stands a chance of failing, simply because a little hypocrisy is good in art. A little hypocrisy, or maybe a little humility.

Leo McCarey

The industrial machine known as Hollywood is formidable. Some people manage to be just as strong as the machine, but some people are broken by it. McCarey is one of those people who never were broken. While working within this machine, McCarey managed to produce absolutely personal products. A McCarey film is absolutely recognizable, not only technically, but also by the kind of spirit that he gives to his characters and situations. I think he is a genuinely great director.

Swamp Water

I was learning English at the time. I understood it, I could say a few words, but I couldn't speak it, and the actors were nice enough to help me a great deal. In conversation, they helped me find the right expressions, they helped me make the necessary changes in the text. There was a great deal of collaboration with the actors. There is one thing that I'm very thankful to Zanuck for. He said to me, "Jean, if you want to succeed in America, you have to work with stars. Seeing as how I like you, take your pick, I'll give you the best stars we have." I answered him, "No." He asked, "Why not?" I told him, "Because if you give me actors whose success is guaranteed, they're exactly like ducks: You throw water on them and they never get wet, they're impermeable, they're protected by their success. I would rather have people who are still hesitant so that I can work with them, so that I can direct them. That's my profession, that's what interests me." So he allowed me to pick some unknowns but gave me very well-known people like Brennan and the old Huston for the supporting roles.

Aside from that, filming in France or in America . . . Listen: I'll use the example of a writer. He's in the habit of writing with a fountain pen, and then he happens to arrive in a country where there is no ink. He has to write with a pencil, and so he writes with a pencil. Then, say, he arrives in an extremely up-to-date country in which only typewriters are used, and so he learns to type. All this will not essentially change what he writes; it may only change the form slightly.

Stars

You know, being a star has many advantages, but it also has many dangers, drawbacks, and deceptions. The truth is, I know that if I had a son or a daughter, and if he or she were to say to me, "Daddy, I want to be an actor or an actress," I would say, "I beg of you, go sell socks, do anything, but don't get into that profession, or if you do, be a supporting actor, don't be a star." All the stars I know (and very honestly, it's not because they're capricious or vain, no . . .) are very unhappy people. You see, the writer manages only with great difficulty to express what's in his head. He may never manage exactly, nor does the painter, but he comes very close. When you write, there is a moment

Dana Andrews in *Swamp Water*.

when you say to yourself: Hey, I've created a sentence that really and truly corresponds to my inner feelings, and maybe to a certain knowledge of the world. The actor never gets to this point; he's always frustrated. He never reaches the goal he has fixed for himself. And I believe that it's an extremely exhausting exercise to have to go from one personality to another.

The Diary of a Chambermaid

In its conception, and I think in the final product as well, the film was a kind of vain race on the part of people who represent a society that is already dead: It's a ghost race. These people represent a bourgeoisie that no longer exists, for the bourgeoisie that replaced it is a business bourgeoisie, an active bourgeoisie, a bourgeoisie that earns money, that declares war, that orders films, that makes films, that lives it up and does so openly. The bourgeoisie in *The Diary of a Chambermaid* is the bourgeoisie of the nineteenth century, which was in the process of crumbling in its uselessness and its desire to do nothing. I take a few of its representatives and make them run after one another in a kind of pursuit, a vain pursuit with no goal. The truth is that *The Diary of a Chambermaid* is, in a different form and a few years later, the same subject as *The Rules of the Game* (*La Règle du jeu*).

Actors

Of course, my Camilla, or my Eléna, are mysterious characters, but so are all women who are courted, who put up a kind of barrier, and who are all the more mysterious because of their candid conversation. Candid words openly express only the feeling of the moment. Behind this feeling of the moment lies a latent feeling, which remains a mystery. There is a great danger in acting, in the profession of an actor or an actress, which is the pleasure of acting out the moment. One must be very wary of that. You must act out the moment, but only after having acted out the character as a whole; one must begin with the character. If you act out the moment, you will come to the conclusion that a girl playing the role of a mother who has lost her child must cry, and this may be a great mistake. If you act out the character, her reaction at that moment may be laughter, and this laughter will be honest. The truth is that one must do what Stanislavski did, the actors must live. That's why films shot on location are generally better, because the actors leave their spouses, their children, their eldest who was left back in high school, the swimming pool, domestic worries. In short, they're at a hotel, they're cut off from life, and they're surrounded by other actors, they're surrounded by the film, so it's easier to become the char-

Paulette Goddard, Judith Anderson, Francis Lederer, and Florence Bates in *The Diary of a Chambermaid*.

acters that they're supposed to represent, and they can allow themselves to go so far as to laugh at tragic moments and to cry at comic ones.

When I shoot a scene, I always try to escape the moment. Many directors believe in the moment. Maybe they're right, but I don't agree with them. I know that in general the stage setting consists of saying, "OK, now your child is dead, you're torn apart, cry!" That may be the truth, but it's not my truth. I'm convinced that there are a thousand truths, billions of truths, as many truths as there are inhabitants of the earth. Mine is to believe in the individual, in general, and not in the moment.

The Elusive Corporal (*Le Caporal epinglé*)

My saddest film is *The Elusive Corporal,* despite my desire to make people laugh. I think it's sort of creepy, don't you? In a story as formless as – I was going to say the invasion of France in 1940 – but I could say the history of the world since 1939. In this kind of shapeless lump of chewing gum, I have the impression that purely human values, like, let's say, simply the pleasure of being with a friend, stand out. When you come right down to it, this may be what so many directors are seeking today, an explanation, an order in this chaos.

Aside from that, I thought that it would be better if *The Elusive Corporal* were acted by a younger troupe. I was afraid it would be somewhat heavy if we gave it to actors who had already been anchored too long to their routines. So I began to write the script with Spaak, and then some personal matters came up, he couldn't stay in Paris, and the subject was only beginning vaguely to emerge. So I worked on it on my own. And then after a few days, I felt a danger lurking, that of inaccuracy. I had to have some extremely elaborate scenes, but they had to be based on specifics. So I asked Guy Lefranc to come help me, to help me with my script and all the extremely tiring, picky work of dealing with details. Having been a prisoner of war, he knew the subject through and through, and he was able to take control of everything concerning exterior truth. Freed from this enormous concern, I was able to take some stabs in a more poetic direction. With an associate who took care of reality, I was able to go farther with my side of things, to try something a bit freer than this exterior realism, that is, something more fantastic. It happens that the unbelievable side of the prison camp in *The Elusive Corporal* is as true as can be... yet it's a creation of the human mind. The characters who say, "Hey, we're going to put some barracks here" are absolutely crazy. Why here? And why metal wires? It has nothing to do with life, it's solely an invention of man's insanity. And already this framework lent itself to and pushed me toward the fantastic. But if a taste for the fantastic means "Do you believe in ghosts?" I definitely believe, if not in ghosts, at least in spirits.

The *auteur*

The problem of the film *auteur* is not really a problem. I believe that in many cases, the author of a screenplay should be the director of the film. Similarly, there are many cases in which, in my opinion, the director has all the talents necessary to write the script, and if he did, he would communicate with the audience much more closely and much more securely. Moreover, the problem of the *auteur* is not a problem, it's a fact. The world evolves, and what we pretentiously call art evolves as well: I, too, would obviously rather live in a period when the creator didn't count. Primitive art is great art. The art of Greek statuary, hundreds of years before Jesus Christ, when each statue was anonymous; the art of the cathedrals – we don't know who sculpted the St. Peter or the Angel Gabriel, we just don't know. It's an Angel Gabriel among thousands of Angels Gabriel; nevertheless, the personality of its creator shines through. We feel the hand of its creator in each stroke, yet we don't know his name. There is a creator and there isn't. I obviously like this kind of primitive art immensely, but the existence of such an art requires conditions that we can't satisfy right now. It requires, first of all, that religion and life be closely intertwined. All primitive peoples live by religion: Eating is a ritual; making love is a ritual; hunting is a ritual; and all these connections between religion and life give the expression of life, which is art, a religious meaning that can be absolutely grandiose. Hence our passion for African sculptures, the sculptures of New Guinea, for primitive Egyptian art, hence our passion for all primitive art.

When it comes to the *auteur*, we become much more demanding; we require that he gather all the elements that were gathered by an entire tribe or by an entire nation. Therefore... there are very few good *auteurs*. And if we look at it from a practical point of view, how can we have many good films? The adversaries of the idea of a *auteur* in film are right. We want to have many good films, and we want to give each movie theater in the world one film a week, but it's obviously almost impossible to find that many people who are both writers and directors. I look at it from another point of view; I use a timeless perspective. The thousands of films that come out in the theaters every week don't interest me, not at all. What interests me is the occasional *Citizen Kane*, the occasional *Gold Rush* or the occasional *David and Lisa*. It's then that I know that the *auteur* is necessary. I know that Chaplin's masterpieces were made possible only because he conceived them, wrote them, acted in them, filmed them, edited them, did the music, did everything. I have one man's expression before my eyes. It happens that that's the way it is, the author's expression in the twentieth century is like that. If we read, for example, *Bonjour tristesse* by [Françoise] Sagan, it may be because Miss Sagan is talented, but that's not the reason for her success. The reason for her success is that she is there, present on her pages. We can touch her, we can talk to her, and she speaks to us. And that's all. The rest doesn't count; her book could be bad, and it would be just as good. It may be a reaction against the masses. We live in a time when we have ten thousand cars on a road, a little red light flashes on, and everyone stops, all ten thousand. What is the reaction to this? It's a wild, exaggerated trend for the individual; in film, a wild, exaggerated trend for the *auteur*. I neither approve nor disapprove of it, I observe it, that's all.

Have we lost sight of it today? Are we no longer certain? Have we insisted on it strongly enough? It is a fact that at *Cahiers*, film was never viewed from an essentially theoretical standpoint, from a well-formed and ready-made aesthetic, and even less from a strictly ideological orientation. Before these constructs could intervene, the essential factor came into play, something more in the realm of the passions, a violent affection that took hold of us and attracted us to certain films, to certain works, to certain cinematic practices, and not to others. It is from this standpoint, from this confused world of taste, that the elaboration of a theory of film was developed, at every period of the magazine. From the point of view of reason, didn't the "politique des auteurs" – to limit ourselves just to this – have all the wobbliness, the deformity, of a construct based on love?

In everyone's eyes, Renoir's films were the elected object of this passion. *Cahiers* was never able to speak about him other than in the mode of love, that is, drunk with a sense of identification and possession. So much the better, of course, especially since if I had to summarize Renoir's art, I would say that it was the attempt and the desire to create this agitation brought on by love in each of the film's viewers, to bring about the familiarity and complicity of the viewer with the characters, and to carry this familiarity and complicity to the height of the ambiguous conflict of these characters, fictional beings, over whom, by the strangely reversible nature of the Renoirian apparatus, the viewer believes he has control.

Despite the vicissitudes of *Cahiers de cinéma* from the time of its founding to the present, its references to Renoir, unlike those to other directors, seem to me to have been constant and to have been accorded no cultural evaluation or admiration, nothing that assigns to the films the impoverished stature of an art object, nothing to envelop the work in an all-engulfing commentary. His place has been both central and diffuse. In short, there has been no critical distance. I say this – aside from what one could say about the functioning of Renoir's films, about his aptitude for arranging this fog or this decline in perspective – because we perceived and received in his films, beyond the notion of film or of a work, something of the truth of film.

Some films were received at the *Cahiers* like letters in a correspondence among filmmakers (and this did not exclude us), whose essentials focused not on styles, manners, methods, or subject matter but on the need to push cinematic representation ever further off its hinges, to carry it to its extreme, and at the same time impossible, limit, where the full art of the image would splinter into lightning fragments of a tangible truth of beings and things. The close-up of Sylvia Bataille's face in *A Day in the Country* (*Une Partie de campagne*) moves me more than do the close-ups of Falconetti, so overwhelming nonetheless, in Dreyer's *Joan of Arc,* but they both represent the same decisive cinematic act, when what Renoir calls "the veil"* is torn away between performance and reality, between our gaze and the truth of the other being. Need we repeat how often *The Golden Coach* (*Le Carrosse d'or*), the height of theatrical illusion, strikes us with flashes of truth all the more thunderous as they come to us from the other side of this veil, from the reverse side of realism? And as for the repeated inscription of death and destruction on the body of Pierre Renoir as Louis XVI in *La Marseillaise,* doesn't it surprise us with a truth that, sprung from a form that is even more twisted with fiction – that of historic reconstruction – is the truth of a body, a class, a society, and a principle (royalty)?

An anthology of such moments could go on forever,† and so I shall mention only the extraordinary link of Françoise Arnoul (Nini) during the dance lesson in *French Cancan,* when she rushes from the back of the field toward the foreground – toward the camera along its axis – right to where our gaze awaits her, and after two somersaults we see her collapse. By the break of the cut and the violence of the link (from close to far away), the dramatic tension of the scene is unexpectedly destroyed. Instead of approaching the character to show us further traces of trauma on her face or in her eyes (as a lazy shooting script would have done), the camera jumps to the opposite corner of the room. Suddenly, the frame is very wide and frustrates our gaze, which

*See the first interview with Jacques Rivette and François Truffaut.

†André Bazin's collection of works on Renoir (*Jean Renoir,* ed. Champ Libre) cites a few others and defines them superbly: "Renoir doesn't choose his actors, as in the theater, by their conformity with a task, but as a painter does, because of what he knows that he will force us to see in them. That is why the most beautiful acting moments are almost indecently beautiful, why the trace they leave in our memory is only that of their brightness, so glaring it forces us to lower our eyes. The actor is pushed beyond himself, surprised in a kind of nakedness of being that has nothing to do with dramatic expression and that is undoubtedly the most decisive light that of all the arts, film, along with painting, can cast on man's body."

seeks to contemplate her pain from up close. This unites the effect of a temporal and spatial expansion with the shock of the distance (the scene resonates, reverberates), but it is contrary to all feelings of continuity. The space imposed on us immediately turns into its opposite: The character races toward the lens, our gaze finds itself replaced at the center of the drama, it becomes the target of Nini's trajectory. Target and trap, pole of attraction, magnetic and captivating surface. As if sucked into the frame, drawn by the spectator's visual desire, Nini, as she runs to hide her pain from the eyes of the other characters, throws herself on us, abandons herself to us.

I should say that this moment makes us aware, it illustrates the mix of conflict and alliance – both merciless in Renoir – between the interests of the spectator and those of the character, according to a dialectic of the demands of fiction and those of cinematography. Is it an exaggeration to see this scene as a mini model of Renoir's device by which, in most of his films, he tries to capture the viewer's gaze directly, with all its desire and fantasies of control, in the production of dramatic effects? I don't think so. Renoir's art lies in placing the spectator in the position of a director. We maintain an ambiguous relationship with the Renoirian characters: The color and the sound of his films, the logic of conflicts and destiny make us sense, before the signs are clearly visible, what will happen to these characters, and at the same time, the flashes of truth that reveal them and deliver them to us defenseless reinforce the blindness of our love for them. We have the impression of lucidity and the feeling of impotence, together. We want to see them survive the difficult tests by which fiction tries to tear them apart (and which we know will inevitably tear them apart), but we enjoy the moment that this tearing apart alone can create. The dense lives of these characters make us love them, only to suffer and rejoice all the more at their loss.*

I cannot resist mentioning another shot in which both the director's desperation and sadism grip the spectator. It's the moment in *La Vie est à nous* in which René, the unemployed engineer (Julien Bertheau) secretly leaves his friend Ninette (Nadia Sibirskaya). The camera occupies the artificial space of the "fourth wall": Ninette turns her back on the scene and faces the audience, in a position and according to a composition all the more unreal as she is shown, throughout the action, busily cooking something on the stove. The lens runs into this stove in the foreground. Ninette moves about facing us and speaks to Julien. We catch her determination to be carefree, her desire for peace. Behind her, in the field (once again used in an antinaturalist manner

*See Jean-Louis Comolli's article on *A Day in the Country* (*Une Partie de campagne*) in no. 299 of *Cahiers*.

as a theatrical element that dramatizes the space by including it in the field of a symbolic "off camera": what one of the characters doesn't see the other doing), René is preparing to flee. He crosses the screen laterally and disappears. By means of this angle and composition, which are not in the least natural, we are able to observe, simultaneously and head-on, the characters' two contradictory actions. But most of all we see how much this young woman is blinded, we see her blindness visually materialized, if I may say, by the fact that she doesn't see what we see and that we see her not seeing at the very moment we see what she is losing. The violence of the scene lies in our being able to seize the two images simultaneously, the truths of each character, which neither character wants to see in the other. The viewer is in the place of the master of ceremonies, in the place of the director, except that we must also assume that this mastery has its price: the conflict between the desire for it to stop and for it to continue; the tension, the contradiction between our feelings of revolt against the visible cowardliness of the man (Ninette would have to turn around in order to see him also as he is) and the pleasure of seeing and knowing more than the abandoned woman does, the complicity with the negative character (he will be absolved only by joining the Communist party) against the positive character, of being able to witness the destruction of innocence.

If so many Renoirian characters, illegitimate ones included,* are likable, I do not believe that this is due to a humanism, to which the filmmaker's twisted game has too easily been reduced. After all, they must be likable for the viewer to rejoice at their loss. I cannot explain Renoir's insistence, in his interviews, on the theme of equilibrium or, rather, on the theme of reequilibrium, in any other way: a balancing act by which a gap is both corrected and created between, as he says, "the two sides of the scale": successive components or moments in a scene, dramatic effects, characters. But it is not merely a question of using an aesthetic principle. The ruptures, contrasts, and gaps also affect the viewer's perspective, the workings of his relationship with the characters and the goals of the film, and bring him to bet simultaneously or alternatively on two outcomes, either recognition or ruination, the desire to be another and the desire for the Other. This can lead to the most political of consequences: Renoir's films are the only ones in which the contradictory representation of opposing classes is not a caricature, a reduction, or dull. We become sensitive to all that separates the Marseillais worker from the courtesan from Koblenz (*La Mar-*

*This is an obligatory reference to the "ignoble (and sublime) Batala" in *The Crime of Monsieur Lange* (*Le Crime de Monsieur Lange*). But we could also include Gaby (Andrex) or Albert (Max Dalban) in *Toni*, and so on.

seillaise), precisely because they both seize us with such strong accents of truth. History functions as fiction: We know who will lose and who will win, but we will win (or lose) either way.

According to the logic of such a system, the more the film's viewer finds *something of himself*, the more of himself he must leave behind. It is performance pushed to the point of consumption. We know how hard Renoir worked: The preceding interviews highlight the role of improvisation in his work, that is, his grasp of opportunities, his capacity to capture and absorb what a certain location, certain lighting, a certain body could contribute. And if it is true that he seemed less to direct his actors than to let himself be guided by them, to give them free rein, to take them as they gave themselves, should we not see a kind of metaphysical correspondence between his manner of seeming to delegate the control of a scene and the subsequent functioning of the film apparatus, which in Renoir's films feeds off the viewer's own emotions?

Films are listed by final shooting dates, rather than release dates. American release titles of French films are given in parentheses.

1924

Catherine* or *Une vie sans joie
Screenplay: Jean Renoir
Adaptation: Jean Renoir, Pierre Lestringuez
Director: Albert Dieudonné
Directors of photography: Jean Bachelet, Alphonse Gibory
Production company: Films Jean Renoir
Cast: Catherine Hessling,* Albert Dieudonné, Eugénie Naud, Louis Gauthier, Maud Richard, Pierre Champagne, Pierre Philippe,† Oléo, Georges Térof, Jean Renoir
First shown: 9 November 1927 at the Max Linder

La Fille de l'eau
Screenplay: Pierre Lestringuez
Adaptation: Jean Renoir
Director: Jean Renoir
Assistant director: Pierre Champagne
Directors of photography: Jean Bachelet, Alphonse Gibory
Production company: Films Jean Renoir, Maurice Rouhier, Studio Films
Cast: Catherine Hessling, Pierre Philippe, Pierre Champagne, Van Doren, Harold Lewingston, Pierre Renoir, André Derain, Maurice Touzé, Georges Térof, Mme. Fockenberghe, Henriette Moret, Charlotte Clasis
First shown: April 1925 at the Ciné Opéra

1926

Nana
Screenplay: Pierre Lestringuez, from the novel by Emile Zola

* Jean Renoir's wife.
† Alias Pierre Lestringuez.

Adaptation: Jean Renoir
Director: Jean Renoir
Assistant directors: André Cerf, Pierre Lestringuez
Directors of photography: Edmond Crown, Jean Bachelet
Camera: Charles Raleigh, Alphonse Gibory
Editing: Jean Renoir
Production company: Films Jean Renoir
Cast: Catherine Hessling, Jean Angelo, Werner Krauss, Valeska Gert, Pierre Philippe, Claude Moore (*alias* Autant-Lara), Pierre Champagne, André Cerf, Pierre Braunberger, Raymond Turgy, Raymond Guérin-Catelain, Jacqueline Forzane, Harbacher, Nita Romani, Jacqueline Ford, René Koval, Marie Prévost
First shown: Aubert Palace

Charleston **or** ***Sur un air de charleston***
Screenplay: Pierre Lestringuez, from an idea by André Cerf
Director: Jean Renoir
Assistant director: André Cerf
Director of photography: Jean Bachelet
Music: Clément Doucet
Production company: Néo-Film
Producer: Pierre Braunberger
Cast: Catherine Hessling, Johnny Huggins, Pierre Braunberger, Pierre Lestringuez
First shown: 19 March 1927 at the Artistic or the Pavilion

1927

Marquitta
Screenplay: Pierre Lestringuez
Adaptation: Jean Renoir
Director: Jean Renoir
Directors of photography: Jean Bachelet, Raymond Agnel
Production company: Artistes Réunis*
Cast: Marie-Louise Iribe, Jean Angelo, Pierre Philippe, Pierre Champagne, Lucien Mancini, Henri Debain
First shown: 13 September 1927 at the Aubert Palace

La P'tite Lili
Screenplay: Alberto Cavalcanti
Director: Alberto Cavalcanti
Director of photography: Jimmy Rogers
Editing: Marguerite Renoir†
Music: Yves de la Casinière, Darius Milhaud
Production company: Néo-Film

* Founded by Marie-Louise Iribe (see cast); at the time she was Pierre Renoir's wife and Lestringuez's sister-in-law.
† Real name Marguerite Mathieu but known as Renoir; lived with Jean Renoir 1935–40.

Cast: Jean Renoir, Catherine Hessling, Guy Ferrand, Roland Caillaux, Eric Aaes, Jimmy Rogers, Dido Freire,[*] Jean Storm, Alain Renoir
First shown: 1 October 1927 at the Ursulines

1928

***La Petite Marchande d'allumettes* (*The Little Match Girl*)**
Screenplay: Jean Renoir, from the story by Hans Christian Andersen
Directors: Jean Renoir, Jean Tedesco[†]
Assistant directors: Claude Heymann, Simone Hamiguet
Director of photography: Jean Bachelet
Producers: Jean Renoir, Jean Tedesco
Cast: Catherine Hessling, Jean Storm, Manuel Raabi, Amy Wells
First shown: 31 March 1928 at the Alhambra (Geneva)

Tire au flanc
Screenplay: Jean Renoir, Claude Heymann, André Cerf, from a comedy by André Mouexy-Eon and A. Sylvane
Director: Jean Renoir
Assistant directors: André Cerf, Lola Markovitch
Director of photography: Jean Bachelet
Production company: Néo-Film
Producer: Pierre Braunberger
Cast: Georges Pomiès, Michel Simon, Fridette Faton, Félix Oudart, Jeanne Helbling, Catherine Hessling, André Cerf, Jean Storm, Paul Velsa, Manuel Raabi, Maryanne, Esther Kiss, Max Dalban, Zellas, Kinny Dorlay
First shown: December 1928 at the Electric

Le Tournoi* or *Le Tournoi dans la cité
Screenplay: Henry Dupuy-Mazuel, André Jaeger-Schmidt
Adaptation: Jean Renoir
Director: Jean Renoir
Assistant director: André Cerf
Directors of photography: Marcel Lucien, Maurice Desfassiaux
Camera: Joseph-Louis Mundwiller
Editing: André Cerf
Production company: Société des films historiques
Producers: M. de Maroussem, François Harisparu
Cast: Aldo Nadi, Jackie Monnier, Enrique Rivero, Blanche Bernis, Suzanne Després, Manuel Raabi, Gérald Mock, William Aguet, Max Dalban, Viviane Clarens, Janvier, Narval, the Cadre Noir de Saumur

1929

Le Bled
Screenplay: Henry Dupuy-Mazuel, André Jaeger-Schmidt

[*] Niece to director Alberto Cavalcanti; later married Jean Renoir.
[†] Manager of the Théâtre du Vieux-Colombier, where a small film studio was set up; *see* text pp. 63–4.

Director: Jean Renoir
Assistant directors: André Cerf, René Arcy-Hennery
Directors of photography: Marcel Lucien, Léon Morizet
Camera: Boissey, André Bac
Production company: Société des films historiques
Cast: Jackie Monnier, Diana Hart, Enrique Rivero, Alexandre Arquillière, Manuel Raabi, Renée Rozier, Jacques Becker, Berardi Aïssa, Hadj ben Yasmina, M. Martin
First shown: 11 May 1929 at the Marivaux

Le Petit Chaperon rouge
Screenplay: Alberto Cavalcanti, Jean Renoir, from the story by Charles Perrault
Director: Alberto Cavalcanti
Assistant directors: Pierre Prévert, André Cerf
Directors of photography: Marcel Lucien, René Ribault
Camera: Jimmy Rogers
Editing: Alberto Cavalcanti
Production company: Societé Française de gestion cinématographique, Jean Renoir
Cast: Catherine Hessling, Jean Renoir, André Cerf, Pablo Quevedo, La Montagne, Odette Talazac, Pierre Prévert, Viviane Clarens, Pola Illery, Amy Wells, M(me). Nekrassof, Raymond Guérin-Catelain
First shown: 14 May 1930 at the Tribune Libre du Cinéma

1930

Die Jagd Nach dem Glück (***La Chasse à la fortune,*** or ***La Chasse au bonheur***)
Screenplay: Lette Reiniger, Karl Koch, from idea by Alex Trasser
Directors: Rochus Liese, Karl Koch
Director of photography: Fritz Arno Wagner
Music: Theo Mackeben
Production company: Comenius Film GmBH
Cast: Jean Renoir, Catherine Hessling, Alexander Murski, Bertold Bartosche, Mme. Jean Tedesco, Amy Wells
First shown: 25 May 1930 at the Marmorhaus (Berlin)

1931

On purge bébé
Screenplay: Jean Renoir, from the play by Georges Feydeau
Director: Jean Renoir
Assistant directors: Claude Heymann, Pierre Schwab
Directors of photography: Théodore Sparkhul, Roger Hubert
Editing: Jean Mamy
Music: Paul Misraki
Production company: Braunberger–Richebé
Cast: Jacques Louvigny, Marguerite Pierry, Sacha Taride, Michel Simon, Olga Valéry, Fernandel, Nicole Fernandez
First shown: late June 1931 at the Roxy

La Chienne
Screenplay: Jean Renoir, André Girard, from a novel by Georges de la Fouchardière
Dialogue: Jean Renoir
Director: Jean Renoir
Assistant directors: Pierre Schwab, Pierre Prévert
Director of photography: Théodore Sparkhul
Camera: Roger Hubert
Editing: Denise Bactheff, Paul Fejos (rough cut); Jean Renoir, Marguerite Renoir (final cut)
Music: Eugénie Buffet, Toselli, others
Production company: Films Jean Renoir, Braunberger–Richebé
Producer: Charles David
Cast: Michel Simon, Janie Marèze, Georges Flamant, Madelaine Bérubet, Pierre Gaillard, Jean Gehret, Alexandre Rignault, Lucien Mancini, Romain Bouquet, Max Dalban, Pierre Destys, Henri Guisol, Jane Pierson, Courme, Argentin, Mlle. Doryans, Sylvain Itkine, Colette Borelli
First shown: 19 November 1931 at the Colisée (preview at the Nancy)

1932

***La Nuit du carrefour* (*Night at the Crossroads*)**
Screenplay: Jean Renoir, from a novel by Georges Simenon
Director: Jean Renoir
Assistant directors: Jacques Becker, Maurice Blondeau
Directors of photography: Marcel Lucien, Georges Asselin
Camera: Paul Fabian, Claude Renoir
Editing: Marguerite Renoir, Suzanne de Troye, Walter Ruttmann
Production company: Europa Films
Director of production: Jacques Becker
Cast: Pierre Renoir, Georges Térof, Winna Winfried, Georges Koudria, Dignimont, Jean Gehret, Jane Pierson, Michel Duran, Jean Mitry, Max Dalban, Roger Gaillard, G. A. Martin, Boulicot, Manuel Raabi, Lucie Vallat
First shown: 18 April 1932 at the Théâtre Pigalle

***Boudu sauvé des eaux* (*Boudu Saved from Drowning*)**
Screenplay: Jean Renoir, from a play by René Fauchois
Adaptation: Jean Renoir
Dialogue: Jean Renoir
Director: Jean Renoir
Assistant directors: Jacques Becker, Georges Darnoux
Director of photography: Marcel Lucien
Camera: Georges Asselin, Jean-Paul Alphen
Editing: Marguerite Renoir, Suzanne de Troye
Production company: Société Sirius (Films Michel Simon)
Directors of production: Jean Gehret, Marcel Pelletier
Cast: Michel Simon, Charles Granval, Marcelle Hainia, Sévérine Lerczinska,

Jean Dasté, Max Dalban, Jean Gehret, Jacques Becker, Georges Darnoux, Jane Pierson
First shown: mid-November 1932 at the Colisée

1933

Choutard et Cie
Screenplay: Jean Renoir, from a play by Roger Ferdinand
Dialogue: Roger Ferdinand
Director: Jean Renoir
Assistant director: Jacques Becker
Director of photography: Joseph-Louis Mundwiller
Camera: René Ribault, Claude Renoir
Editing: Marguerite Renoir, Suzanne de Troye
Production company: Films Roger Ferdinand
Cast: Fernand Charpin, Jeanne Lory, Jeanne Boitel, Georges Pomiès, Max Dalban, Louis Seigner, Dignimont, Fabien Loris, Malou Treki, Louis Tunk, Robert Seller
First shown: March 1933

1934

Madame Bovary
Screenplay: Jean Renoir, from the novel by Gustave Flaubert
Adaptation: Jean Renoir, Anne Mauclair, Karl Koch
Dialogue: Jean Renoir
Director: Jean Renoir
Assistant directors: Pierre Desouches, Jacques Becker
Director of photography: Jean Bachelet
Camera: Alphonse Gibory, Claude Renoir
Editing: Marguerite Renoir
Music: Darius Milhaud, Donizetti
Production company: NSF
Director of production: Robert Aron
Cast: Pierre Renoir, Alice Tissot, Valentine Tessier, Héléna Manson, Max Dearly, Daniel Lecourtois, Fernand Fabre, Léon Larive, Pierre Larquey, Louis Florencie, Romain Bouquet, Robert le Vigan, Georges Cahuzac, Alain Dhurtal, André Fouché, Georges de Neubourg, Edmond Beauchamp, Robert Moor, Henri Vilbert, Monette Dinay, Marthe Mellot, Maryanne, René Bloch, Pierre Bosy, Max Tréjean, Albert Lambert, Christiane Dor, Odette Dynès, Paulette Elambert
First shown: 4 January 1934 at the Ciné Opéra

1934

Toni
Screenplay: Jean Renoir, Carl Einstein
Dialogue: Carl Einstein, Jean Renoir

Director: Jean Renoir
Assistant directors: Georges Darnoux, Antonio Canor
Director of photography: Claude Renoir
Editing: Marguerite Renoir, Suzanne de Troye
Music: Paul Bozzi
Production company: Films d'aujourd'hui
Director of production: Pierre Gaut
Cast: Charles Blavette, Jenny Hélia, Célia Montalvan, Max Dalban, Edouard Delmont, Andrex, André Kovachevitch, Paul Bozzi

1935

***Le Crime de Monsieur Lange* (*The Crime of Monsieur Lange*)**
Screenplay: Jacques Prévert, Jean Renoir
Adaptation: Jacques Prévert, from a story by Jean Castanier and Jean Renoir
Dialogue: Jacques Prévert, Jean Renoir
Director: Jean Renoir
Assistant directors: Georges Darnoux, Jean Castanier
Director of photography: Jean Bachelet
Camera: Champion
Editing: Marguerite Renoir
Music: Jean Wiener, Joseph Kosma
Production company: Obéron
Director of production: Geneviève Blondeau
Producer: André Halley des Fontaines
Cast: Jules Berry, René Lefèvre, Florelle, Nadia Sibirskaya, Sylvia Bataille, Henri Guisol, Marcel Levesque, Odette Talazac, Maurice Baquet, Jacques Brunius, Marcel Duhamel, Jean Dasté, Paul Grimault, Guy Decomble, Henri Saint-Isles, Fabien Loris, Claire Gérard, Edmond Beauchamp, Sylvain Itkine, René Génin, Janine Loris, Jean Brémaud, Paul Demange, Charbonnier, Marcel Lupovici
First shown: October/November 1935 at Billancourt studios

1936

***La Vie est à nous* (*People of France*)**
Screenplay: Jean Renoir, Paul Vaillant-Couturier, Jean-Paul le Chanois, André Zwobada
Directors: Jean Renoir, André Zwobada, Jean-Paul le Chanois
Assistant directors: Henri Cartier-Bresson, Jacques Becker, Marc Maurette, Jacques B. Brunius, Pierre Unik, Maurice Lime
Directors of photography: Louis Page, Jean-Serge Bourgoin, Jean Isnard, Alain Douarinou, Claude Renoir, Nicolas Hayer
Production company: French Communist party
Cast: Jean Dasté, Jacques B. Brunius, Pierre Unik, Max Dalban, Madeleine Sologne, Fabien Loris, Emile Drain, Charles Blavette, Jean Renoir, Madeleine Dax, Roger Blin, Sylvain Itkine, Georges Spanelly, Fernand Bercher, Eddy Debray, Julien Bertheau, Nadia Sibirskaya, Marcel Lesieur, O'Brady, Marcel

Duhamel, Jacques Becker, Claire Gérard, Jean-Paul le Chanois, Charles Charras, Francis Lemarque, Teddy Michaux, Simone Guisin, Henri Pons, Gabrielle Fontan, Gaston Modot, Léon Larive, Pierre Fervall, Tristan Sevère, Guy Favières, Muse d'Albret
First shown: before the war (via *Ciné Liberté*); first shown commercially 12 November 1969 at Studio Git-le-Coeur

***Une Partie de campagne* (*A Day in the Country*)**
Screenplay: Jean Renoir, from a story by Guy de Maupassant
Director: Jean Renoir
Assistant directors: Yves Allégret, Jacques Becker, Jacques B. Brunius, Henri Cartier-Bresson, Claude Heymann, Luchino Visconti
Director of photography: Claude Renoir
Camera: Jean-Serge Bourgoin, Albert Viguier, Eli Lotar
Editing: Marguerite Renoir, Marinette Cadix, Marcel Cravenne
Music: Joseph Kosma, Germaine Montero
Director of production: Roger Woog
Producer: Pierre Braunberger
Cast: Sylvia Bataille, Jeanne Marken, Gabriello, Georges Darnoux, Jacques B. Brunius, Paul Temps, Gabrielle Fontan, Jean Renoir, Marguerite Renoir, Pierre Lestringuez
First shown: 8 May 1946 at the Raimu

***Les Bas-Fonds* (*The Lower Depths*)**
Screenplay: Eugène Zamiatine, Jacques Companeez, from the play by Maxim Gorki
Adaptation: Charles Spaak, Jean Renoir
Dialogue: Charles Spaak, Jean Renoir
Director: Jean Renoir
Assistant directors: Jacques Becker, Joseph Soiffer
Director of photography: Fedoze Bourgassoff, Jean Bachelet
Camera: Jacques Mercanton
Editing: Marguerite Renoir
Music: Jean Wiener
Production company: Albatros
Director of production: Vladimir Zederbaum
Producer: Alexandre Kamenka
Cast: Louis Jouvet, Jean Gabin, Suzy Prim, Vladimir Sokolov, Junie Astor, Robert le Vignan, Gabriello, Camille Bert, Léon Larive, Fernand Bercher, René Génin, Maurice Baquet, Jany Holt, Paul Temps, Lucien Mancini, Henri Saint-Isles, René Stern, Sylvain, Robert Ozenne, Alex Allin, Annie Ceres, Nathalie Alexieff, Jacques Becker
First shown: December 1936 at the Max Linder

1937

***La Grande illusion* (*Grand Illusion*)**
Screenplay: Charles Spaak, Jean Renoir
Dialogue: Charles Spaak, Jean Renoir

Director: Jean Renoir
Assistant directors: Jacques Becker, Robert Rips
Director of photography: Christian Matra
Camera: Claude Renoir, Eranest Bourreaud, Jean-Serge Bourgoin
Editing: Marguerite Renoir, Marthe Huguet
Music: Joseph Kosma
Director of production: Raymond Blondy
Producers: Frank Rollmer, Albert Pinkevitch
Cast: Erich von Stroheim, Jean Gabin, Pierre Fresnay, Marcel Dalio, Julien Carette, Gaston Modot, Jean Dasté, Georges Péclet, Jacques Becker, Sylvain Itkine, Dita Parlo, Werner Florian, Claude Sainval, Michel Salina
First shown: June 1937 at the Marivaux

La Marseillaise
Screenplay: Jean Renoir, with Karl Koch, Nina Martel-Dreyfus
Dialogue: Jean Renoir
Director: Jean Renoir
Assistant directors: Jacques Becker, Claude Renoir, Claude Renoir l'aîné, Jean-Paul Dreyfus, Louis Demazure, Marc Maurette, Antoine (Tony), Francine Corteggiani
Directors of photography: Jean-Serge Bourgoin, Alain Douarinou, Jean-Marie Maillols, Jean-Paul Alphen, Jean Louis
Editing: Marguerite Renoir, Marthe Huguet
Music: Lalande, Grétry, Mozart, J. S. Bach, Rouget de l'Isle, Joseph Kosma, Sauveplane
Production company: GGT, then Société de production et d'exploitation du film *La Marseillaise*
Directors of production: André Zwobada, A. Seigneur
Cast: Pierre Renoir, Lise Delamare, Léon Larive, William Aguet, Elisa Ruis, Germaine Lefébure, Marie-Pierre Sordet-Dantès, Yveline Auriol, Pamela Stirling, Genia Vaury, Louis Jouvet, Jean Aquistapace, Georges Spanelly, Pierre Nay, Jaque Catelain, Edmond Castel, Werner Florian-Zach, Aimé Clariond, Maurice Escande, André Zibral, Jean Ayme, Irène Joachim, Jacques Castelot, Andrex, Charles Blavette, Edmond Ardisson, Paul Dullac, Jean-Louis Allibert, Fernand Flament, Nadia Sibirskaya, Jenny Hélia, Gaston Modot, Julien Carette, Séverine Lerczinska, Marther Marty, Odette Cazau, Edmond Beauchamp, Blanche Destournelles
First shown: 9 February 1938 at the Olympia

1938

Le Bête humaine (The Human Beast)
Screenplay: Jean Renoir, from the novel by Emile Zola
Dialogue: Jean Renoir
Director: Jean Renoir
Assistant directors: Claude Renoir, Suzanne de Troye
Director of photography: Curt Courant
Camera: Claude Renoir l'aîné, Jacques Natteau, Maurice Pecqueaux, Guy Ferrier, Alain Renoir

Editing: Marguerite Renoir, Suzanne de Troye
Production company: Paris Film Production
Director of production: Roland Tual
Producer: Robert Hakim
Cast: Jean Gabin, Simone Simon, Fernand Ledoux, Julien Carette, Colette Régis, Jenny Hélia, Gérard Landry, Jacques Berlioz, Léon Larive, Georges Spanelly, Jean Renoir, Emile Genevois, Jacques B. Brunius, Marcel Perez, Blanchettes Brunoy, Claire Gérard, Tony Corteggiani, Guy Decomble, Charlotte Clasis, Marceau, Georges Peclet
First shown: 29 December 1938 at the Madeleine

1939

La Règle du jeu (The Rules of the Game)
Screenplay: Jean Renoir, with Karl Koch
Adaptation: Jean Renoir
Dialogue: Jean Renoir
Director: Jean Renoir
Assistant directors: Karl Koch, André Zwobada, Henri Cartier-Bresson
Director of photography: Jean Bachelet
Camera: Jacques Lemare, Jean-Paul Alphen, Alain Renoir
Editing: Marguerite Renoir, Marthe Huguet
Production company: Nouvelles editions françaises
Director of production: Claude Renoir l'aîné
Cast: Marcel Dalio, Nora Grégor, Roland Toutain, Jean Renoir, Mila Parély, Odette Talazac, Pierre Magnier, Pierre Nay, Anne Mayen, Richard Francoeur, Claire Gérard, Tony Corteggiani, Roger Forster, Nicolas Amato, Paulette Dubost, Gaston Modot, Julien Carette, Eddy Debray, Léon Larive, Jenny Hélia, Lise Elina, André Zwoboda, Camille François, Henri Cartier-Bresson

1940

La Tosca
Screenplay: Luchino Visconti, Jean Renoir, Karl Koch, from the play by Victorien Sardou
Director: Karl Koch (five shots by Jean Renoir)
Director of photography: Ubaldo Arata
Editing: Gino Bretone
Music: Giacomo Puccini
Production company: Scalera Films
Cast: Michel Simon, Imperio Argentina, Rossano Brazzi, Massimo Girotti, Clara Candiani, Andriano Rimaldi, Juan Calvo, Nicholas Perchicot
First shown: 30 September 1942 at the Lord Byron, Paris

1941

Swamp Water
Screenplay: Dudley Nichols, from a story by Vereen Bell

Director: Jean Renoir
Directors of photography: Peverell Marley, Lucien Ballard
Editing: Walter Thompson
Music: David Rudolph
Production company: 20th Century–Fox
Producer: Irving Pichell
Cast: Dana Andrews, Walter Huston, John Carradine, Eugene Palette, Ward Bond, Guinn Williams, Anne Baxter, Virginia Gilmore, Walter Brennan, Mary Howard, Russell Simpson, Joseph Sawyer, Paul Burns, Dave Morris, Frank Austin, Matt Williams
First shown: 5 December 1941

1943

This Land Is Mine
Screenplay: Dudley Nichols, Jean Renoir
Dialogue: Dudley Nichols
Director: Jean Renoir
Assistant director: Edward Donohue
Director of photography: Frank Redman
Editing: Frédéric Knudtsen
Music: Lothar Perl
Production company: RKO
Producers: Jean Renoir, Dudley Nichols, Eugène Lourié
Cast: Charles Laughton, Kent Smith, Maureen O'Hara, George Sanders, Walter Slezack, Una O'Connor, Philip Merivale, Nancy Gates, Thurston Hall, Ivan Simpson, Georges Coulouris, Wheaton Chambers, John Donnat, Franck Alten, Leo Bulgakov, Cecil Weston
First shown: 17 March 1943

1944

Salute to France
Screenplay: Philip Dunne, Jean Renoir, Burgess Meredith
Directors: Jean Renoir, Garson Kanin
Assistant director: Harry Gerson
Director of photography: George Webber
Editing: Helen Van Dongen (supervisor)
Music: Kurt Weill
Production company: Office of War Information
Cast: Burgess Meredith, Claude Dauphin, Philip Bourneuf, Jose Ferrer (narrator), and many others
First shown: December 1944/January 1945

1945

The Southerner
Screenplay: Jean Renoir, from the novel *Hold Autumn in Your Hand* by George Sessions Perry

Adaptation: Hugo Butler
Dialogue: Jean Renoir (advised by William Faulkner)
Director: Jean Renoir
Assistant director: Robert Aldrich
Director of photography: Lucien Andriot
Editing: Gregg Tallas
Music: Werner Janssen
Producers: David L. Loew, Robert Hakim
Cast: Zachary Scott, Betty Field, Jay Gilpin, Jean Vanderbilt, Beulah Bondi, J. Carroll Naish, Percy Kilbride, Blanche Yurka, Charles Kemper, Norman Lloyd, Estelle Taylor, Noreen Nash, Jack Norworth, Paul Harvey, Nestor Paira, Paul Burns, Dorothy Granger, Earl Odgkins, Almira Sessions
First shown: 30 April 1945 at the Four–Star Theater, Beverly Hills

1946

Diary of a Chambermaid
Screenplay: Jean Renoir, Burgess Meredith, from the play by André Heuzé, André de Lorde, and Thielly Nores, after the novel by Octave Mirbeau
Director: Jean Renoir
Assistant director: Joseph Depew
Director of photography: Lucien Andriot
Editing: James Smith
Music: Michel Michelet
Producers: Benedict Bogeaus, Burgess Meredith, Corley Harriman, Arthur M. Landau
Cast: Paulette Goddard, Burgess Meredith, Hurt Hatfield, Reginald Owen, Judith Anderson, Francis Lederer, Florence Bates, Irene Ryan, Almira Sessions
First shown: 1948

The Woman on the Beach
Screenplay: Jean Renoir, Franck Davis, J. R. Michael Hogan, after the novel *None So Blind* by Mitchell Watson
Director: Jean Renoir
Assistant director: James Casey
Directors of photography: Harry Wild, Leo Tover
Editing: Roland Gross, Lyle Boyer
Music: Hans Eisler
Production company: RKO
Producers: Jack J. Gross, Will Price
Cast: Joan Bennett, Charles Bickford, Robert Ryan, Nan Leslie, Walter Sande, Irene Ryan, Glenn Vernon, Frank Dorien, Jay Norris
First shown: 14 May 1947

1950

The River
Screenplay: Rumer Godden, Jean Renoir, from the novel by Rumer Godden
Director: Jean Renoir

Assistant director: Forrest Judd
Director of photography: Claude Renoir
Camera: Romananda Sen Gupta
Editing: George Gale
Music: traditional Indian, Weber
Production company: Oriental International Film Inc.
Producers: Kenneth McEldowney, Kalyan Gupta, Jean Renoir
Cast: Nora Swinburne, Esmond Knight, Arthur Shields, Thomas E. Breen, Radha Shri Ram, Suprova Mukerjee, Patricia Walters, Adrienne Corri, Richard Foster, Penelope Wilkinson, Jane Harris, Jennifer Harris, Cecilia Wood, Ram Singh, Nimai Barik, Trilak Jetley, narrated by June Hillman
First shown: 19 December 1951 at the Madeleine and the Biarritz, Paris

1952

***Le Carrosse d'or* (*The Golden Coach*)**
Screenplay: Jean Renoir, Renzo Avenzo, Giulio Macchi, Jack Kirkland, Ginette Doynel, from the play *Le Carrosse du Saint-Sacrement* by Prosper Mérimée
Director: Jean Renoir
Assistant directors: Marc Maurette, Giulio Macchi
Directors of photography: Claude Renoir, Ronald Hill
Camera: Rodolfo Lombardi
Editing: Mario Serandrei, David Hawkins
Music: Antonio Vivaldi, Archangelo Corelli, Olivier Mettra
Production company: Panaria Films–Hoche Productions (French–Italian coproduction)
Director of production: Valentino Brosio, Giuseppe Bardogni
Producers: Francesco Alliata, Ray Ventura
Cast: Anna Magnani, Duncan Lamont, Odoardo Spadaro, Riccardo Rioli, Paul Campbell, Nada Fiorelli, Georges Higgins, Dante, Rino, Gisela Mathews, Lina Maregno, Ralph Truman, Elena Altieri, Renato Chiantoni, Giulio Tedeschi, Alfredo Kolner, Alfredo Medini, John Pasetti, William Tubbs, Cecil Mathews, Fedo Keeling, Jean Debucourt
First shown: 27 February 1953 at the Olympia and the Paris

1954

French Cancan
Screenplay: Jean Renoir, from an idea by André-Paul Antoine
Adaptation: Jean Renoir
Dialogue: Jean Renoir
Director: Jean Renoir
Assistant directors: Serge Vallin, Pierre Kast, Jacques Rivette, Paul Seban
Director of photography: Michel Kelber
Camera: Henri Tiquet, Vladimir Lang, Georges Barsky
Editing: Boris Lewin
Music: Georges Van Parys and music hall songs
Choreography: Georges Grandjean

Production company: Franco London Films–Jolly Films
Director of production: Louis Wipf
Cast: Jean Gabin, Maria Felix, Françoise Arnoul, Jean-Roger Caussimon, Gianni Esposito, Philippe Clay, Michel Piccoli, Jean Parédès, Albert Rémy, Lydia Johnson, Max Dalban, Jacques Jouanneau, Jean-Marc Tennberg, Valentine Tessier, Hubert Deschamps, Franco Pastorino, Dora Doll, Annick Morice, Michèle Nadal, Anna Amendola, Anne-Marie Mersen, Sylvine Delannoy, Pâquerette, Léo Campion, Gaston Gabroche, Jaque Catelain, Pierre Moncorbier, Jean Mortier, André Numès fils, Robert Auboyneau, Laurence Bataille, Pierre Olaf, Jacques Ciron, Claude Arnay, R. J. Chauffard, France Roche, Michèle Philippe, Gaston Modot, Jacques Hilling, Patachou, Edith Piaf, André Claveau, Jean Raymond
First shown: 27 April 1955 at the Biarritz, the Paris, the Gaumont-Palace

1956

***Eléna et les hommes* (*Paris Does Strange Things*)**
Screenplay: Jean Renoir
Adaptation: Jean Serge, Jean Renoir
Dialogue: Jean Renoir
Director: Jean Renoir
Assistant director: Serge Vallin
Director of photography: Claude Renoir
Editing: Boris Lewin
Music: Joseph Kosma, Georges Van Parys
Production company: Franco London Films–Films Gibé–Electra Compagnia Cinematrografica
Cast: Ingrid Bergman, Jean Marais, Mel Ferrer, Jean Richard, Magali Noël, Juliette Gréco, Pierre Bertin, Jean Claudio, Jean Castanier, Elina Labourdette, Dora Doll, Frédéric Duvallès, Jacques Jouanneau, Mirko Ellis, Jacques Hilling, Renaud Mary, Gaston Modot, Jacques Morel, Michèle Nadal, Albert Rémy, Olga Valéry, Léo Marjane
First shown: 12 September 1956

1959

Le Testament du Dr. Cordelier
Screenplay: Jean Renoir, from the novel *Dr. Jekyll and Mr. Hyde* by Robert Louis Stevenson
Dialogue: Jean Renoir
Director: Jean Renoir
Assistant directors: Maurice Beuchey, Jean-Pierre Spiero
Director of photography: Georges Leclerc
Camera: Bernard Giraux, Jean Graglia, Pierre Guégen, Pierre Lebon, Gilbert Perrot-Minot, Arthur Raymond, Gilbert Sandoz
Editing: Renée Lichtig
Music: Joseph Kosma
Production company: RTF Sorifrad–Compagnie Jean Renoir

Director of production: Albert Hollebecke
Cast: Jean-Louis Barrault, Teddy Bilis, Michel Vitold, Jean Topart, Micheline Gary, André Certes, Jacques Dannoville, Jean-Pierre Granval, Gaston Modot, Jacqueline Morane, Ghislaine Dumont, Madeleine Marion, Primerose Perret, Didier d'Yd, Jaque-Catelain, Régine Blaess, Raymond Jourdan, Sylviane Margolle, Céline Salles, Raymone, Jaque Catelain
First shown: 16 November 1961 at the George V, Paris

***Le Dejeuner sur l'herbe* (*Picnic on the Grass*)**
Screenplay: Jean Renoir
Dialogue: Jean Renoir
Director: Jean Renoir
Assistant directors: Maurice Beuchley, Francis Morane, Jean-Pierre Spiero, Hedy Naka, Jean de Nesles
Director of photography: Georges Leclerc
Camera: Ribaud, Jean-Louis Picavet, Andreas Winding, Pierre Guégen
Editing: Renée Lichtig, Françoise London
Music: Joseph Kosma
Production company: Compagnie Jean Renoir
Director of production: Ginette Doynel
Cast: Paul Meurisse, Catherine Rouvel, Fernand Sardou, Jacqueline Morane, Jean-Pierre Granval, Robert Chandeau, Micheline Gary, Frédéric O'Brady, Ghislaine Dumont, Ingrid Nordine, André Brunot, Hélène Duc, Jean Claudio, Jacques Dannoville, Marguerite Cassan, Charles Blavette, Paulette Dubost, Michel Péricard, Roland Thierry, Dupraz, Lucas, Régine Blaess
First shown: 11 November 1959 at the Marignan, the Français

1962

***Le Caporal épinglé* (*The Elusive Corporal*)**
Screenplay: Jean Renoir, Guy Lefranc, from the novel by Jacques Perret
Dialogue: Jean Renoir
Directors: Jean Renoir, Guy Lefranc
Assistant directors: Marc Maurette, J. E. Kieffer
Director of photography: Georges Leclerc
Camera: Jean-Louis Picavet, Gilbert Chain, Antoine Georgakis, Robert Fraisse
Editing: Renée Lichtig, Madeleine Lacompère
Music: Joseph Kosma
Production company: Films du Cyclope
Director of production: René G. Vuattoux
Producers: G. W. Byer, Georges Glass
Cast: Jean-Pierre Cassel, Claude Brasseur, Claude Rich, O. E. Hasse, Jean Carmet, Jacques Jouanneau, Cornelia Froboess, Mario David, Philippe Costelli, Raymond Jourdan, Guy Bedos, Gérard Darrieu, Sacha Briquet, Lucien Raimbourg, François Darbon
First shown: 23 May 1962 at the Ermitage, the Français, the Miramar, the Wepler Pathé

1968

La Direction d'acteur par Jean Renoir
Renoir directs Gisèle Braunberger through an excerpt he translated from *Breakfast with the Nikolides* by Rumer Godden
Director: Gisèle Braunberger
Director of photography: Edmond Richard
Editing: Mireille Mauberna
Producer: Roger Fleytoux

1969

***Le Petit Théâtre de Jean Renoir* (*The Little Theater of Jean Renoir*)**
Comprises four short films: "Le Dernier Réveillon," "La Cireuse électrique," "Quand l'amour meurt," and "Le Roi d'Yvetot"; was originally conceived in five parts as *C'est la revolution*!
Screenplay: Jean Renoir
Adaptation: Jean Renoir
Dialogue: Jean Renoir
Director: Jean Renoir
Assistant director: Denis Epstein
Directors of photography: Georges Leclerc, Antoine Georgakis, Georges Liron
Camera: Henri Martin, Claude Amiot
Editing: Genevieve Winding, Gisele Chezeau
Music: Jean Winer, Joseph Kosma, Octave Crémieux
Production company: Son et Lumière
Director of production: Robert Paillardon
Cast: Nino Formicola, Milly-Monti, Roger Trapp, Robert Lombard, André Dumas, Roland Bertin, Paul Bisciglia, Marguerite Cassan, Pierre Olaf, Jacques Dynam, Denis de Gunsburg, Claude Guillaume, Jean-Louis Tristan, Jeanne Moreau, Fernand Sardou, Françoise Arnoul, Jean Carmet, Dominique Labourier, Edmond Ardisson

The Christian Licorice Store
Director: James Frawley
Cast: Jean Renoir (as himself)

1978

Julienne et son amour
Published screenplay.
Henri Veyrier, Paris.

1981

Œuvres de cinéma inédités
Published screenplay.
Cahiers du cinéma, Gallimard, Paris.

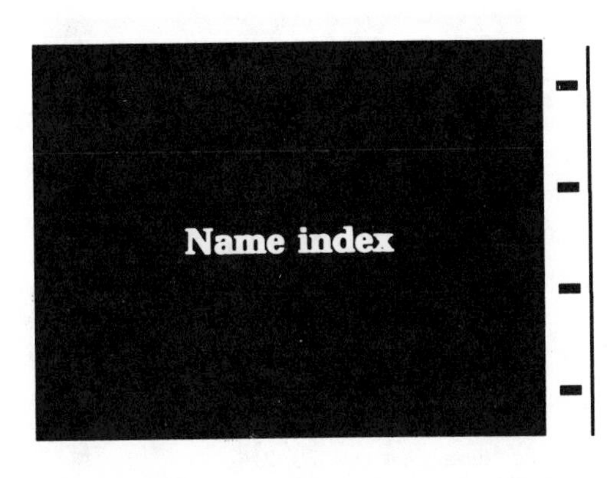

This index lists people, periodicals, organizations, studios, and so on. Abbreviations: f, photo; n, note.

Andersen, Hans Christian, 65
Anderson, Judith, 26f, 255f
Andrews, Dana, 13, 253f
Andrex, 85, 137, 142, 262n
Andriot, Lucien, 5
Angelo, Jean, 221
Antoine, André, 79–80, 100
Argentin, Imperio, 9f
Aristotle, 24
Arnaud, François Thomas Marie de Baculard d', 142
Arnoul, Françoise, 99f, 117f, 260
Astruc, Alexandre, 3n
Aubert Palace (film theater), 73

Baal, 120
Bach, Johann Sebastian, 34, 96, 118
Bachelet, Jean, 192, 229
Ballard, Lucien, 14
Barnes, Alfred C., 24
Barrault, Jean-Louis, 214f
Bataille, Sylvia, 89, 176, 250, 260
Bates, Florence, 255f
Baxter, Anne, 13, 14f
Bazin, André, 3n, 260n
Bazin, Janine, x, xii, 147, 168, 181f
Beatles, 122
Beaumarchais, Pierre Augustin Caron de, 191, 237
Becker, Jacques, xi, 233, 248
Bédier, Joseph, 22
Beethoven, Ludwig von, 167
Bennett, Joan, 27, 28, 29, 30
Bergman, Ingrid, 69, 90, 101, 102f, 103, 104, 245, 246f, 247
Berry, Jules, 144, 227
Bertheau, Julien, 261
Bertin, Pierre, 247
Bertini, Francesca, 80
Berubet, Madelaine, 173
Billancourt (studio), 82
Billis, Teddy, 214f
Blavette, Charles, 85, 176, 178f
Bogeaus, Benedict, 25
Bondi, Beulah, 20
Boucher, François, 156
Bouguereau, Adolphe William, 209
Boulanger, Georges Ernest, 245–7
Bourgoin, Jean-Serge, 139
Bourelly, Léon, 176
Boyer, François, 18
Braque, Georges, xii
Braunberger, Pierre, 63, 87, 89, 113, 169, 170
Braunberger–Richebé, 73
Brecht, Bertolt, 82, 135, 227
Brennan, Walter, 13, 252
Bresson, Robert, 118
Briquet, Sacha, 148f
Brosset, Colette, 113
Brown, Clarence, 169
Brunius, Jacques B., 86, 87
Buñuel, Luis, ix

Cahiers du Cinéma, vii, viii, ix, x, xi, xii, 1, 189, 248, 259, 261n
Camus, Albert, 111
Carette, Julien, 150f, 234
Carmet, Jean, 117f

Caron, Leslie, 106, 109
Cartier-Bresson, Henri, 87, 160–1, 233
Cassan, Marguerite, 115f
Cassel, Jean-Pierre, 148f
Castanier, Jean, 227
Castro, Guillén de, 233
Cellini, Benvenuto, 22
Cézanne, Paul, fils (*son* of the painter), 60, 166, 180
Champagne, Pierre, 58f, 61f, 68f, 221
Chaplin, Charles, 25, 82, 169, 251
Charles X, 203
Chateaubriand, François René, 142
Chevalier, Maurice, 163
Cinémathèque (film theater), 184
Circle (stage group), 30
Clair, René, 74, 250
Clariond, Aimé, 142, 143f
Clay, Philippe, 99f
Clement, René, 18n
Cocteau, Jean, 171
Coldefy, Jean-Marie, 147
Colisée (film theater), 237
Columbia Pictures, 21
Combat, 208f
Comolli, Jean-Louis, 261n
Companeez, Jacques, 89
Copeau, Jacques, 127
Cori, Adrienne, 38f
Corneille, Pierre, 233
Corteggiani, Francine, 133, 135

Dalban, Max, 85, 262n
Dalio, Marcel, 136, 150, 192, 193, 195, 196f, 198f, 199, 200, 202, 238f
Danton, Georges-Jacques, 142
Darnous, Georges, 88f
Darrieux, Danielle, 111
Dasté, Jean, 150f
Daudet, Alphonse, 18
Dearly, Max, 81, 225, 227
Degas, Edgar, 119
Delahaye, Michel, xi, xii, 1, 195
Delamare, Lise, 93, 130, 140, 142
Deutschmeister, Henry, 98, 245, 247
Dhéry, Robert, 113
Dietrich, Philippe-Frederic, Baron de, 134
Don Quixote, 124
Dreyer, Carl, 260
Dullea, Keir, 248n
Dunne, Philip, 18
Durbin, Deanna, 15
Duvivier, Julien, 90

Einstein, Albert, 116
Einstein, Karl, 84–5
Eustache, Jean, 168

Fernandel, 71–2
Fernandez, Nicole, 172f
Ferrer, Mel, 69, 101, 104
Feydeau, Georges, 73, 214
Félix, Maria, 99f
Field, Betty, 20, 240
Fieschi, Jean-André, xi, 1
Figaro, 207f, 209f
Film Group, 30
Flaherty, Robert, 184
Flamant, Georges, 215
Flaubert, Gustave, 224, 237
Florelle, 86f
Fouché, André, 226f
French Institute, Calcutta, 242
Fresnay, Pierre, 217

Gabin, Jean, 4n, 90, 91, 150f, 217f, 229, 231, 232, 234, 235f, 236
Gaillard, Michel, 175
Garbo, Greta, 153
Gaumont-Palace (film theater), 23, 215
Gaut, Pierre, 83, 84, 91, 176
General Service (studio), 25
Gélin, Daniel, 70f
Goddard, Paulette, 25, 26f, 218, 255f
Godden, Rumer, 31, 32, 35, 36, 37, 241, 250
Goethe, Johann Wolfgang von, 140
Goldoni, Carlo, 8, 42
Gorki, Maxim, 176, 229, 231, 232
Granval, Charles, 225f
Granval, Jean-Pierre, 187f
Gréco, Juliet, 103, 104, 105f, 245
Grégor, Nora, 192, 201f, 203f, 205
Grétry, André Ernest Modeste, 134
Griffith, D(avid) W(ark), 81, 169
Gross, Jack J., 28
Guitry, Sacha, 181
Guynemer, Georges, 125

Hakim, Robert, 19–20, 96, 239
Hal Roach (studio), 33
Henri IV, 156

Hessling, Catherine, 58f, 59f, 66f, 68f, 221
Hitchcock, Alfred, ix
Hitler, Adolf, 141
Homer, 127, 189
Hugh Capet, 205
Huston, Walter, 13, 252

Iribe, Marie-Louise, 61f
Ivory, James, 119, 120

Jeu de Paume (museum), 166
Jouanneau, Jacques, 247
Jouvet, Louis, 119, 140, 142, 223f, 229, 230f, 231, 232
Julius II, 164

Kamenka, Alexandre, 89, 231
Kazan, Elia, 104
Kerans, James, vii
Kinkéwitch, Albert, 91
Koch, Karl, 8–9, 133, 135
Korner, Charles, 16, 31
Kosma, Joseph, 89
Koster, Henry, 15
Koudria, Georges, 222f
Krauss, Werner, 221

La Fouchardière, Georges de, 215
Labarthe, André S., xii, 168
Labourier, Dominique, 117f
Larive, Léon, 131f
Laughton, Charles, 18, 19f
Le Vigan, Robert, 223f, 229, 230f, 231
Leblond-Zola, Denise, 3
Lederer, Francis, 255f
Lefèvre, René, 86f, 227
Lefranc, Guy, 256
Leonardo da Vinci, 22
Lestringuez, Pierre, 221
Levesque, Marcel, 228f
Lewton, Val, 27
Linder, Max, 158
Loew, David, 20–1, 239, 240
Louis XVI, 95, 127–30, 133, 135, 138, 204–5, 218, 260
Louis-Philippe, 58–9
Lourié, Eugène, 17, 67, 69
Louvre, 189
Lucullus, Lucius Licinius, 75
Ludmilla Tcherina Ballet, 162
Lurçat, Jean, 157

Macchi, Giulio, 42
McCarey, Leo, 251–2
McEldowney, Kenneth, 241
Magnani, Anna, 41, 219, 242–5
Marais, Jean, 103, 245
Marat, Jean-Paul, 142
Marceau, Felicien, 111
Mareschal, Pierre, 168
Marèze, Janie, 194
Margolin, Janet, 248n
Marie Antoinette, 23, 130–2, 133, 138, 205
Marivaux, Pierre Carlet de Chamblain de, 4, 8, 43, 58, 78, 191, 237
Marley, Peverell, 13n
Mathilda of Flanders, 156, 157
Matisse, Henri, 51, 151
Maupassant, Guy de, 57, 113, 232, 250
Medici (family), 42
Meerson, Mary, 96
Meredith, Burgess, 18, 25, 218
Meurisse, Paul, 108, 111, 113
Mérimée, Prosper, 242–3
Michelangelo Buonarroti, 164
Mirbeau, Octave, 218, 219
Modot, Gaston, 150f
Molière, 41, 43, 119, 233, 237
Monde, 55, 71
Monogram Pictures, 27
Montaigne, Michel Eyquem, seigneur de, 170, 249
Morane, Jacqueline, 187f
Moreau, Jeanne, 138
Morgan, Michèle, 108
Mortier, Jacques, 83
Moulin Rouge, 169
Mozart, Wolfgang Amadeus, 22, 35, 57, 167
Museum of Modern Art, 53
Musset, Alfred de, 4, 191, 237
Mussolini, Benito, 8

Narboni, Jean, xii
Nazimova, Alla, 37
Neau, André, 168
Nehru, Pandit Motilai, 31, 241
New Yorker, 31
Niblo, Fred, 169
Nichols, Dudley, 11, 16, 106, 107
Noames, Jean-Louis, xii, 248

Offenbach, Jacques Levy, 101, 169
Office of War Information, 18

Olaf, Pierre, 113
Olivier, Laurence, 151
Ophuls, Max, 69
ORTF, 147

Pagnol, Marcel, viii, 176–7
Panaria Company, 42
Parély, Mila, 202, 238f
Pasquet, Marinette, 168, 181f
Paulhan, Jean, xii
Perrault, Charles, 108
Perret, Mme. (wife of dir. Léonce), 170
Perry, Frank, 248n
Perry, George Sessions, 19, 239
Petit, Roland, 106
Peupliers (studio), 176
Philippe, Pierre, 58f, 61f
Philips Company, 63, 64
Picasso, Pablo, 11, 104, 180, 221
Pierry, Marguerite, 72
Pinsard, Armand, 90–1, 92, 126
Pius XII, 153
Plato, 24
Point, 1
Pomiès, Georges, 63
Prévert, Jacques, 85–6, 89, 227
Prim, Suzy, 223f, 230f

Rabelais, François, 170
Radha Shri Ran, 34, 37, 38f, 42, 98, 242, 250
Raleigh, Charles, 65
Raphaël Sanzio, 60, 165, 209
Ray, Man, 68–9
Reichenbach, François, 180
Reininger, Lotte, 9
Renoir, Claude, 87, 175, 216, 236, 241, 242, 243, 245
Renoir, Jean, vi(frontis.), 33f, 38f, 102f, 108f, 162f, 177f, 181f, 183f, 187f, 196f, 198f, 201f, 203f, 217f, 244f; also text throughout
Renoir, Pierre, 40, 78f, 81, 93, 131f, 133, 222, 223, 260
Renoir, Pierre-Auguste, 60, 159, 167, 181, 250
Rivette, Jacques, x, xi, xii, 1, 147, 183, 260n
RKO, 16, 27, 28
Robespierre, Maximilien Marie Isidore, 142
Roederer, Pierre Louis, 139
Roland Petit Ballet, 106
Rollmer, Frank, 91
Ronsard, Pierre de, 170
Rouget de L'Isle, Jean-Claude, 134
Rouvel, Catherine, 184, 187f
Rubens, Peter Paul, 51
Ryan, Robert, 28, 29, 30

Sagan, François, 258
Saint-Exupéry, Antoine de, 15
Samson, 208
Sarah Bernhardt Theater, 162
Sardou, Fernand, 117f, 187f
Sartre, Jean-Paul, 114
Schufftan, Eugene, 67
Schumann, Robert, 35
Scott, Zachary, 20, 219, 239
Sennett, Mack, 5, 40
Shakespeare, William, 41, 97, 109, 119, 161, 231, 233, 249
Sibirskaya, Nadia, 128f, 261
Signoret, Simone, 113
Simenon, Georges, 109, 222, 223
Simon, Michel, 9f, 63, 64f, 75, 76, 77, 120, 168, 171–3, 174, 175, 176, 177f, 194, 215, 223–4
Simon, Simone, 27, 53, 96, 184, 234, 235f
Société des films historiques, 93
Socrates, 121
Sokoloff, Vladimir, 229
Solignac, Guy, 168
Spaak, Charles, 89, 90, 91, 229, 256
Stanislavski, Konstantin, 254
Sully, Maximilien, de Béthune, 156

Talazac, Odette, 195
Tcherina, Ludmilla, 162
Technicolor, 34, 50, 54, 241, 242
Tedesco, Jean, 63
Temps, Paul, 231f
Tessier, Valentine, 81, 225, 226f
Thalberg, Irving, 70
Theodorakis, Mikis, 162
Tourneur, Jacques, 27
Toutain, Roland, 193, 202, 238
Truchy, Alex, 128f
Truffaut, François, xi, 1, 141, 260n
Turgenev, Ivan Sergeyevich, 106
Twentieth Century–Fox, 10, 11, 15

United Artists, 21
Universal Pictures, 15

Valentino, Rudolph, 169
Valery, Olga, 72
Venice Film Festival, 239
Verdi, Giuseppe, 41
Verrier, Anne-Marie, 233
Vidal, Henri, 108f
Vieux-Colombier, Théâtre du (used as studio), 63, 64, 158
Visconti, Luchino, 87, 233
Vivaldi, Antonio, 41–2, 96, 118, 243
Von Stroheim, Erich, 169, 170, 217f, 221

Walters, Patricia, 38f
Wanger, Walter, 28
Warner Bros., 239
Watteau, Jean-Antoine, 156
Weber, Carl Maria Friedrich Ernst von, 35
Welles, Orson, ix
Werner, Oscar, 113
Western Electric, 25
Wilhelm II, 92–3
William the Conqueror, 156
Willkie, Wendell, 22
Winfried, Winna, 222
Wise, Robert, 28

Zanuck, Darryl F., 10–11, 13, 15, 16, 252
Zola, Emile, 3, 57, 96, 98

Title index

This index lists works cited in the text; unless otherwise indicated, they are Renoir films. Abbreviations: f, photo; n, note.

Angèle (dir. Pagnol), 85, 176
Amours de Toni, Les, see Toni
Around the World in 80 Days (dir. Todd), 67

Baby Doll (dir. Kazan), 104
Bas-Fonds, Les, see The Lower Depths
Belle Equipe, La (dir. Duvivier), 90
Bête humaine, La, see The Human Beast
Bled, Le, 60, 64, 73, 93, 266
Bonjour tristesse (Sagan novel), 258
Boudu Saved from Drowning (Boudu sauvé des eaux), 223–4, 267
Braconniers, Les (The Poachers) (unfilmed Renoir screenplay), 106–7
Breakfast with the Nikolides (Godden novel), 36

C'est la révolution!, see The Little Theater of Jean Renoir
Cahiers de revendications (of the States-General), 129
Capitaine Georges, Le (Renoir novel), 205, 206
Caporal épinglé, Le (Perret novel), 256; *see also The Elusive Corporal*
Caprices de Marianne, Les (Musset play), 4, 237
Carola (Renoir play), vii, 110f, 111
Carosse d'or, Le, see The Golden Coach
Carosse du Saint-Sacrement, Le (Mérimée play), 242–3
Cat People (dir. J. Tourneur), 27
Catherine or *Une vie sans joie*, 264
Cathédrale, La (Zola novel), 3
César (dir. Pagnol), viii
Ceux de chez nous (dir. Guitry), 181
Chair et cuir (Marceau play), 111
Charleston or *Sur un air de Charleston*, 265
Chienne, La, 72, 73–5, 76, 111, 171–3, 174, 175, 194, 213–15, 219, 223, 224, 266–7
Choutard et Cie, 267–8
Cid, Le (Corneille play), 233
"*Cinéastes de notre temps*" (Bazin–Labarthe TV series), 168
Citizen Kane (dir. Welles), 16, 257
"Crème de beauté, La" (unfilmed; intended for *C' est la révolution!*), 207
Crime of Monsieur Lange, The (Le Crime de Monsieur Lange), 77, 85–7, 106, 144, 227, 228f, 229, 262n, 268–9

David and Lisa (dir. Perry), 248, 257
Day in the Country, A (Une Partie de campagne), 87, 88, 112, 232–3, 250, 260, 261n, 269
Diary of a Chambermaid, 21, 24–5, 26f, 27, 218–19, 254, 255f, 273
Direction d'acteur par Jean Renoir, La (dir. G. Braunberger), 277
"Duchesse, La" (unfilmed; intended for *C'est la révolution!*), 207

Egg, The (L'Oeuf) (Marceau play), 111
"Electric Waxer, The" ("La Cireuse électrique") (2nd in *The Little Theater...*), 115f, 207
Eléna et les hommes, see Paris Does Strange Things

Elusive Corporal, The (Le Caporal épinglé), 147–8, 149, 165, 239, 256–7, 276
Etang tragique, L', see Swamp Water

Fanny (dir. Allégret; Pagnol screenplay), viii
Faute de l'Abbé Mouret, La (Zola novel), 3
Femme sur la plage, La, see The Woman on the Beach
Feu aux poudres, Le (Renoir ballet), 162
Fille de l'eau, La, 57, 67, 264
"First Love" (Turgenev story), 106
"Four Winds, The" (Andersen story), 65
Forbidden Games (dir. Clement), 18n
French Cancan, 98–100, 219, 220f, 221, 260, 274–5

Gold Rush, The (dir. Chaplin), 257
Golden Coach, The (Le Carosse d'or), xi, 41–2, 43, 44–8, 49, 98, 219, 242–5, 260, 274
Grand Couteau, Le (The Big Knife) (Renoir adaptation of Odets play), 69, 70f, 75
Grand Illusion (La Grande Illusion), 53, 83, 88, 90–3, 111, 122, 126, 135, 136, 149, 150f, 175, 216, 217f, 250–1, 270

Hard Day's Night, A (dir. Lester), 122
Histoire du vitrail, L' (Zola novel), 3
Hold Autumn in Your Hand (Perry novel), 239
Human Beast, The (La Bête humaine), xi, 1, 3n, 53, 88, 95–7, 98, 184, 234, 235f, 236, 239, 271

Iliad, The (Homer epic), 127
Invitation to the Dance (Weber music), 35

"Jean Renoir le patron" (TV), 168–210
"Jean Renoir vous parle de son art" (TV), 147–67, 213
Joan of Arc (dir. Dreyer), 260
Jofroi (dir. Pagnol), 176
Joie de vivre, La (Zola novel), 3
Julienne et son amour (unfilmed Renoir screenplay), 277
Julius Caesar (Shakespeare play), 105, 108–9

"King of Yvetot, The" ("Le Roi d'Yvetot") (4th in *The Little Theater...*), 117f

"Last Class, The" (Daudet story), 18
Little Match Girl, The (La Petite Marchande d'allumettes), 63–5, 66f, 67, 71, 158, 265
Little Theater of Jean Renoir, The (Le Petit Théâtre de Jean Renoir), xi, 1, 112–16, 117f, 137, 207, 276–7
Lola Montès (dir. Ophuls), 69
Louisiana Story (dir. Flaherty), 184
Lower Depths, The (Les Bas-Fonds), 60, 77, 87, 88, 89, 91, 96, 176, 229, 230f, 231–2, 269–70
Lucia de Lammermoor (Donizetti opera), 80

Madame Bovary, 80, 81, 82, 224–7, 268
Marius (dir. Korda; Pagnol screenplay), viii
Marquitta, 60, 61f, 67, 265
Marseillaise, La, xi, 88, 93, 94–5, 124, 125–37, 138–40, 141–2, 143f, 205, 216, 218, 260, 262, 270–1
"Marseillaise, La" (Rouget de L'Isle song), 134, 175
Merchant of Venice, The (Shakespeare play), 231
Midsummer's Night Dream, A (Shakespeare play), 161
Mocedades del cid, Las (Castro play), 233
Mona Lisa (Leonardo painting), 189, 190
"Monday Tales" (Daudet story), 18
Monsieur Beaucaire (dir. Olcott), 169

Nana, xi, 25, 57, 60, 75, 169–71, 221, 264
Night at the Crossroads (La Nuit du carrefour), 77, 78f, 222–3, 248–9, 267

Odyssey, The (Homer epic), 127
Œuvres de cinéma inédités (unfilmed Renoir screenplays), 277
"Oh Richard! Oh My King" (aria from opera *Richard Coeur de Lion)*, 134
On purge bébé, 71–3, 171, 172f, 175, 214, 266
Orvet (Renoir play), xi, 4n, 53, 105–8, 109

Paris Does Strange Things (Eléna et les hommes), xi, 69–70, 71, 75, 100–4, 105f, 245–7, 275
Paris-Province (unfilmed Renoir screenplay), 110

Partie de campagne, Une, see A Day in the Country
People of France (La Vie est à nous), 261, 269
Petit Chaperon rouge, Le (dir. Cavalcanti), 266
Petit Théâtre de Jean Renoir, Le, see The Little Theater of Jean Renoir
Petite Marchande d'allumettes, La, see The Little Match Girl
Picnic on the Grass (Déjeuner sur l'herbe), 184–6, 187f, 276

Règle du jeu, La, see The Rules of the Game
Religieuse, La (dir. Rivette), 134
Richard Coeur de Lion (Grétry opera), 134
River, The, xi, 31–7, 38f, 39–40, 44, 49, 51, 55, 69, 97, 98, 106, 119, 240–2, 274
Robe, The (dir. Koster), 18
Rules of the Game, The (La Règle du jeu), xi, 1, 4, 5–7, 8, 10, 24, 42, 47f, 48, 49, 88, 97, 98, 135, 136, 190–204, 236–9, 254, 271

Salute to France, 18, 272–3
Secret Game, The (Boyer novel), 18
Shakespeare Wallah (dir. Ivory), 119
Shoulder Arms (dir. Chaplin), 67
Singe vert, Le (Mortier novel), 83
Song of Roland (French epic poem), 22, 118, 154
Southerner, The, 5, 18–21, 219, 239–40, 273
Stranger, The (L'Etranger) (Camus novel), 111
Sur un air de Charleston, 265
Swamp Water (L'Etang tragique), 10–11, 12f, 13–15, 240, 252, 253f, 272

Tempest, The (Shakespeare play), 249
Terre des hommes (Wind, Sand and Stars) (Saint-Exupéry novel), 15–16
Testament of Doctor Cordelier, The (Le Testament de Doctor Cordelier), 184, 213, 214f, 275–6
This Land is Mine, 16–18, 19f, 272
Three Smart Girls (dir. Koster), 15
Tire au flanc, 61–3, 64f, 81, 171, 265
Toni, 77, 83–5, 90, 91, 93, 126, 176–8, 215–16, 219, 262n, 268
Tosca, La (dir. Koch), 7–8, 272
Tour de Nesle, La (Dumas père play), 41
Tournoi dans la cité, Le, 60, 61, 62f, 64, 73, 93, 265–6
Trois Chambres à Manhattan (Simenon novel), 109

Vie est à nous, La, see People of France
Vie sans joie, Une, 264

Woman on the Beach, The (La Femme sur la plage), xi, 16, 27–30, 32, 48, 273